Beautiful pages by Judith Tendler

Edited by Nicoletta Stame

A Colorni-Hirschman International Institute e-book series
1 - For a Better World, First Conference on Albert Hirschman's Legacy, 2017
2 - Beautiful Pages by Judith Tendler, 2018

BEAUTIFUL PAGES by JUDITH TENDLER
edited by Nicoletta Stame

1ˢᵗ edition october 2018

©Italic Digital Editions S.R.L. 2018
Via Benedetto Croce 34 – 00142 Roma
www.italicdigitaleditions.it

ISBN: 9788898156528

Table of contents

"Judith Tendler's fine insight into the differential characteristics and side-effects of thermal and hydropower, and of generation and distribution, contributed in many ways to the formation of my views".

A.O. Hirschman, *Development Projects Observed* (1967:xi)

"What if the fortress of underdevelopment, just because it is so formidable, can not be conquered by frontal assault? In that unfortunately quite common case, we need to know much more about ways in which the fortress can be surrounded, weakened by infiltration and subversion, and eventually taken by similar indirect tactics and processes. And I suggest that the major contribution to our knowledge of economic development must now come from detailed studies of such processes".

A.O. Hirschman, Foreword to J. Tendler's *Electric Power in Brazil* (1968).

Nicoletta Stame

Introductory note

Judith Tendler (1938-2016) was a development economist who, as consultant for international development agencies, combined in an original way scholarship in the social sciences and professional work. From field observation she was able to extract theoretical concepts that she used in her fruitful and extraordinary "teaching cum research", especially with graduate students at MIT. Since her Ph.D. dissertation, conducted under the supervision of Albert Hirschman, she worked out her unconventional way of looking at reality: she suggested to "look at any successes with a sense of awe (…) explaining what is happening against a background of what is predictable and what is a surprise"

Judith left an enormous body of work that is still little known. Apart from three books (*Electric Power in Brazil*, *Inside Foreign Aid*, *Good Government in the Tropics*) and a few articles, most of her work is confined to grey literature. Yet, she was proud of it, and on the occasion of her Festschrift, in 2011, she listed 81 papers, organized in chronological order. This material is now available on the website of A Colorni-Hirschman International Institute www.colornihirschman.org.

This material may be studied for different purposes: either for relevant topics (development, specific economic sectors, the public sector, kinds of interventions) or in order to grasp her methodology (comparative analysis, what she called "lesson learning evaluation research"). Or more generally to assimilate her way of looking at the world of development: discovering what worked unexpectedly, and trying to provide an explanation for it.

As a first taste of the wealth of insights that Judith's work can offer, we have decided to select some beautiful pages from her professional writings[1]. In contrast to the usually formal and compliant style of similar documents, Judith utilized these occasions to develop what she had understood while working at the project sites themselves. This evidence was used to challenge received ideas and advance new ones, and to show things in a different light than usual; she ruminated on the surprises she had found, always in search of what might work for development and for improving people's lives – with much solicitude for the poor.

Her papers were full of minute observations of particulars, which were given a special role in her theoretical reconstruction, and in her suggestions on how to help future project designs. At the same time, in the abstracts, executive summaries or conclusions of each work she provided sweeping syntheses of the main messages. This collection draws mainly from such summarizing pages.

---

[1]   By re-utilizing a well-known stratagem from Italian culture invented by Gaetano Salvemini – the famous anti-fascist and 'meridionalist' who taught history at Harvard in the thirties of the last century – when he edited *Le più belle pagine di Carlo Cattaneo* – 1922 (1993).

COMMENTS ON EVALUATIONS OF BID-FINANCED RURAL CREDIT PROGRAMS IN SIX COUNTRIES

Judith Tendler
Center for Latin American Studies
University of California, Berkeley

September, 1970
Draft

Programs

in Six Countries   Judith Tendler
                    September, 1970
                    Draft

Evaluation of BID-Financed Rural Credit

I - Introduction

The information gathering and discussion of the country studies seems
to be underlain by a concept of agricultural development that is unrecognized
as such by the analyst because it has become such a habitual way of discussing
development. The implicit presence of this concept seems to obstruct somewhat
the utilization of the rich raw materials that the country projects have
generated. Namely, the development "lens" through which the individual
projects are described and evaluated seems to be that of "prerequisites" and
"balanced growth," with its corollary explanations of "vicious circles" and "low-
level equilibrium traps," which can be broken only by "big pushes" o   one or
all fronts. Through this type of evaluative "lens," agricultural development
cannot occur without the prior existence of the "prerequisites " of agricultural
credit, literacy, transport infrastructure, well-functioning market facilities,
competitive rather than predatory intermediaries, land ownership, clear title
to it, minimum economic-size land units, agricultural extension, etc.

The result of this way of looking a t things is that one has ready-
made explanations of failure and success, of a kind which occur throughout the
country studies. As will be seen in the examples of this text, failure is
"obviously" a result of the lack of one of the well-known prerequisites, or is
an exception to the rule, caused by an unpredictable factor such as natural
disaster. Success, according to this approach, is the obvious result of agricultural credit having been the last of the prerequisites to be put into place. Or
it, also, is an exception to the rule--like the successful ACAR borrower who

achieved what he did "despite" the fact that he was illiterate (Braz, p. 31, pars. 1-3), or the other ACAR beneficiaries who were highly successful "in spite of" the fact that they didn't keep books (p. 33, par. 3). Or success is described as the result of a massive "big push"--like the corn program in Nicaragua (pp. 19-20, par. 1). The massiveness of the push is enough to explain the success, according to this concept of development, and hence further exploration of the elements of the success is not carried out.

The clearest outcropping of the "prerequisites" approach appears in the Guatemala study, where the growth potential of rural credit candidates is said to be a function of "size of farm, quality of land, land tenure system, entrepreneurial capacity (education and cultural aspects), location with respect to transport systems (marketing, access to credit, technical assistance, and suppliers of inputs, etc.)..." (pp. 25-26, last par). Yet the farmer who scored well in these attributes, one would think, would not need the assistance of a subsidized rural credit program. Hence this list is a description more of success than of the path that leads to it.

In general, the problem of such an analytic frame of mind behind this kind of evaluation is that one knows, by definition, the answers to why things worked or didn't work before one starts. The evaluation tends, therefore, toward categorization rather than toward a more open-ended and analytic exploration. One tallies up the problems and the achievements, and then places them into their appropriate box: existence of the classic prerequisites, lack of them, big pushes, exogenous circumstances, and exceptions to the rule. It has long been recognized, however, that prerequisites often turn out to be the result rather than the cause of development, that progress on one front often sparks-- rather than being dependent on--progress on another front, that "big push" successes often turn out to be a function of factors unrelated to the push, and that exceptions to the rule often, upon close examination, lead to the discovery of new "rules." In short, because we are still struggling to discover the possible sequences of agricultural development, an agricultural credit evaluation is an occasion to search for such sequences in the rich material that the projects provide.

It might be argued that an agricultural credit evaluation cannot take upon its shoulders the whole burden of agricultural development. But the course of these projects is, willy nilly, being profoundly affected by the forces involved in such development and, just as important, is generating precious information about it. Hence one is, at the least, forced to work into the design of an agricultural credit project what is being learned about these forces of development. After all, it is often suggested that provision be made in assisted rural credit programs for forces that are even more remote than those of development--i.e., it is often suggested that the forces of weather be incorporated into rural credit policy by building crop insurance features into credit programs.

These opening paragraphs are meant less as a critique than as an explanation of the approach that underlies most of the comments that follow. In Section II, I have dwelled on some cases of success and failure. In Section III, I have tried to approach some of the substantive questions raised in the draft outline of the final report. Section IV takes care of some miscellaneous items.

II - Success and Failure

It might be useful to make a reference list of expected problems or failures, those that appear in every textbook on agricultural development, and are familiar to those working in the field: inadequate marketing organization, inordinate price fluctuation, oligopsonistic marketing structures, lack of transport infrastructure, illiteracy, etc. Such traditional-type failures are

reported, for example in the Guatemala paper (p. 21, pars. 1, 3). Because
these problems are so familiar and common, there is perhaps little need to spend
much time on them in explaining the causes of problems in the evaluated projects.
It may be more useful to find out if these problems were recognized at the
time the loan was conceived, if attempts were made to overcome them, and what
happened to the attempts. Most important are the suggestions that the experience
generates as to how these problems can be overcome, or circumvented, the next
time around. Take marketing, for example. In the case of Nicaragua, marketing
was a problem even though a government marketing entity existed (pp. 35-37, #2).
Might it not be helpful, the next project around, to give equal financial and
technical importance in an agricultural credit loan to the marketing institution
in existence? (This credit-marketing "package" approach is also suggested, in
general, in the outline of the final report, p. 7, F.)

In contrast to "unsurprising" failures, considerable attention should be
given to the unexpected cases of failure, where all or most of the prerequisites
were in place. Take the case of the coffee farms subject to the erradication
program in Minas Gerais--and the subsequent decay of the area (Braz, p. 6, par. 1).
Here one had all the prerequisites one would want--one of the richest regions
of the state of Minas, a previously successful agricultural experience with
coffee, and erradication payments high enough to induce people to pull out
their trees. If a smooth switch to another crop had been made, and the area
had continued to flourish, then this would have been hardly noticed, or
explained as a "natural" success--due to the prerequisites that were already
there. Because the failure is unexpected, then, one wants to know more about
the anatomy of it. Did the region decay as a result of bad luck by the ex-
coffee farmers with new crops? Or did it decay as a result of abandonment?--
i.e., the coffee farmers took their erradication payments and invested them in

commerce and industry? The latter phenomenon might be considered much less

of a problem result than the former.

The same kind of analytic approach should be taken with the success

stories that appear in the country studies. They are important not so much

because they happened, but for what they can tell us about what we are trying

to do--i.e., bring about agricultural development through credit programs. Thes e

successes should be examined minutely to see if cause-and-effect sequences can

be discovered which will help in the better designing of future loans.

One important feature of this success-story kind of information is that

it is often attainable by very informal methods, with little need to resort to

quantitative data that may be difficult to obtain and of dubious value. Most

of the success stories are given straightforward descriptive treatment in the

country studies, with little discussion of, or conjecture about, what brought

them about. In some cases, a success story is not even presented as such--since

the success takes the form of the absence of one of the traditional problems

that usually bog down agricultural credit programs. For example, the marketing

problem is not mentioned in the success story of a massive corn-incentive

program in Nicaragua (pp. 19-20, par. 1) until much later in the paper (pp. 36-37,

par. 3). In the meantime, one wonders how this considerable increase in

corn output (yields were almost doubled) was handled by the existing marketing

system--in that the lack of an adequate or equitable marketing system, or the

clogging of it caused by significant increases in output, are the most commonly

cited problems of agricultural credit programs.. If the marketing system had

given no problems, then that in itself would have been a success story. It is im-

portant in such cases to find out why, since this will help provide an under-

standing of how to decrease the probability that there will be no problems

in this area in future projects. I want to go over briefly some cases of success that I foundnin the country studies, listing the questions or possible explanations that came to mind. Most of the success stories, are my questions about them, are discussed in the more extensive topic-oriented Section III.

A. In the conclusion of the Panama paper, it is said that one of the most "positive and interesting" aspects of the IFE credit program is the mobilization of local resources at the public sector level--and at the private level, in the form of the savings and labor of the beneficiaries (p. 18, #5). I didn't see this mentioned in the text, and would normally assume that it refers to an extra financial and physical effort made by the farmer-borrowers in the use of their additional credit funds. But since this would be the result of any credit program, I thought the sentence might refer to a result peculiar to this specific program. If this was the case, what form did this effort take?

Also, what was the extent of, and what explains the considerable independent financial support of the program by the government--in view of the fact that governments usually don't tend to devote much financial attention to agriculture, and that this tendency is sometimes reinforced when it is known that foreign aid institutions will finance agricultural programs. Did the national financial support of the program represent a significant marginal increment in the public expenditure usually devoted to agriculture? Or was this support taken from other areas in agriculture where it was usually spent?

B. The Guatemala study points out that the BID-financed program with SCICAS had little significant global impact. But where SCICAS combined forces with INTA, the colonization entity, and the Ministry of Agriculture--such as in the corn-promotion program, significant increases in production were achieved (p. 24, #3).

13

Why the difference in the BID-SCICAS and the SCICAS-INTA-MAG programs? Was it anything to do with the crop involved? The amounts of money spent? The types of farmer worked with? The marketing structure? Did the results of the corn-promotion program "stick" after the massive efforts receded? Were any positive changes caused by the program in marketing facilities, the intermediary system, in marketing margins, in price fluctuations, in demand and supply of public services such as health and educaton. Who were the farmers who responded to the corn incentives? Were they already planting corn, and just planted more? O r did they switch from something else? Was the major part of their living derived from corn as a result of the program? Did one noticedany corresponding changes in their standard of living, aspirations, or attitudes toward education, health and technology in general--as a result of their successful experience with corn? On the institutional level, how is it that three government agencies worked so well together, when the contrary is usually the case? What was the mechanism of that cooperation, and what were the incentives that kept it going? Why was a completely local effort more successful than the foreign-financed effort?

C. In the annex on cooperatives, the Guatemala study refers to some of the cooperatives financed by BID-SCICAS in the department of El Progresso. One cooperative succeeded in stabilizing the price of yuca flour, another in strengthening theprices of fruits and vegetables. Some borrowers were converting from corn to fruits and vegetables and tobacco (p. 1 of annex, pars. 1, 3, 6). The report also says that many of the borrowers "have not legalized their occupation of the land, mainly because they haven't been very interested in doing so," that there is considerable population pressure on the land, which is not of as good quality as that of the altiplano, that there is considerable illiteracy, and that the land parcels are quite small (5-10 manzanas) for properties that are without irrigation (pp. 1-2 of annex, pars. 5, 7, 8).

One wants to know first the anatomy of the two cooperative successes cited, particularly in view of the fact that progress was made in the absence of secure land title, literacy, and adequate-size properties--all of which are usually considered basic requisites of agricultural development for the peasant farmer, and whose absence is often cited as the reason when an agricultural credit program has problems.

D. The Paraguay study gives a rather bleak description of the fortunes of the BNF program with IBR colonists. Parenthetical mention is made of an exception to this problem picture--the successful tobacoo farmers of the Pastoreo colony-- but no further mention or analysis is made (p. 20, par. 1). One wants to know the elements of this success, and how it happened midst a general pattern of failure. Did it have anything to do with the crop involved?

E. The Nicaragua study mentions briefly, as one of the positive aspects of the program, the fact that there was a 120% increase in the storage of the produce of the assisted farmers, and that this implies a certain strengthening of the peasants' bargaining power in the market, given the fact that their credit position made it possible for them to hold out longer than they normally could
(p. 26, par. 2).** One wants to know more about this--since marketing usually turns out to be such a problem, and since peasants are considered to be generally victimized by the marketing interemediary. Was the more than doubling of storage accomplished by using existing facilities with excess capacity? Or were new

---

**Doesn't this conflict with the report, cited above, on the miserable failure of the marketing entity (p. 36, pars. 2, 3)?

facilities built? If the latter is so, were these facilities built in conjunction with the credit program, in anticipation of the need to store produce in order to make good on the returns of the credit program? Or were they built independently? If the former is true, how was the provision of the new storage facilities handled, both institutionally and financially? Was there any organization among the peasants--such as cooperatives--which aided the storage procedure? If not, might this experience teach something about how to overcome the marketing problem without resorting to cooperatives, when the conditions for successful cooperative organization do not exist?

In drawing up amortization schedules for the rural credit program, did the lending institution allow time for withholding the produce from the market immediately after the harvest, instead of requiring that amortization payments begin immediately? This question is important, in that the other studies almost uniformly express concern about the post-harvest amortization requirement that puts the farmer at the mercy of post-harvest prices, and allows him no time to hold out for better prices. (See further discussion of this in section on "Delinquency" below.)

F. The conclusions of the Nicaragua study refer to the fact that the rural credit program had quite an impact through significant increases in the production of basic grains during the period of the program--an increase that was even more impressive, given the less-than-proportional weight (in relation to share of grain production) of the peasant sector in the ownership of land and water (p. 46, #3). This type of accomplishment, the paper says, was a primary concern of the government, upon initiating the program.

I don't recall that this particular aim of the program was mentioned in the text, nor the successful result. The case is important for several reasons. It may show that when government credit institutions are concerned with obtaining increases in output on a national level--in contrast to concern with improvements

in the productivity and conditions of a group of small farmers--the final
result may be a much greater increase in the welfare of the small farmer
than would result from a program based specifically on welfare concerns. This
might tend to happen because the government's own finances and performance are
at stake when it is concerned about deficient levels of total production and
resulting importations of foodstuffs, with corresponding drains on the balance of
payments. Hence it may throw much more of its power and resources behind the
attempt to make such a program succeed. The equity-oriented small farmer program,
in contrast, may be undertaken or supported by a government for a variety of
other reasons--paternalism, moral pressure, pockets of rural discontent, a desire
to be modern, interest by foreign lending agencies--motivations which are
likely to be accompanied by much less financial and political power than that
associated with a government's concern for its country's food-producing defi-
ciencies and the consequent balance-of-payments problems.

As a corollary to the above, it may be that small farmer programs spurred
by a primary concern about output increases have significant external "social"
economies when the peasant sector accounts for a major part of the production
of the crop in question for the local market. This seems to have been the
case in the Nicaragua report, where the peasant sector had a much greater-than-
proportional share--in relation to its possession of land and water--in the
production of grains. Specifically, the importance of the peasant sector's
production--and credit-financed production increases--in the share of global production may increase, beyond a threshhold point, the attractiveness and perceived
feasibility and economic rationality, to the peasants, of organizing. This would
be a function of the potential economic power resulting from the large amount
of production involved, its significant impact in the marketing system, on
price levels, and on consumer welfare. The peasant groupings made feasible
through this mechanism--whether formal or informal--might serve the purposes of

increasing bargaining power in buying and selling, or in demanding more of a
share of the sponsoring government's public services and public investment
capital. The government, in turn, is more likely to consider a peasant group
that is producing a large portion of one of the country's basic foods as a
force to be contended with. The peasant sector, to complete the circle, is
aware of this, and hence its expectations of achieving its organized demands
would be correspondingly greater. The peasant's perception of his potential
bargaining power, in short, is an important variable in determining his willingness
to form and participate in groups such as cooperatives. The success or failure
of cooperative efforts, which is touched upon at various points in the country
studies, may thus be related to a factor which has nothing to do with the
members' administrative ability, the presence of a cooperating spirit, literacy,
etc.

While all this may seem a quite obvious association of social welfare
with economic power, this line of reasoning has quite specific implications for
rural credit programs. That is, many programs, including those evaluated in
the country reports, have attempted to get small farmers to diversify their
production, to switch from traditional crops to commercial export crops, or to
try new crops for which local conditions seem propitious but which, at the
moment, are imported. Many of these hoped-for switches--no matter how valid from
a pure efficiency point of view--may involve the entry of the peasant sector
into a much larger "pond" of production. That is, they would involve a
diminution of one of the peasant sector's few sources of potential power--the
share of his production of a particular crop in the country total. Switching
to tried-and-true commercial export crops may mean merging his share of production
with that of the large, established commercial producers. This might not only
reduce the potential political and economic value of his high share of total
production of a traditional crop; but it would also merge him into a group of

farmers much more politically powerful than he, and with demands upon the public sector and political interests directly contrary to the interest of his, the peasants', sector. A similar result might occur from encouraging the peasant to switch from a high-proportion traditional crop to an import-substituting crop. This also could represent a diminution in the peasant sector's economic power, since his production can always be supplemented or replaced by imports. Finally, diversification out of crops in which peasant production accounts for a high proportion of total consumption can also mean a diminution in the peasant sector's potential group power, given the decrease in the share of total production of the traditional crop. To put the argument conversely, and in a more positive way: when the peasant sector produces a high percentage of a certain widely consumed crop, this could be considered as the foundation for a certain type of development, involving the building up of organizational and bargaining power based on the economic significance of his production. His situation would be improved via a socio-political route--rather than by an economic route (e.g., diversification) which might be much more difficult, since it would not have, and indeed would destroy, an already existing foundation for development.

Because of the considerations outlined above, it would be useful, if possible, to get some estimate of the share of peasant sector production in the total domestic consumption of various crops in countries with BID-financed rural credit programs. This should be a particularly important variable to watch, in trying to explain the successes and failures of cooperative efforts in these programs.

In general, one would like to know if such a significant increase in the output of the peasant sector brought about any changes in the conditions of that sector--with respect to marketing structure, organizational efforts, land tenancy, water rights, literacy, etc. If the increase was accomplished without any such accompanying socio-economic change, then this might constitute evidence against the suggestions I have made regarding the efficacy of output-increasing programs vs. small-farmer-oriented programs.

G. The Brazil study describes the success story of an "exceptional" ACAR beneficiary in the municipio of Betím, who "can neither read nor write" (p. 31, par. 2). Similarly, the Guatemala paper described a cooperative success story in a region with a high degree of illiteracy (p. 2 of annex, par. 1). The Brazil paper refers to the same municipio of Betím, in which "only six ACAR borrowers keep books," and in which "the majority have no more than two years of primary education...despite (italics mine) the high degree of commercialization of the agricultural activity of the zone and the influence of the city (Belo Horizonte)" (p. 31, par. 1). Further reference is made to the fact that few borrowers of ACAR keep books, even though the agency distributed simple accounting pamphlets to its beneficiaries. There is no empirical data, the paragraph continues, which can assist cattlemen in choosing "the optimal combination of feed grains that would maximize their profits." A following paragraph reports that an indirect measure of the income level of the region can be taken from the fact that eighty to ninety percent of the beneficiaries submitted income tax returns in 1969, such submission being obligatory for annual incomes above US$1,000 (p. 33, par. 4).

It seems that these cases of success without literacy or bookkeeping are treated as exceptions, rather than as unsurprising outcomes. That they crop up so frequently--note the number of times they appear in the country reports--leads one to believe that literacry, and the attendant bookkeeping, may not be as much a prerequisite for, or a feature of, small-farmer development as is assumed. Again, the interest in literacy, and the pursuit of it, may more often be a result, rather than the cause, of the kinds of development successes described here. If a small farmer credit program brings about limited success to a beneficiary, and in the process a demand for literacy is generated--if not for the farmer himself, then for his children--then that is a major indirect benefit of the program. It provides knowledge, as well, about sequences of development that are different from what is normally expected. In order to learn more about these sequences and possible causal relationships, it would be useful to build into future loans a feedback on the educational aspirations and activities of the success beneficiaries vs. the failure beneficiaries. Moreover, if illiteracy were to be accepted as a constant in an agricultural credit program, rather than as a target for change, then this recognition might eliminate unnecessary, and therfore costly, attempts to help beneficiaries put their business down on paper (e.g., the fruitless attempts of ACAR mentioned above). Such recognition might lead to the redesigning of rural credit programs so that they would be more accessible to, and operatable by, the illiterate beneficiary.

H. The Brazil study describes how as soon as the Caixá Econômica started to lend to fruit and vegetable growers through the ACAR program, this provoked the interest of other banks, who also started to lend to the ACAR beneficiaries. The result of this large supply of credit, the study says, was that Belo Horizonte and the area surrounding it no longer have to import fruits and vegetables from outside the state, whereas almost all such produce was previously imported from the state of São Paulo. The study also notes that many of the horticulturists moved upward in social class (p. 24, par. 1)p. 57, #7).

One wants to know more about this success. Were the horticulturists growing these products before the ACAR program? Why were they selected as ACAR beneficiaries? Because of an already demonstrated entrepreneurial potential? Or because the ACAR technicians felt that horticulture would be a good thing to introduce into the region, given the obvious comparative advantage of close location for this type of produce? DID ACAR try to prmmote the use of improved inputs, or fixed investment? Or were they interested in financing more

of the same--i.e., increasing the amount of existing production through the

cultivation of new lands, rather than through the use of new techniques?

Was the horticulture output increase spurred by a "boom" atmosphere, which

might explain why the private banks came in so quickly on the heels of the initial

ACAR efforts? There seems to be some evidence of this, to the extent that the

horticulturists, the paper says later on, are switching to other, mechanized

crops, because of the "increased minimum wage," which has made less economic

the labor-intensive horticulture crops (pp. 30-31, par. 4). It is a little diffi-

cult to accept the minimum-wage-increase as the reason for this switch to mechani-

zation, since various studies of the real wage question in Brazil indicate that,

at best, real wages have remained the same since 1964, and, more likely, have

declined.** Indeed, the horticulture boom seems to have taken place precisely

at the time when real wages were rising in Brazil, between 1959 and 1965.***

This paradox might be explained by the fact that minimum wages only started to

be enforced in this region during the period in question. But the study itself

states that this was a region where the minimum wage is already strictly observed,

and where farm-labor unions function well (p. 30, last par). All this leads one

to believe that the minimum-wage explanation of the switch out of horticulture

to mechanized crops is not valid. It also supports the impression that the

original increase in horticulture production may have been part of a boom,

**For example, Peter Gregory, "Evolution of Industrial Wages and Wage Policy in
Brazil, 1959-1967," unpublished ms. for USAID, Sept. 1968. Gregory's data
is limited to industrial wages in Rio and São Paulo, but it is virtually
impossible to get adequate data on wages outside this sector and area.

***It is not clear to me from the paper just exactly when the boom took place.

22

latched on to, and reinforced by the commercial credit institutions of the region. The switch to mechanization and other crops, then, might be explained in terms of the fact that the original horticulture was not carried out in an economically (or socially) viable way, and as soon as the boom mentality petered out, growers switched to more economic pursuits.

This suggested explanation, of course, does not deny any value to the complete growth sequence. For it seems that the impulse of the boom, if that was the case, was strong enough--and the growers capable enough--so that when the bubble busted, they were financially and entrepreneurially capable of switching to another activity--an activity which involved, furthermore, a higher percentage of fixed and semi-fixed cost, and therefore credit. Hence I would tend to point out the commendable aspects of this switch--in terms of successful development sequences--in addition to the treatment in the text, where the switch is considered in terms of its negative aspects--i.e., an abandonment of the original horticulture, a slowing down of the horticulture growth rate before production supplied completely the Belo Horizonte market, and ensuing unemployment problems (p. 30,31, last par). Actually, the boom-like quality of this story, and the financial and entrepreneurial agility of the growers in switching from one production technique to another, leads one to believe that these growers may have initially been advanced enough to have access to the commercial credit system without the benefit of ACAR--a feature often characteristic of ACAR beneficiaries, as reported throughout the Brazil study (e.g., p. 56, #6).**

**One cannot help but be reminded of the contrasting case in the same study of the region subject to coffee erradication, which subsequently fell into decay (pp. 5-6, par. 3). It is necessary to know more about the antecedents of these two opposite results in order to understand why they could occur.

Another reason for analyzing the desirable "horning in" by commercial banks on an ACAR-sponsored program is for what it can·tell us about the mobilization of private domestic resources for agricultural development, let alone for small-farmer-oriented agricultural development. (I assume that the private banks financed these horticulture operations out of their own resources, rather than from a foreign or state-supplied line of credit.) In general, in both the country studies and the outline of the final report, the subject of domestic resource availability for agricultural credit seems to be missing--treated as if it were a constant rather than a variable. Resources seem to be assumed very scarce, attention is therefore concentrated on the most efficient manner in which to spend them, preoccupation is expressed over the cases where it seems they have not been spent well.

The only attention paid to domestic credit resources as a variable appears in the Brazil study, and focuses on the legally lower interest rate for agricultural credit, which acts as a disincentive away from directing commercial credit toward agriculture (see "Interest Rate" Section below). But the interest rate question is a problem in itself. It frequently takes on the knowledge-impeding quality of a "prerequisite:" one can't even start to think about domestic resource mobilization for agriculture, according to this approach, until one starts to pay a decent interest rate. Yet the Brazil study itself cites two cases where commercial banks participated in programs with subsidized interest rates--the horticulture case at hand, and the general phenomenon of private banks entering into working agreements with ACAR(p. 20, par. 1).

It is important to understand these cases thoroughly, precisely because they seem to demonstrate--in their superficial form--that the subsidized, or negative real interest rate is not always a barrier to commercial credit mobilization for agriculture. Why wasn't it a barrier in these cases? Can the experience gained here be applied in other cases, where it may be easier to recreate conditions similar to those surrounding the ACAR experience, than to make any headway in the interest rate problem?

In sum, the commercial banks' interest in the ACAR horticulture program and in other ACAR programs is important to understand because (1) it can tell us something about domestic resource mobilization for agriculture in the private sector and through the market mechanism, and (2) it may show that the interest rate problem is not as significant in determining the supply of credit to the agricultural sector as is usually thought.[**] Conversely, there may be mechanisms other than the interest rate--or better, in addition to it--through which commercial banks become interested in agricultural credt, which may neutralize the barrier-creating problems of unreasonably low interest rates in the mobilization of domestic credit for the agricultural sector.

[**] For example, Dale W. Adams, "Agricultural Credit in Latin America: External Funding Policy," Studies in Agricultural Capital and Technology, Occasional Paper No. 9, The Ohio State University, April 1970.

25

THE TROUBLE WITH GOALS OF SMALL FARMER CREDIT PROGRAMS

(AND HOW TO GET OUT OF IT)

Judith Tendler

Center for Advanced Study in the Behavioral Sciences

Stanford, California

September 1973

For Office of Program and Policy Coordination of the Agency for
International Development, Spring Review of Small Farmer Credit Programs

In reading the Spring Review evaluations, one is
impressed with the number of important achievements
which receive little attention. Because these items
have not caught the fancy of the evaluator, they are
not presented in enough detail to give an idea of
what brought them about. It is not that resoundingly
successful programs are being described as failures.
Rather, the decisionmaker, implementer or evaluator
seems to be watching his program through a lens of
traditional evaluating criteria which tend to block
the perception of significant developments. This precludes any questioning about how these developments
came about, and how the lessons they teach might be
fed back into the program. Hence the small farmer
credit program that is a mixed outcome of success and
failure--as most such programs are--is often deprived
of positive feedback about its own, sometimes unexpected, outputs. In this paper, then, I want to
(1) show how it is that objectives have come to cause
such problems of perception, and (2) point to some
of the unnoted lessons that seem to be emerging from
the small farmer credit experience.

I - Goals and Their Problems

The objectives or goals of small farmer credit programs (SFCPs), and the concerns about their performance, seem to fall into three broad categories. One
has to do with the economic efficiency of the activities financed by credit, a second with the ability of
the program to serve a hitherto neglected portion of
the rural population, and the third with the viability
of the institution through which SFCP funds are administered. The three can be referred to as the pursuit
of efficiency, equity, and institutional viability.
They are basic to almost all small farmer credit pro-
grams--explicitly, or implicit in the position taken
on certain issues, as discussed below.

Confronting Goal Conflicts

Most of the issues around which the evaluation of SFCPs
has revolved--default, interest rate, supervision,
profitability, lending criteria, technology, etc.--do
not belong exclusively in any one of the above three
categories. Indeed, different policy positions with

respect to any particular issue were expressed frequently in the Spring Review workshops, depending on the goal context from which a person was speaking. Substantial default rates, for example, were considered highly undesirable, and to be avoided at all costs, when one was concerned about institutional viability. At the same time, however, persons felt strongly about taking a soft stand on default, when speaking out of an equity concern for accomplishing a transfer of income that was considered otherwise difficult.

Similarly, raising of the interest rate on small farm credit from subsidized to market levels can be persuasively argued, when one has the viability of the credit institution in mind. Such a measure also fits within the pursuit of the efficiency goal: a profitable technology should be able, by definition, to withstand a market rate of interest. The interest rate, however, is also very much at the center of equity concerns: subsidized interest rates on small farmer credit, despite the drawbacks, are considered one of the few politically feasible avenues of subsidy in existence.

The issue of lending criteria also elicited varying responses in the workshops, depending on the goal context of the moment. With institutional viability in mind, the credit institution's preoccupation with the borrower's repayment capacity was considered justifiable. The issue takes on a slightly different cast when couched in terms of efficiency goals: if the technology is right, repayment, supposedly, will be no problem. Ability to repay will be a function of the successful application of a profitable technology, and not necessarily of the pre-existing repayment capacity of the borrower. Thus, the repayment capacity problem, according to the efficiency-minded, gets solved if proper attention is paid to profitable technology.

A look at the repayment issue through equity "lenses" brings yet a different response. Lending criteria based on concerns about institutional viability would be seen as resulting in the exclusion of the less-established farmer, thus undermining the basic strategy of such programs. Moreover, the efficiency argument about repayment criteria and profitable technology is looked at as unrealistic: lending institutions, when given the chance, will always select the more established farmer in order to increase the probabilities that their books will look good, thereby insuring their own survival. From the equity point of view, then, institutional behavior will be determinant--profitable technology or no. The problem must be faced head on, from this point of view, by the imposition on the institution of rigorously equity-oriented criteria of lending.

Much of the controversy in the discussion of SFCP lending results from the different answers that these three different goals evoke. Indeed, the disappointing results of many SFCP programs, and their evaluations, may be caused to some extent by the failure to recognize that their underlying goal structure is quite problematic. It is not that the basic goals of efficiency, equity, and institutional viability are mutually exclusive, or highly incompatible. Rather, the pursuit of any one of these goals will often require significant compromise of another, or a reworking of program design so as to cause less damage to the compromised goal. If these goals continue to be put together in SFCPs as an inseparable threesome, then there needs to be some recognition and working out of the problems that result from that combination.

The pairing of the equity and efficiency goals is particularly problematic. The CADU project in Ethiopia provides a classic example of the kind of problem that can result from failure to recognize and accept the difficult challenge of combining two goals (Ethiopia, Holmberg). CADU was one of the few programs which was successful in promoting the adoption of modern inputs and increasing the yields of farmers. At the same time, it was just as much a disaster in that the adoption of modern techniques and resulting increases in outputs led to an increase in the value of land, great interest in increased production by large landholders, and the resulting eviction of smallholders by those who wanted to consolidate their lands, and cash in on the new innovations.

The central importance of this CADU outcome is that the disaster was a direct result of the success. An improvement in terms of efficiency was the direct cause of a loss in equity. It is not that such an outcome is unusual. To the contrary, its very expectedness needs to be made explicit at the time the objectives of such a program are being laid out, so that various decisions can be made: whether there are ways of lessening the equity loss; whether certain losses in equity are a reasonable cost to pay for the projected gains in efficiency; whether there are other equity gains that might counterbalance the direct equity losses; whether there are ways of building into the program an assurance of these gains; and whether the equity-efficiency conflict might be diminished by, for example, altering the chronological sequence of the program design.

The CADU program, like many others, couldn't have asked these questions because it was not recognized that it had set out to achieve potentially conflicting goals-- equity and efficiency. To unite them without considering their incompatibility is to set oneself a terrible trap: one raises the expectation that they are compatible and easily achieved together. This precludes the possibility of working on program designs that seek to minimize their incompatibility. Hence small farmer credit programs frequently end up being damned for having failed on one of the two counts--because, as is rarely noted, it may have been successful on the other.

The evaluation of the agricultural credit scheme of Sri Lanka is another example of this unavoidable damning (Sri Lanka, Gunatilleke). In contrast to CADU, the Sri Lanka program is criticized on efficiency grounds, though it seems to have made notable progress on equity grounds (see p. 12 below). Similarly, the High Yielding Varieties (HYV) programs made their success on efficiency grounds and, like CADU, were criticized for failing on equity grounds (e.g., India, Hendrix, Sen). Given the technology of the HYV--the need for irrigation and the special sensitivity of output to divergence from recommended input proportions--it should have come as no surprise that the benefits of the Green Revolution were found to have been limited mostly to large farmers. Again, the equity-efficiency conflict was a foreseeable one, yet wasn't faced up to at the start.

Another variation on the equity-efficiency bind can be found in the frequent exhortations to the efficiency-oriented credit banks to become more "development promoting"--for example, the Brazilian Bank of the Northeast (Brazil, Meyer), the Caja Agraria in Colombia (Colombia, Tinnermeier), and the Coop Credit Societies in India (India, Abraham). Or, development promoting banks are exhorted to behave in a more efficient way. Again, both objectives had been initially pronounced as if they were perfectly marriageable forms of institutional behavior, thus precluding discussion of whether and how they could be brought to- gether: should the functions of small farmer programs be divided up between efficiency-oriented institutions and development promoting institutions? Are there cases of successful institutions which combined both modes of behavior?

Because of the censure of SFCPs that occurs on either equity or efficiency grounds, one often does not get to find out about the part of a program that was successful. The program or institution, in turn, doesn't get to sense its own strengths, since failure on one count is taken as a generalized failure overshadowing any inter- stitial successes.

An interesting aspect of the equity-efficiency question is that at the same time that development planners are weaving the two warring objectives into the rhetoric of a small farmer program, they often are admitting to themselves and colleagues that they constitute an irrec- oncilable dichotomy. For political reasons, however, the dichotomy can not be brought into the open. One acts publicly, then, as if the two goals belong together, directing institutions to implement them jointly and reprimanding them when they don't. The problem is never aired, as a result, and there is no chance for explora- tion of a middle ground where the two goals might be found to conflict less.

For example, the recent literature on peasants and small farmer credit indicates that equity and efficiency need not be as opposed as everyone privately thought. The small farmer was found to respond to innovations, given the right market signals. Rural savings, as well, were found to materialize more readily than was thought, given such signals. The major defaulters in many credit programs turned out to be the large farmers*--a remark- able reverse in the equity-vs-efficiency picture of the small farmer as poor defaulter and "welfare recipient." Default, in these cases, turned out to be a function of the possession of economic power, not of the lack of it. Findings like this would tend to tone down the assumed incompatibility of the equity-efficiency goals, or would help program designers to accomplish such a toning down.

---

*E.g., Ethiopia, Holmberg; India, Shah.

How is it that these goals came to be so blithely
paired, with no attention paid to the task of recon-
ciling them? It is not unusual, of course, that in
order to garner as much political support as possible,
public sector programs are couched in objectives that
are difficult to achieve. It may be, however, that
the lack of confrontation of this particular issue has
more to do with the basic political and economic questions that cannot be avoided when one really gropes
with the question. That is, if one feels that equity
and efficiency are quite dichotomous for a small farmer
program, then one may have to entertain the idea of
major diversions from the market mechanism in order to
achieve any gains in equity. Or, pursuit of the efficiency goal could mean that equity proponents will have
to be pacified with claims of a filter-down effect
which, everyone knows, will not satisfy such proponents
and, moreover, will not necessarily take place. Or, if
one accepts the idea of non-market intervention, and
sets a standard minimum coverage of the population compatible with equity considerations, then the cost may
turn out to be much greater than what a country has
shown itself willing to devote to the agricultural population. Or, a small farmer program successful on equity
grounds may signify an unavoidable change in the power
structure of a region. The prospect of such change may
not be tolerated by those with power to approve and fund
the program; witness the fate of the Farm Security Administration in the United States (FHA, Hartman).

It is sometimes easier not to face these issues, and to
think that one can proceed as in the past by relying on
accepted market modes and at the same time aiming oneself in the general direction of the small farmer.
This way one doesn't run up against the supposition that
the existing economic system might not be able to make
inroads into the problem. As one evaluator said, agricultural credit "has the advantage of being relatively
politically neutral" (GURU, Davis). Exposing the equity-
efficiency conflict, however, requires serious consideration of difficult questions such as land reform. This
was the case with CADU in Ethiopia, though recognition
of the problem was accounted for in somewhat superficial
terms: land reform was considered an essential that
would be required at a later stage of the program. When
"later" came, it turned out that the first stage of the
program had, by its very success, helped to mobilize
the opposition to land reform. Had the question been

grappled with more seriously, the program's designers might have predicted that such an outcome was inevitable, and, as a result, might have planned a different sequence for their program.

The difficulties of coping with equity-efficiency issues have been compounded by the policies of international lending institutions. Donor agencies, by requiring both equity and efficiency objectives in small farmer programs, have become like a microcosm of a nation's polity, generating conflicting demands from all sides. It is ironic that the development assistance world should have come to burden the decisionmaking process of developing countries with an intensification of the political problems that arise from trying to meet conflicting demands. Granted, the donor organizations may have their own political constituencies making equity demands from one side and efficiency from the other. But these organizations would better play their role by assisting borrower countries to work out the reconciliation of such demands, instead of encouraging their superficial and problematical pairing.

Goals After the Fact: The Coverage Criterion

Evaluation of SFCPs often contains criticism that amounts to an after-the-fact setting forth of objectives. The major example of such an "implicit objective" is the frequent statement that a certain program reached "only" a certain percent of the population. For example, in El Salvador, it was reported that "only 30-40% of small farmers" adopted hybrid corn (GURU, Davis). In Colombia, the INCORA program covered "only a little over 2%" of small farmers (GURU, Rochac). In Sri Lanka, the credit schemes "reached only 20-25%" of the farming population (Sri Lanka, Gunatilleke). In Brazil, the ACAR program of Minas Gerais covered "only 5%" (Brazil, Meyer).

The implicit objective behind these statements was that the program should have covered substantially more population than the percentages achieved. Such goals, however, are rarely stated as objectives at the beginning of agricultural credit programs--in part, perhaps, because of the above-mentioned avoidance of the equity-efficiency issue and the broad questions

it raises. If these judgments are to be applied retro-
actively, however, then a program should know about
such directives from the start. Granted, it may be
politically difficult to start out a bold new program
saying that one expects to reach, say, "only" 20% of
the farm population. But it is important to have some
kind of understanding about what the resources at hand
can buy.

If it costs several times more to get a fuller coverage
of the farm population--and if that higher sum is completely beyond the realm of possibility--then this conclusion in itself is an important piece of information
about the program to be undertaken. Such a conclusion
might force policymakers and program designers to consider totally different approaches to the problem at
hand; or might encourage the consideration of a separate
and different type of program for the untouched segment
of the population. Or a minority percent of the target
population might be considered adequate as a first step
toward learning about the costs, problems, and successes
of such an approach (as is suggested with reference to
the 2% coverage in one of the Colombia papers, GURU,
Davis).

Similarly, it may be that structural changes are hoped
to be induced by the program in other parts of the
economy: for example, the HYV programs in Pakistan increased the importance of the labor which handled the
new technologies--namely the tractor drivers and the
pump drivers. This led to an increase in the social
importance of the members of these groups; the pump
drivers came to be called "the controllers of the water"
(Bangladesh, Myers). The CADU project in Ethiopia increased the demand for casual labor (Ethiopia, Holmberg).
The credit program in Uganda made economic, from the
demand side of things, the operation of a government-
operated tractor-hire service (Uganda, Frederickson).

The above examples of changes were not, it seems, anticipated or programmed in any way. It is important to
be alert to such developments as they occur, however,
for a little marginal effort by program implementers
could push them further than they might go on their own.
If planners had to consider the percent-effectiveness
question at an earlier stage of the program, they might
build into the program design support for those induced

effects considered desirable. The occurrence of such effects, in turn, might make justifiable a program that couldn't pass muster on percent-effectiveness grounds.

The post-hoc application of a percent-covered criterion tends also to obscure what actually worked and what didn't. After all, the 30-40% coverage achieved in the El Salvador case doesn't really seem like a failure at first glance. Perhaps the failure was actually in the area of not knowing how to change techniques for the remaining 60-70%, after having experienced a whopping success with the first forty. It is important to know whether that first forty was a success or not, how it was accomplished, and what stopped the program from moving on to the rest.

Goal Addiction

The equity-efficiency issue is part of a more general obscuring of certain developments that occurs when programs are measured against their stated goals. Goals sometimes become overly fixed, even if midstream readings indicate that the course might be altered somewhat, or that progress in an unexpected area might be pursued further and traded for lack of progress in a goal-related-area. There is sometimes not enough "displacement of goals," one might say, in contrast to the frequent case where public programs are criticized because of goal displacement--that is, diversion from original objectives toward ends considered less worthy.

The CADU study provides an example of what may be an excess of loyalty to goals. In the early stages of the project, it was decided that cooperatives would be promoted only later on, after the credit and modern input programs were well grounded. This sequence would unburden the first phase of the program from the difficult institutional task of cooperative organization. When CADU finally initiated promotion of coops, however, it found little interest among the beneficiary population. Hence that aspect of the program was considered a failure, something to which more funds and hard work would have to be devoted (Ethiopia, Holmberg, Cohen).

One of the rare cases of a cor_____ive reevaluation
of goals and means in midstream is also found in the
CADU study. The study notes that grazing land was
converted to wheat land by small farmers in the project area, resulting in wheat monoculture. This
development could have been considered a setback in
terms of the project's goal of diversifying agricultural production in the area and developing livestock
production, considered by CADU to be most economically
suited to the region. CADU reported, however, that
it did not view this development unfavorably. The
initial capital requirements for establishing cattle
grazing production units were perhaps unrealistically
high for people coming up from small farmerdom. The
more divisible, less capital-intensive wheat, CADU
reasoned, could be a vehicle by which incomes would
increase to the point where investment in cattle capital was more feasible (Ethiopia, Holmberg).

The move to wheat, then, was not looked at as a step
backward, or away from the cattle goal, but as a move
which would ultimately facilitate the development of
cattle grazing. This perception of possible sequences
of development, and the altering of programs in accordance with new information from the program itself about
such sequences, seems to have occurred rarely, and to
have been hindered by an excessive adherence to initially stated goals.

Another totally different example of change in mid-
stream--with a somewhat different lesson--is the CIBA-
BIMAS contract in Indonesia for aerial application of
pesticides and bulk supply of other inputs (Indonesia,
Hansen). Before the Indonesian government entered into
the contract with CIBA, it was encountering various
problems in an HYV rice program it was sponsoring. The
pesticide aspect of the program in particular had not
been working well; farmers either didn't see the reason
to use them, or didn't use and maintain well their hand
spraying equipment. Other problems related to the in-
stability of input and output prices and faulty delivery
systems for inputs. In response to these problems, the
government entered into a contract with the foreign
firm CIBA for the provision and delivery of seeds and
fertilizers, and for aerial spraying with pesticides.
The contract specified fixed prices for the inputs, and
delivery provisions which were supposed to work much
better than the previous ones. The aerial spraying, of
course, was to solve the pesticide problem in one fell
swoop.

There was tremendous resistance to the CIBA program on the part of the farmers, and the contract was terminated two years after its signing. The farmers had objected to the arbitrary decisions that the technology of aerial spraying imposed on their activities, and also to the nature of the input packet which they had to use: the proportions of fertilizers were rigidly fixed according to an average formula and allowed no variation in accordance with the soil composition of any particular plot. Many peasants also disliked the new seeds. When the government terminated the CIBA contract, the packet program (now including pesticides) was replaced by a more flexible system permitting the peasant to select his input proportions within a maximum and minimum range. In addition, the government had promoted research into the development of a miracle-rice variety more adapted to consumer tastes and the production conditions of the country.

The BIMAS story is remarkable in that it reveals two major policy changes in midstream in response to feedback from the program: the decision to undertake the contract with CIBA and the decision to abandon it. As the story is told in the BIMAS paper, however, it is presented as the story of failure. Hence one obtains only scant information at the end as to the lessons learned and how they were applied in the post-CIBA program. In comparison with other studies of small-farmer programs, however, the BIMAS story stands out as a remarkable case of sequential learning and action.

Goal-Unrelated Achievements

There are many useful pieces of information about agricultural development and program strategies that seem to be lost because they don't directly pertain to the original objectives of the program, or because they don't fit the standard criteria by which such programs are judged (percent effectiveness, default rate, increases in output, etc.), or because failure has occurred with respect to an important objective, and everything else that happened is considered secondary.

The Colombia paper, for example, reports that the credit program probably brought about no significant changes in income or productivity levels "with the possible exception of small potato growers and small farmers in the

37

more heterogeneous farm size areas where the new technology has become available" (Colombia, Tinnermeier). Why potatoes? Did heterogeneity play a role? How precisely did the new technology impact on this development? Is there anything about this exception which sheds light on the reasons for lack of significance in the bulk of the program?

As another example, the Sri Lanka paper emphasizes that the two primary objectives of the cooperative program were not achieved--increased productivity and income, and the relief of indebtedness (Sri Lanka, Gunatilleke). In other places, however, it is reported that the government's agricultural credit schemes "have improved the condition of the farmer in that he is less dependent on middlemen and traders;" and that these schemes have resulted in "the enlargement of the functions of new institutions at the village level, the cooperative society and the Rural Bank." Moreover, "the expansion of the economic activities of these institutions has given them a crucial role in the village economy." The paper laments that the program has caused a "transfer of incomes" and sometimes inflation; yet "all critics are agreed that the agricultural credit scheme cannot be withdrawn because its function of meeting part of the requirements of working capital in the peasant sector is too vital."

These achievements are not of easy accomplishment! Their absence is the frequent plaint of the evaluations of other programs. Yet, because the program is considered in a general context of failure to meet efficiency goals, major gains with respect to both equity and institutional viability don't receive proper attention. They don't get to be considered as an output of the project, to be fed back into it through modifications of existing design.

The CADU paper, as another example, briefly covers some interesting areas of information which merit more thorough treatment. CADU was quite careful about the type of equipment it promoted. It shied away from sophisticated equipment and stuck close to the simple tools to which farmers were already accustomed--mainly, plows and oxcarts. It also embarked upon the production of improved versions of these implements, as well as introducing simple harrows and threshers (Ethiopia, Holmberg). This story stands in marked contrast to the more typical tale of the imported tractors, trucks, and sprayers, which sit unused because of the lack of a spare part, of local maintenance know-how, or of maintenance capacity--as occurred, for example, in the Thai program (Thailand, Gamble).

One wants to know more about CADU's approach in this venture, and what secondary effects in input markets occurred or were anticipated. It would be highly useful to donor organizations, moreover, to know how the decision to proceed in this way could have emerged unscathed in a program sponsored by a developed country with a sophisticated equipment-producing industry!

II - Lessons and Designs

In the last section, it was seen that an excess of attention paid to fixed objectives may result in the failure to observe, chronicle, and explain, seemingly isolated instances of success and failure. If such cases aren't likely to get their due, then certainly the probability is even lower that anyone's attention will be caught by the emergence of certain patterns that can explain, in a different way, a group of such isolated instances. In this section, therefore, I would like to suggest some different ways of putting together the isolated cases of success and failure that have surfaced in the Spring Review. Hopefully, the lessons learned in this way would be taken advantage of in future designing and redesigning of SFCPs.

Technological Compulsion

It is difficult to capture the considerations in this section in one word, or to separate them neatly from each other. As the examples below will indicate, they have to do with the way in which the characteristics of a certain crop influence the structure of production and marketing which, in turn, bears on the possibilities for successful small farmer development. Another explanatory factor, sometimes related to the factors discussed in this section, is the market power that certain arrangements or policies bestow on previously powerless individuals or institutions.

Rather than find a word that describes what these various factors are, it is easier to describe what they do.

39

I would call their action "technological compulsion."
"Technology" conveys their material or physical nature--
as opposed to economic, institutional, or policymaking
impacts. "Compulsion" indicates that they are now determining certain outcomes of SFCPs, rather than being
determined by them, or leading a neutral existence. The
fortuitous nature of their determining influence could
be reduced considerably if the■ compelling power of
these factors were recognized and harnessed in service of
outcomes that they are now bringing about, willy-nilly.

Input Technology. We return again to the story of BIMAS
in Indonesia, and the aborted attempt to use aerial
spraying on many production units (pp. 10-11 above). Some
of the reasons for this failure are made clearer by comparing the technology of aerial spraying with that of
another agricultural input, irrigation. Likewise, the
comparison also serves to teach something about the role
that irrigation can play in the determination of SFCP
success, as illustrated by the case of Comilla in Bangladesh.

One of the factors that undermined the attempt to introduce aerial spraying in Indonesia was the existence of an
alternative way of spraying, which didn't involve the
coercion that spraying did. Even though hand spraying
hadn't worked well, the existence of this alternative
made it possible for the peasants to feel that they were
being treated arbitrarily. In irrigation agriculture,
however, there is little alternative to some sort of
organization of water supply as a way of obtaining water.
The choice is not between efficient, coercive irrigation
and less efficient, more individualistic acquisition of
water--but between irrigation or no water at all. Of
course, varying degrees of organization of water supply
are possible--from pumps and tubewells to large-scale
projects. But the alternative of cheap individual provision and voluntary participation does not exist in the
same way that it does in aerial spraying.

A government that is sponsoring irrigation agriculture is
not as vulnerable to accusations of coercion as is a government promoting aerial spraying, since in irrigation
there is often no other way. The technology of aerial
spraying, in other words, turned out to be too "permissive," given the government's desire to maintain individual farm units and given the power of the peasant to

resist. Aerial spraying might have been looked upon more benignly if, as in irrigation, it meant the coming of a technology that couldn't be applied in any other way.

In contrast to BIMAS in Indonesia, the integrated rural development program at Comilla, in Bangladesh, must have had the technology of one of its main inputs on its side--namely, the "compulsion" of irrigation agriculture. Many of the Comilla project's cooperative associations were organized around the acquisition and operation of a tube-well or hydraulic irrigation pump. Each pump or well would support from 30 to 50 family farms. The availability of the wells at the time when Comilla was organizing, and the subsidization of their acquisition cost by the government, was a powerful organizing incentive for families with contiguous farms. Since it was technologically and economically more efficient for all contiguous farms in a prescribed area to participate, moreover, there was considerable social pressure exerted on individuals who refused to join, or who, once having joined, refused to contribute their share toward maintenance expenses. The technology of the input, in short, mobilized social and political forces pressing for participation.

Once these small groups were organized around the acquisition and operation of an irrigation pump, other things started to happen. The technology of water distribution allowed easy diversion by more zealous users, or non-members. Technology, then, did not help settle these particular questions arbitrarily; to the contrary, it opened them up, and hence required the formation of some type of institution that could arbitrate. As a result, small councils were formed by each association, which met periodically to adjudicate such disputes. The councils eventually got into other matters of adjudication, unrelated to the dividing of the waters. The cooperative associations, as well, took on a range of activities and functions unrelated to irrigation--mainly, the channeling to their members of agricultural credit. Though the availability of credit was probably an important incentive for organizing into groups, it certainly could not have had the compelling influence and the specific organizational results that the availability of pumps and tubewells had.

In the Comilla case, then, the technology of irrigation agriculture had forced a form of organization and self-government. This type of irrigation, that is, required

41

a group which was large enough to achieve the benefits
of size (qualification for agricultural credit and inputs at favorable prices), small enough to facilitate
group organization and action, and spatially close
enough for familiarity and social pressure to ease the
difficulty of enforcing compliance with group action.
Familiarity and social pressure, moreover, would also
play the important role of helping the agricultural
credit institution to determine creditworthiness efficiently, and to bring about repayment.

The tubewell experience can be seen as a variation on
the theories of Karl Wittvogel, who first brought to
light the "technological compulsion" of irrigation
agriculture in his researches on large-scale hydraulic
projects in Ancient China. Whereas Wittvogel emphasized the centralized despotic control permitted by
large-scale irrigation works, Comilla illustrates the
contrasting results from the use of irrigation technology on a smaller scale. Pumps and tubewells, that is,
contributed to a political development that was more
decentralized and pluralistic, in contrast to the large-
scale control facilitated by large-scale irrigation.

A recurrent theme of the Spring Review was the problem
of achieving small farmer participation in group formation. The Comilla experience has shown that irrigation,
by forcing this issue somewhat, provides a setting in
which such group formation is more likely to be achieved.
Indeed, the efforts of the Bangladesh government to
replicate its successful Comilla project throughout the
country may fall short in cases where pump or tubewell
irrigation is not a feature of the program. It is possible that no substitute will be found for the compul-
sory role that was played by irrigation technology in
the formation of the Comilla cooperatives.

Usually, irrigation is considered a costly way to bring
agricultural development to a region. The technological determinism described above, however, is a significant compensating benefit for any irrigation program
involving small farmers. Conversely, alternative approaches to small farmer development have their own high
costs--namely, the difficulty of bringing about the
group action often necessary for program success. Any
consideration of irrigation should include these particular costs of the no-irrigation alternative--or the
benefits inherent in the coercive element of the technology.

The Geography of Supplier and Consumer. The marketing problem seems to be one of the most difficult ones facing small farmer credit programs. It has become a kind of catch-all explanation of failure. The marketing system is said to be incapable of distributing a large increase in production caused by a successful credit program, the power of the marketing intermediary is said to eat away at any new profits the small farmer might attain, and the marketing system is said to force the farmer to sell when prices are low, instead of providing him with the power, in the form of storage facilities, to withhold his supply until prices improve.

Perhaps the marketing system has become a convenient scapegoat for SFCP failure, since it represents a different stage of the production process not taken on directly by the small farmer program. If an agricultural production program fails, it is often blamed on the market; but if the program succeeds, one doesn't hear about how the marketing system facilitated this success. In a sense, the marketing system gets the worst of both worlds: it gets credit for the failure of a program directed at the previous stage of production, and doesn't get any credit for such a program when it succeeds. Whatever the reason for the marketing pessimism that pervades most evaluations of small farmer development, it certainly seems to have prevented the analysis of marketing situations that, despite their imperfections, worked reasonably well.

It is in marketing that some of the technological factors related to crop seem to play an important role. One of the Spring Review studies, for example, mentions a highly successful program of development of commercial dairy enterprises in parts of dryland India (Gujarat). The program concentrated first on the development of market outlets and collection facilities for milk, and only later focused on the means of increasing production (GURU, Hendrix). Commercial dairy operations in general seem to be one of the few areas where agricultural cooperatives have been successful. This leads one to believe that there may be something characteristic of milk production that explains this success. It may be that the "compulsion" that this product exerts on its producers to gather together at a central point to deposit the raw product, and to do so before the product perishes, explains in some way the greater success rate of dairy-promotion efforts. If this is the case, one ought to look at other agricultural products with this "coercive potential" in mind.

The study of cooperatives, and their varying degrees of success and failure, is in particular need of such an approach. Such ventures are usually explained in terms of the absence or presence of effective cooperative leadership and of the proper kind of cooperative organization.* But it may be that the product itself is sometimes determining the degree of success or failure, despite the absence or presence of the right kind of organization and leadership.

Another example of the way a product's "geography" determines institutional success or failure is that of coffee in Costa Rica. One of the constant criticisms of small farmer credit programs is that the traditional credit institution's mode of operations makes it too risky to lend to the small farmer. It is too centralized and bureaucratized to be familiar with a myriad of small farmers and their creditworthiness. Likewise, it doesn't hold the local power over its client that the local moneylender does. Hence the small farmer and the credit institution end up avoiding each other mutually--the small farmer because of the geographic and cultural distance between him and that institution, and the institution because of the risks that this distance requires it to take.

In Costa Rica, the characteristics of highland coffee production have compensated somewhat for this problem of distance between traditional institution and small farmer. The country's coffee quota is allocated among its 127 processors, rather than among producers or exporters. Central Bank credit for purchase of this coffee is likewise distributed among the processors, who advance it, in turn, to their grower-suppliers, many of whom are small farmers. Although this system creates some monopsony power on the part of the processor over his small-farm supplier, it nevertheless decentralizes the banking function in an efficient way. Credit is dispensed throughout the coffee-producing area in 127 branch-bank-like channels. The lender-borrower relation is less distant and formal, and the lender-processor, by nature of his business, is well acquainted with

---

*Tom Carroll's analytical paper is a notable exception.

the creditworthiness of the small growers in his region.
Moreover, the small farmers do not necessarily limit
themselves to coffee. Their secure credit arrangement
in coffee allows them to engage in other cropping activi-
ities where credit arrangements are not as easy.

Hence the Costa Rican coffee processors' position in the
production process, and in the countryside, suits them
well for being credit intermediaries between the banking
system and the small farmer. Indeed, the guaranteed
access to credit and marketing that this system provides
to the smaller coffee farmer has probably played a role
in bringing about the greater equality of land and income distribution in Costa Rica, as compared to other
Central and South American countries. (Also important,
of course, is the suitability of coffee and the Costa
Rican terrain to small- and medium-size production units.)*

Two other considerations of a "spatial" nature, and bearing on the credit and marketing issue, emerged in the
Spring Review workshops. It was pointed out in Nairobi
that for one particular region of the country, marketing had not been a problem of the SFCP, because all the
produce of the region was consumed right there. More
generally, this might suggest that credit programs promoting the financing of subsistence crops do not run up
against the marketing problem as much as those that finance cash crops. Because the former product is consumed
in the very region in which it is produced, the demands
made on the marketing system are minimized.

Put in another way, one could say that the demands made
on the marketing system by a region switching from subsistence to cash cropping, as promoted by many SFCPs, are
maximized. One may increase the probability of marketing
failure, then, by promoting the production of the crop
(cash) which, from an economic point of view, makes more
sense. The greater economic benefit of the cash crop
over the subsistence may be outweighed by the higher
probability of failure due to marketing problems. Conversely, the lesser economic desirability of the subsistence crop is counterbalanced by the higher probability
of marketing success.

---

*This description is based on my A.I.D. memorandum "Agri-
cultural Sector Loan for Costa Rica," July 1969.

45

This kind of calculation might be a more realistic way of seeking solutions to the marketing problem, than the often ill-fated attempts to mount integrated production-marketing schemes. Such an approach also counteracts the fatalistic frame of mind with which SFCP evaluators tend to look at the marketing system, for it requires that they identify those situations in which the marketing system is working, or is likely to work, well.

The cash-vs-subsistence argument can go the other way, if one is concerned with the potentials for success of cooperative organization, and is sensitive to the effects of spatial relationships between supplier and consumer. It was pointed out in Nairobi that the only successful cooperative marketing organizations seemed to be those dealing with cash crops for which the final consumer was located at some distance from the producer. This distance, it was suggested, made monopoly of marketing possible. Such monopoly, in turn, was considered basic to the success of a marketing cooperative.* In the case of subsistence crops, that is, the geographical proximity or interspersing of supplier and consumer makes for relatively easy entry into the marketing business and for considerable difficulty in the enforcement of monopoly. With great distances separating supplier and consumer-- and a product that perhaps requires some processing at a central point--monopoly would be relatively easy to enforce, and the attraction of would-be entrepreneurs to marketing would be diminished by higher entry and operating costs. These types of conditions, then, may be at least as important a part of the explanation of successful cooperatives as those relating to cooperative leadership and organization.

Market Power and Economies of Scale

Most justifications or evaluations of SFCP's contain an ode to the powerlessness of the small farmer in the market for inputs and outputs, and an excoriation of those who exert power over him: the moneylender, the impersonal commercial bank, the marketing intermediary, the local merchant. Many of the consequent proposals dealing with this problem focus on reducing the economic power of those who have it, rather than increasing the power

---

*Tom Carroll goes one step further and suggests that existing marketing groups are the best base for any credit cooperative.

of those who don't--e.g., introducing a small farmer
bank as competition to the moneylender, decentralizing
and personalizing the commercial bank, building roads
so as to break the monopoly conferred by local isolation on the marketing intermediary and local merchant.
It may be just as important, and sometimes more realistic, to aim at increasing the economic power of the
small farmer, rather than concentrating solely on measures that take power away from those who have it.

The story of the BIMAS-CIBA contract exemplifies a notable attempt to overcome problems of small farmer powerlessness in the market (pp. 10-11 above). Aerial spraying and other aspects of the BIMAS-CIBA program were
ways of reaching toward technological economies of scale
that were otherwise unattainable if one were to preserve
the small farmer as the unit of production. Moreover,
to substitute the Government of Indonesia for the small
farmer as purchaser of inputs was to attempt to match
the market power of the seller with a buyer whose power
was infinitely greater than that of the small farmer.
The prices resulting from such a transaction, and their
stability, would no doubt be more favorable with such a
balanced matching of buyer and seller power.

It is not clear whether the CIBA contract would have
worked if it had been designed or timed differently, or
if the political situation had been different. Though
this particular try did not work, it was still a profound and novel attempt to reach for technological economies of scale accessible only to the very large farmer
and the collectivized or colonized economy--and to make
them available to the small farmer, without forcing him
into large productive enterprises.

Another powerful and unlikely agent to which one might
hitch the small farmer, as a way of remedying his powerlessness, is the large farmer himself. This is rarely
proposed, of course, since the large farmer usually ends
up gaining even more power in such situations, at the
expense of his smaller colleague. After all, large-farmer
shouldering aside of the smaller farmer in SFCPs was a
constant theme in the Spring Review. There may still be
some ways, however, of exploiting the large farmers for
their market power without, at the same time, being exploited by them. For example, the CADU program strictly
limited its credit to a target population which was below
certain maximum levels of landholding and income. At the
same time, the program allowed large tenants and landowners

47

to buy inputs on a cash-basis-only from CADU (Ethiopia,
Cohen). (Small farmers could buy these inputs on credit.)
Although the paper does not say, it seems plausible that
CADU may have done this to achieve economies of scale in
buying inputs. By bringing the larger farmers into the
picture in a limited way, the program was able to create
external economies--a buying population large enough to
make possible the provision of a certain level of services at certain prices. Since the input-buying program
is not described in this particular light, one does not
find out whether the approach worked well, or whether it
amounted to putting in the lion with the lambs.

Another example of the acquisition of market power through
scale economies in purchasing was given in the Nairobi
Workshop. One participant related how changing economic
conditions in parts of Swaziland had caused the heads of
farm families to seek salaried labor elsewhere, leaving
their wives to tend the farm. Since plowing was an activity not traditionally carried out by women, there
arose a demand for some kind of plowing arrangement that
would replace the work of the men. Since the interested
farms were located in the same area, the rental of such
services became economically feasible, and their supply,
potentially profitable. Tractor-hire service eventually
materialized.

Considered on its own, the migration leading to the emergence of tractor-hire service in this area might have
appeared economically and socially disruptive. But these
developments ended up making it possible for the small
farm community to avail itself of an important and modern
agricultural input.

Similar results were achieved, in a less fortuitous way,
in Uganda. The organization of credit societies in that
country with certain input-purchasing practices made it
attractive for the government-operated tractor-hire service to make itself available to these societies (Uganda,
Frederickson). The tractor service looked more favorably
on requests for service from credit society members because of the guarantee of a larger income owing to less
traveling, larger plots, and certainty of payment. (At
the completion of a plowing job, the credit society would
transfer loan funds directly to the government account,
thus avoiding the necessity of cash collections from individual farmers; each member's loan account with the
society would then be debited with the cost of the plowing job.)

These examples, in a sense, represent the capturing of scale economies that was sought after, and lost, by the Indonesian government in its contract with CIBA for aerial spraying. The importance to small farmer development of the acquisition of such market power is not, of course, a new idea to those in agricultural credit. Rather, it seems that market power is now being conferred on certain groups almost fortuitously, outside the strategies of small farmer programs. Because these situations aren't being recognized for the power they may confer, the possibility of deliberately bringing them about is being lost.

Political Significance

It is rather strange that the Spring Review paid almost no attention to the question of mobilizing resources for small farmer programs. The point of inquiry seemed to have started after the funds were granted, and concern revolved around how the monies were spent and repaid. Yet many issues which did receive the spotlight-- the interest rate, default, lending criteria--gained much of their importance from the fact that they were crucial to the credit institution's supply of funding, and hence to its institutional survival.

It seems that funding out of domestic and foreign public sector resources would get at least equal billing with interest and amortization payments in the discussion of institutional survival. After all, it was never stated or implied that SFCP programs were to sustain themselves, or have significant impact, on a once-for-all injection of government capital. Even if there had been some illusion that interest and amortization payments would take over fully after the first shot of government funds, the SFCP experience to date has certainly shown this to be unrealistic. The question of how a program obtains subsequent doses of funding from an often apathetic sponsoring government, in sum, seems to have been given short shrift. The Spring Review, by concerning itself with interest and amortization questions to the neglect of outside funding, may have been overcome by the same kind of "banker's mentality" for which the small farmer credit institutions were so often criticized. I conclude this paper, therefore, with an emphasis on the question of funding.

Whether or not an agricultural credit program will continue to obtain the public funding that it requires will be very much a function of its political importance to government leaders in the borrowing country. When one runs across the subject of political significance in the Spring Review evaluations, however, it usually takes on a negative light--political meddling, high defaults, "welfarism" (e.g., Sri Lanka, Gunatilleke). At the same time, it is not recognized that some of the shortcomings of programs in other countries may be due to the lack of political importance of the agricultural sector.

The story of the BIMAS program in Indonesia is a good example of the impact that political significance can have. One striking thing about that story, in contrast to the other SFCP evaluations, is that the program was so involving of the peasant population that it could provoke the widespread resistance that it did. One is impressed that this resistance, in turn, could claim the political attention that it did. It is difficult to imagine the president of, say, a Latin American country being impelled by political self-interest to visit the fields and discuss with the peasants their beefs about a credit program--as happened in the Indonesian case.

What happened in Indonesia was a far cry from the quiet projects of many other countries--occupying small corners of their development programs for several years, not achieving much, not provoking resistance, and not changing in response to their failure to achieve. No massive demands are made upon them to change what they are doing, as occurred in the Indonesian case, or to try some things they are not doing.

In general, many of the Asian programs give the impression of stirring things up and having wider and deeper impact than do, say, the programs of Latin America. The latter countries, unlike the former, passed through a long period during which their development hopes were focused on some form of industrialization. Agricultural programs usually came second in such circumstances. Even after the recent shift of policy emphasis from industry to agriculture, the sector never became the focus of profound development aspirations and dramatic rhetoric in the way that industry had been.

In many of the Asian cases, in contrast, one notes immediately the more central position of agriculture in a country's concerns and budgets, the absence of industry as a powerful competitor for development attention, and the political weight of the rural population. Agricultural development policy--even if it has failed or has been ridden with problems--is more a first-class citizen in these countries in comparison to Latin America.

The political importance of SFCPs in the Asian-type situation is not always more advantageous for such programs than the absence of political interest in the Latin American setting. But at the same time, political significance should not always be looked upon as a debit. It can result in greater perceptiveness and responsiveness to problems, as in the Indonesia case, as well as a greater commitment to provide public resources. In this light, the negative results of political significance can be seen as the costs of obtaining a certain type of decisionmaking, and a certain commitment of funds, which are crucial to the success of a small farmer program. Once this aspect is looked at as a cost which yields some benefits, then one can start thinking of ways to minimize the cost, or maximize its potential benefits--instead of turning one's back on it in despair. As soon as it is realized that programs can be damned for not being the object of intense political concern, then one sees the value that can sometimes inhere in political significance.

INTER-COUNTRY EVALUATION OF SMALL FARMER ORGANIZATIONS: HONDURAS

V - What Happens in an Agrarian Reform

Judith Tendler

October 1976

For Office of Development Programs of the Latin America Bureau of A.I.D.

Agrarian Reform as a Development Project

Agrarian reform is a different animal than other kinds of projects that AID supports. When a reform is taking place, and AID wants to lend for it, the reform process should be looked at as the thing being lent to. During a reform, a program to supply an input or the servicing of a particular client will take place only if the reform is properly cared for. The agrarian reform program, moreover, represents much higher stakes for AID than a program of small farmer cooperatives or credit. If the reform works, it will have a much broader impact on small farmers than a successful cooperative or credit program. AID has rarely been able to achieve significant impacts with these latter programs, even when they were successful—as the cases in this and other evaluations show. The stakes are higher for AID in an agrarian reform, then, because of the unique and brief opportunity to have a significant impact on the well being of the small farmer.

All this means that agrarian reform requires a different timing of responses by AID than, say, the kind of institution-building program involved in the BNF small farmer credit program. With a BNF-type program, the institution has considerable time to grow with AID support and assistance. It can even afford the luxury of having serious problems in its first years, because AID is committed to help overcome these problems over a long period of time. By definition, institution-building takes time. Cautious behavior by AID on these occasions is compatible with the task at hand. It does not cause any setbacks.

An agrarian reform project, in contrast, has to achieve highly in its first years, if it is to survive at all. Unlike a small farmer credit program, which has no uphill political battle to fight, it cannot build up its strength in an incremental fashion. It is more like a dam construction project, which has to be finished before the rains come: if not, the rains will make it impossible to work until the next season and will undermine the construction already in place. An agrarian reform, similarly, is vulnerable to the opposition that will mount inevitably if it does not get things in place quickly enough.

The design of AID's involvement with an agrarian reform, then, has to be radically different from that of other projects in more tranquil times. Because a quick and concentrated AID response is important, and because the income redistribution following a successful reform is one of AID's highest priorities at the present time, the Agency should work out a response strategy for any future agrarian reforms that might occur. Such a design should take into account the unique quality of the reform as an assistance project, and its high stakes for AID.

Legislation as precondition or goal? A government committed to an agrarian reform is operating, by definition, in an uncertain political setting. It is the certain and stable political settings, in a sense, that have been associated with the intractability of the rural poverty problem. Instead of seeing a reform process as fraught with riskiness and requiring caution, AID should perhaps reverse its implicit conception of the causality of this situation. AID has the power of making such a government more certain and more stable, that is, by committing itself to the reform. Waiting-and-seeing, in contrast, can in itself lead to enhanced shakiness. Though caution can keep the Agency away from risky investments, it can also keep it away from potentially successful agrarian reforms.

In 1973 and 1974, AID was hesitant to commit so much to a reform that existed on the basis of a temporary decree and a military government of uncertain duration. An immediate AID loan, however, could have been seen as increasing the probability that permanent reform legislation would materialize. Instead, the absence of a permanent law was pointed to by AID officers as a sign of less than full commitment—of an uncertain future. The situation regarding the implementing legislation for the reform law was similar. AID had set up the sector loan so that the loan monies for asentamientos could not start disbursing until issuance of the

implementing legislation defining asentamiento structure and legal
status. This seemed a perfectly reasonable requirement.

In Latin America, implementing legislation is often as
politically significant and controversial as the basic law.
Sometimes it is even more controversial than the law; it can nail
down the situation more tightly than the law itself, which
opponents may have more hopes of evading. The implementing
legislation for the asentamientos was a particularly significant
issue in Honduran politics, since it would define the degree of
control that the government would have over peasant groups. It was
expected to reveal the political cast of the government
according to the amount of state
control that it designated over the groups and their second-level
associations. Hence the implementing legislation was long in
coming—almost a year. During this period, the structure of the
asentamiento and its relation to the government was a hotly
debated issue. Opposition to the reform mounted from peasant
organizations themselves, who feared having to give up control to
the government.

AID did not disburse credit to asentamientos during
this period even after the government came up with the promised
permanent agrarian reform law and with no delay. For AID
had required implementing legislation as a precondition for
disbursement. (This did not affect the other credit lines of
the sector loan to individuals and cooperatives

through the BNF.) AID might have been able, however, to bring about
an event as difficult as the issuance of the implementing legislation
—instead of considering this achievement as a precondition of
lending and as a sign of commitment. It could have designed a
project agreement that did not make loan disbursement contingent
upon a difficult political achievement. AID itself could have
increased the probability of that implementing legislation coming
to light sooner, by arranging to release its credit prior to the
legislation.

With respect to the implementing legislation for
asentamientos, AID has pointed out that it could not lend to groups
without legal title or stature. But the Central Government had
been lending to these groups through the BNF for two years under
such conditions; in lieu of legal title to the land and legal
personality of the group, the Agrarian Institute had guaranteed
the loans. Indeed, even AID 018 funds had been lent to such
groups during 1973. (I do not know how prevalent such cases
were. I found two in my sample of 018 loans.)[1] In Ecuador,
moreover, AID was heavily involved in a program of investment credits
to peasant groups who, like the Honduran asentamientos, did not yet
have legal title.[1a]

AID felt that the delays in issuance of the implementing
legislation, and of the permanent agrarian reform law in 1975, were
signs of an inability of the government to get itself together.

_____
[1]See footnote b to Table 7b, p. 145 of BNF section.
[1a]See PPEA chapter of Ecuador volume.

57

These signs, however, can be interpreted in a different way. The process of achieving consensus within the government on legislation is a highly political and extremely difficult one—even for a military government. The temporary nature of Decree 8, the undefined legal status of the reform groups, and the large amount of government credit immediately committed to them—can be seen as the genius of the reform and not its inadequacy. The half-way quality of these measures allowed the reform to get going without first requiring laws and implementing legislation, the enactment of which would have been much more difficult to pull off.[2]

This stepwise approach allowed the peasants to get a foot in the door. As a result, they became politically stronger. They played an important role in pressuring to keep the pace of expropriation going, and to get the reform law and its implementing legislation issued. Having the peasants identify lands they wanted in "forced rental," moreover, was a way of shifting the burden of identifying expropriable lands from the government to the beneficiary —at a time when it was necessary to settle people fast and the institutional capacity of the government was not up to the task. The reform might never have gotten off the ground, in short, if it had tried to do first things first in terms of legislation.

---

[2] Albert Hirschman describes a similar sequence for the achievement of agrarian reform legislation with respect to the Colombian case. Journeys Toward Progress (New York: The Twentieth Century Fund, 1963), pp. 93-158.

That AID had made the implementing legislation a
precondition of lending to asentamientos contributed in part to a
situation in which the Mission was working with the National
Development Bank, the Ministry of Natural Resources and the
Cooperative Department for a considerable time during which it
was not working with the Agrarian Institute.[3] The latter was the
institution most associated with the reform. This put AID at some
distance from the institutional heart of the reform during the
early implementation period of the sector loan.

Conclusion. AID's relation with the Honduran reform government,
and the design of its sector loan program, were influenced by
apprehension over the risk of investing large amounts on an
unproven reform government and its beneficiary groups. The risk
was indeed there. But I disagree with the implicit assumption

---

[3]The sector loan was authorized in June 1974. The permanent
agrarian reform legislation was issued in January 1975. By August
1975, the implementing legislation had not been issued, and none
of the sector loan funds for credit had started disbursing—for
various reasons, in addition to the one cited in the text. The
Mission was working with the three other agencies because of technical
assistance monies in the sector and previous programs.

that AID's other small farmer projects are less risky. Two years of involvement in agrarian reform certainly gave the Honduran government a track record sufficient enough to warrant a less cautious AID commitment. In Latin America, two years of survival for such a program is a good piece of time.

Looking at the AID decisions to finance other programs in its Honduran history, one finds it difficult to understand why the agrarian reform in particular evoked such caution. AID decided to provide the National Development Bank with $7.9 million in 1969, for example, even though it was fully aware of the fact that the Bank had never made a profit, had a 25% delinquency rate, was against independent audits, had a proven bias toward large borrowers, and was on the record as uninterested in small farmer groups.[4] That was certainly less of a track record for a small farmer credit program, let alone for a bank, than that established by the post-1972 government for agrarian reform. Similarly, FECOAGROH was chosen by AID as the conduit for more than $1 million of credit for small farmer groups and construction of grain storage facilities before it was even created, let alone had a record.[5] The BNF and FECOAGROH decisions, in short, were fraught with considerable risk.

---

[4] See BNF chapter above.

[5] See FECOAGROH chapter above.

I am not saying that AID's decisions to finance the BNF and FECOAGROH were unusual. These kinds of histories are the rule rather than the exception for many foreign assistance projects. I am also not saying that the Honduran agrarian reform government merited full confidence, or exuded certainty and stability. I am saying, rather, that it merited no less confidence than most other programs AID has financed in the agricultural sector. To apply caution to this particular situation was to invoke a decision standard that is almost never used in the Agency's other small farmer programs. There is now enough evaluative evidence on small farmer programs to show that they generally carry substantial risk and uncertainty. Whether it's small farmer credit or an agrarian reform, AID is going out on a limb.

Table 1

Honduras: Comparison of Budgets for National Agrarian Institute (INA)
and Ministry of Natural Resources (MRN), 1966-1974
(dollar thousands)

	Annual budget						
	MRN[a]		INA				
			Internal[b]		Total		
	Value	Annual % change	Value	Annual % change	Value	Annual % change	Ratio of total INA to MRN budget
1968	4,158	--	na	-	1,381	--	0.33
1969	5,670	36.4	na	-	1,873	-35.6	0.33
1970	5,358	5.5	na	-	1,979	5.7	0.37
1971	5,281	1.4	2,216	-	4,691	137.0	0.89
1972	4,514	14.5	2,694	21.6	4,072	-13.1	0.90
1973[c]	6,448	42.8	4,975	84.7	7,129	75.1	1.11
1974	9,516	47.6	3,666	-26.3	6,715	-5.8	0.71

[a]Net of transfers to other government agencies.

[b]The difference between internal resources and total resources is
listed in the data source as "external." This includes foreign
assistance (the IDB was channeling funds through INA) and resources
transferred from other Honduran government sources.

[c]Military coup occurred on November 14, 1972; agrarian reform Decree
No. 8 was issued December 26, 1972. First year of the agrarian
reform is 1973.

Source: Based on data from AID/LA/DR, "Honduras: Agriculture
Sector Program" (21 February 1974), Annex A, p. 5.

Rural Works Programs in Bangladesh:
Community, Technology and Craft

Judith Tendler
June 1979

For the Transportation Department of the World Bank

SUMMARY AND RECOMMENDATIONS

I - The Graft and the Monitoring of Rural Works Programs

Graft is a constant in construction projects in all countries.
Attempts to deal with it through monitoring and supervision have to keep
it within reasonable bounds at a reasonable cost and, at the same time,
not simply drive it underground from whence it will resurface elsewhere
in another form. Project implementation, moreover, may suffer from
successful graft control if past graft has played the role of "incentive"
payments to dedicated workers. Because of this delicacy of the question
of graft, monitoring systems and special institutional arrangements to
inhibit graft should be evaluated as to (1) whether their cost, both
nominal and in terms of encumbered project administration, is less or
more than the resulting decrease in misappropriation; and (2) whether
existing graft is actually harmful to project execution, and whether
decreases in graft will result in an improvement in the quality of
implementation.

Decentralized works projects executed by local bodies are
considered by some to be particularly vulnerable to graft. In Bangladesh,
however, there seems to be no evidence that graft takes a greater share
of project costs than in the case of centrally-executed, larger, and more
capital-intensive construction. Graft in the rural works programs of
Bangladesh, moreover, is not associated with considerable failure of
projects to be started or completed.

The concern for graft, and for the designing of adequate
monitoring and supervision systems, can have a considerable influence on
project design. Over time, for instance, USAID and CARE have tended
toward larger projects in implementing the Food-for-Work program because
this minimizes the demand made on scarce monitoring staff. Earthworks
have been preferred over structures for the same reasons, as well as
road works over water works. Partly for the same reasons, reinforced
concrete bridges have been preferred over brick bridges because brick
"tends to fall down" if not properly built. Finally, structures
projects have been chosen that are concentrated on a few embankments, or
in one geographic area, so as to minimize demands made on the time of
supervisory staff.

In some cases, these kinds of choices result in costlier
projects or contravene program objectives. The preferred larger projects,
for example, may be less within the capabilities of local bodies than
smaller projects; yet local execution is a cornerstone of the rural works

64

programs. Similarly, larger projects are more likely to result in the use of contractors and migrant labor, also contrary to the intentions of the works program. Larger projects, moreover, tend to have lower completion rates than smaller ones.

The preference for earthworks over structures on monitoring grounds has had important cost implications: the construction of many embankments and canals without their appurtenant structures. This reduces the usability and durability of such infrastructural investments, not to mention the damages inflicted on the facility itself and on surrounding agricultural production when embankments are built without drainage. Similarly, though brick bridges may tend to fall down, if their construction is not properly supervised, they cost approximately half as much as the preferred reinforced concrete. Though roads are managerially easier than irrigation works, moreover, the preferences of rural users and the relative economic benefits often run in the other direction. Finally, the most socially profitable set of appurtenant-structure projects--out of all the missing structures that need building in Bangladesh--is not likely to be concentrated on one embankment or in one area. Giving paramount importance to monitoring and supervision constraints in making the above types of decisions will, in some instances, be worth the extra project costs and the compromised project objectives--and, in some instances, will not.

The concern for graft often takes attention away from other problems that, in contrast to graft, are actually impairing project execution. The problem of delays in wheat distribution in Food-for-Work projects is an example. These delays have significantly impaired the rate of project execution and markedly reduced the real wage paid to workers--in that workers frequently have to sell their wheat in advance at a discount as a result of delayed wheat payments.. The issue of paying workers in cash instead of wheat, however, has not called forth the attention and time of the implementing agencies that graft has--though graft has not inflicted as significant costs.

Graft is sometimes given more credit than it deserves for causing certain repeated problems in project execution. The lack of compaction is an example. Though this problem is usually attributed to faulty contractor performance and government supervision, there are also some strong economic arguments for not doing compaction at all on earth roads. The fact that it is not done, then, reflects the force of this economic logic, in part, rather than just graft. Though the two explanations are not mutually exclusive--indeed, each may reinforce the other--the exclusive attention to graft and supervision makes it difficult for attention to be devoted to the economic and technical side of the compaction question. Another frequent problem in works projects, which has an etiology similar to compaction, is the inadequate finishing of embankment slopes.

Graft on works projects takes many different forms and has markedly different effects. If graft is taken out of total wage allocations of an earthmoving project in Bangladesh, for example, the result will be less earth moved and less workers hired than is reported. If graft is taken out of the individual worker's wage, in contrast, the reported amount of earth moved and laborers hired will be accurate, but the worker will receive a lower wage than specified. In the former case, less employment is generated and the donor or government agency finances the graft, since it results in a lower-quality project (less earth moved) for the same money. In the latter case, the worker "finances" the graft, since it results in a lower wage for him. This latter form of graft represents a more regressive form of project financing, especially relevant for a program in which an important objective is to increase the incomes of the rural unemployed.

The underfulfillment of specifications, or overstatement of work done, is a common form of misappropriation in construction projects. The underfulfillment of specifications on earthworks projects has very different implications than that on structures projects. Bridges that threaten to fall down and culverts that do not drain properly can reduce the benefits of the facility of which they are a part and, in the case of inadequate drainage, can cause damage to agricultural production; repair costs will be incurred. A road or flood embankment that is lower than reported, in contrast, will inflict much smaller damages, if any at all.[1]

In various ways, cheating on earthworks is easier to deal with than that on structures. It is easier to measure the cost of underfulfilled specifications on earthworks after the project is

_____

[1]Exceptions are cheating on flood embankments and on the base width of an embankment. In the case of a flood embankment with over-reported measurements, the embankment will not protect from as severe flooding as was planned, though it takes only a small discrepancy between reported and actual heights to generate a significant amount of misappropriable cash, given an embankment of some length. If cheating comes out of the base width of the embankment, as opposed to the height or the crown width, this will make the slopes steeper, and result in erosion, higher maintenance requirements and, perhaps, earlier reconstruction.

completed--i.e., the earth paid for and not there--as opposed to underfulfillment on structures, which may be buried under concrete. Though the cost of cheating on earthworks can be immediately identified by taking one's own measurements after project completion, the cost of cheating on structures may not manifest itself for some time; when it does become manifest, as in a fallen bridge, the real cost can be much greater than the shortfall in the materials used. Finally, it is easier to identify the "cheater" on the earthworks project--he who took the final measurements--as opposed to the structures project, where opportunities abound to blame various parties and uncontrollable forces for things having gone wrong. Since earthworks projects without structures have accounted for at least 80% of the value of rural works programs in Bangladesh in recent years, it is clear that monitoring and supervision demands have been much less than they would be with a program that built earthworks along with their structures.

Though graft may be undesirable, it may also help get projects done. The graft to be earned on rural works projects, for example, is probably one reason why the implementation of the works component of rural development projects frequently goes more smoothly and rapidly than that of other components like agricultural extension, health, and education, where opportunities for graft are less. In construction programs where contracts are let by government field offices rather than headquarters, engineers have been found to prefer living and working in the field rather than the capital city, because of the greater opportunities there for graft. Since the problem of getting professionals to work in the field is a major one for many rural development programs, this constitutes a certain achievement, which might be lost if graft were discontinued.

Many costs incurred by field officers in development programs often go unreimbursed, except through graft payments taken by them. The project-committee members in charge of Food-for-Work projects in Bangladesh, for example, have to advance their own funds for wheat-transport costs, and are not reimbursed for the lodging and food costs of their various trips to requisition and obtain wheat from storage. A successful graft-control program that touches any of these "legitimate" and project-related misappropriations, then, could also result in footdragging on project execution.

Recommendations

Monitoring and supervision strategies should try to focus on those forms of graft that (1) result in delays in project execution and in significant impairment of project quality, and (2) seriously compromise program objectives, such as the graft that is taken out of the individual worker's wage. At the same time, careful attention should be paid to the potential deleterious effect of successful graft control--to the extent that project executors have been using graft payments for project-related expenses. One way of preventing the latter problem is to transfer legitimate graft costs to project financing--through increased salaries or commissions paid to project executors. The remuneration now received by local bodies in executing works projects should be reviewed with this consideration in mind. Any increase in project costs that causes the financing of graft costs to be transferred from workers to project funders is also desirable.

Because graft is good at surviving formal systems of monitoring and sanction, incentives to do things other than misappropriate should be provided outside the formal monitoring system-- incentives that have the effect of raising the opportunity costs of graft. One such incentive would be cash rewards for good performance in project execution and in wage payment, as described more fully in Sections II and IV.

Project types and techniques should be evaluated as to their vulnerability to graft, and as to the costs that graft inflict on projects and project beneficiaries. Just as USAID and CARE have developed a graft-minimizing set of preferences about earthworks projects, a similar evaluation should be made of the experience with structures--because they are more demanding of monitoring and supervision, and because their role in works programs in Bangladesh is on the increase. Where graft costs and vulnerability are high, alternative techniques, project types, or project organization should be sought. Because earthworks and structures vary so considerably in their vulnerability to graft, for example, there is some argument to separate their monitoring and supervision and, as discussed in Section III, even their execution.

If project costs are increased considerably by the choices of less graft-prone alternatives--or project objectives undermined-- then it should be determined whether the diminished vulnerability to graft is worth these costs, and whether there are other, less costly choices. Before deciding that reinforced concrete bridges are preferable on monitoring grounds over brick, for example, one should determine whether brick bridges "tend to fall down" because of contractor irresponsibility or because experience in building them is insufficient. Even if the answer is a mixture of the two explanations, there is still a chance that increased training and supervision will be less costly than the twice-as-costly bridges. The costs to communities of bridges falling down, moreover, may not be as great as the costs to implementing organizations, especially if the communities are instructed in how to prevent such occurrences, or repair them.

Recurrent problems in works projects can be caused by sloppiness, the traditional way of doing things, and lack of experience—in addition to graft. Problems that are usually attributed to graft, but have other less attention-getting causes, will require different approaches than problems caused by graft alone. If the lack of compaction and treatment of embankment slopes can be explained in part by economic logic, for example, then it may be necessary to change specifications and organizational design in a way that adapts to how these tasks are traditionally done. In such cases, a "lowering" of specifications may result not only in diminished project quality but also in real project costs that are lower than (1) providing the supervision or monitoring necessary to guarantee that specifications are properly filled, and (2) ending up with projects for which specifications are routinely and predictably not filled.

The bridges and culverts under construction in a rural works program are numerous, dispersed and, in many cases, of difficult access—making it difficult to meet the greater demands of structures over earthworks for constant supervision. At the same time, bridges and culverts in construction are, like any construction project, out in the open for anyone to see. The villagers in Bangladesh who routinely gather around construction sites should be drawn upon for some of the constant attention that is required by structures projects and yet is so difficult to provide through field organization. Villagers can be instructed in some of the simple operations that should be carried out repetitively during construction, such as the wetting of bricks or concrete. They are well qualified as monitors because they are interested in the project turning out well—since it will serve their village—and because they have a healthy distrust of contractors and local leaders. The villagers are very available, moreover, because they live nearby and because construction takes place during the time of ebb in agricultural activity.

During the appraisal of the proposed project, advantage should be taken of CARE's experience with the monitoring of works projects. In particular, an analysis of CARE's project-by-project data on non-reimbursement for over-reported earthwork could suggest which types of circumstances and projects tend to be associated with graft. These records should also give an idea of whether graft is fairly constant, or whether it varies considerably from one project to the next. A constant level of graft across all projects would require a different approach to monitoring than graft that varied widely between projects.

II - Workers, Wages and Misappropriation

Laborers on works projects often receive lower real wages than specified because of wage payments that are lower than reported, or because of long delays in payment, which necessitate their borrowing at high interest rates or selling their expected wheat payments in advance at a discount. At least a part of this shortfall between real and specified wages usually represents graft payments taken by project executors. The difference can also be seen as the price charged by project executors in rationing out scarce jobs to a highly unemployed labor force.

When contractors delay wage payments--and use their funds to cover other costs or as a hedge against delayed reimbursement--this represents a forced interest-free loan by laborers to contractors. Delay in wheat payments to workers on Food-for-Work projects, in turn, represents the bearing by workers rather than program funders of the costs of inadaquacies in the wheat-distribution system. Financing these costs and graft out of workers' wages compromises the asset-creating objectives of rural works programs as well as the income-redistributing ones, in that lower wages in construction work are associated with decreased productivity.

As noted above, graft taken out of total wage allocations before determining the number of workers to be hired--instead of out of workers' wages--results in less employment, overreporting of earth moved and underfulfilled specifications. This represents higher real project costs, paid for by program funders instead of by workers. Graft through underfulfilled specifications, then, is less regressive than graft taken out of workers' wages. Since earthwork measurements are easy to verify, moreover, it has been possible for USAID and CARE to identify and penalize the graft taken out of total wage allocations-- by refusing to reimburse for shortfalls in reported earthwork specifications. This successful mechanism of post-hoc measurement, however, may also have the effect of driving graft toward the unmonitored area of laborer wages.

Wages paid by the rural works projects of Bangladesh are vulnerable to misappropriation because unemployment is high and workers are willing to be "charged" for obtaining and keeping a job--and because it is difficult for laborers to monitor their own wage payments, which results from a certain confusion as to what is actually owed them. Confusion about the wage payment arises because (1) workers are paid by the task--a given amount of earth moved--rather than on an hourly or daily basis; (2) the completed task is measured for a group of workers, a gang of approximately 20, and the individual's wage is determined by dividing the amount owed the gang by the number of workers in it; (3) payment is made to a gang leader or a labor contractor, rather than to the individual laborer; (4) workers are paid irregularly and often at long intervals, so they do not become accustomed to receiving a certain amount; and (5), most important, the wage is composed of a two-part rate--a basic wage plus a "ration rate" for more arduous work, the latter rate being difficult to calculate. The ration rate can account for a significant share of wages, averaging 20% to 35%, and its payment is often withheld until the project is completed. Because of the ambiguity surrounding the calculation of the ration rate, it is looked upon by implementing agencies as providing an additional opportunity for misappropriation.

The vulnerability of workers to wage misappropriation on the decentralized and labor-intensive works projects of Bangladesh contrasts strikingly with the "natural" monitoring potential of such projects--in contrast to more centralized and capital-intensive projects. In the decentralized projects, graft costs are inflicted on a homogeneous, socially distinct class--local laborers--who work and live together in a small geographical area. This aggrieved party has a substantial self-interest in monitoring the way funds are handled. There is no such aggrieved class resulting from the graft that occurs in centrally-managed capital-intensive projects.

The common practice of withholding part of a worker's payment until project completion results, in part, from the fact that the construction season encompasses one of the peaks in the demand for agricultural labor--the roughly six-week period following the spring rains of April. Project committees and labor contractors feel that workers may leave them during this period, when wages for casual agricultural labor, and demands to work on one's own plot, increase. Thus the timing of the construction season from January to June results in (1) a decrease in the net employment-generating impact of works programs, to the extent that works jobs simply substitute for jobs offered after the spring rains; (2) a reduction in the real wages of workers to the extent that wage payments are withheld from them in order to keep them from leaving during April or May; and (3) increased use of labor contractors and migrant labor, which contravenes the regulations of the Food-for-Work program and the intentions of the Rural

Works Program to give employment to local labor.[1]

Recommendations

Implicit in the following recommendations is the recognition
that formal regulations and sanctions regarding the payment of laborers
cannot be expected to work because of (1) the collusion of workers in
breaching the regulations to protect their wages, as a price for
obtaining and retaining jobs; and (2) the absence of an institutional
mechanism to enforce such regulations. The recommendations fall into
two categories: those that increase the ability of laborers to monitor
their own wage payments, and those that provide incentives to project
executors to pay the specified wage, or decrease the opportunities
to take graft payments out of wages.

Worker Monitoring. Measures should be taken to increase the ability of
workers to know how much payment is owed them. Principally, the
present two-part wage rate--the basic wage plus the ration rate--
should be substituted by a single rate set in accordance with the
conditions of each particular project.

A worker representative should be appointed to the project
committee, perhaps filling the "landless" position on that committee,
and literacy requirements should be waived for this particular position.
The worker representative should be given supervisory or grievance
responsibilities; or, two worker representatives should be appointed,
one for each purpose. These representatives should be paid, as is the
labor supervisor on current project committees. As representatives
of the workers, these committee-members would have a self-interest in
preventing misappropriation, in contrast to existing members of the
project committees, who are drawn from the rural elites. Because of
this "natural" monitoring interest of the workers, the project
committees might succeed in playing the watchdog role intended for them.

_____

[1] The use of labor contractors and migrant labor also deprives rural
works projects of two important sources of pressure to get them started
and completed: (1) the interest of local landowners, who comprise
project committees, in having off-season employment provided for the
local unemployed, so that the latter will be available for agricultural
work during peak periods; and (2) the political benefit to the local
elected officials who control such projects of "doing something" about
extreme local unemployment.

If the mixing of workers and elites on the project committee is unrealistic in the social context of Bangladesh, an alternative grievance mechanism outside the project committee should be considered. The approach taken to the problem should be informed by a more careful investigation of the constraints and possibilities of social organization at the local level. In particular, the allegiances of the gang leader should be assessed, along with his potential for successfully representing the workers. An incentive or payment scheme could be devised that keeps the gang leader on the side of the laborers.

Increased incentives and decreased opportunities. Local bodies are very responsive to unambiguous signals from the central government as to what types of works-project proposals will be approved--especially given that only a small portion of such project proposals is ever approved. Criteria should be introduced for project approval which consider the "wage performance" of a project committee on last year's projects. (Project construction is usually completed at about the same that next year's project proposals are being submitted.) "Wage performance" could be measured in two ways: variation of the actual wage received from the specified wage, and variation in the frequency of wage payments from the specified frequency--e.g., from the once-weekly standard of the Food-for-Work regulations.

Project committees that paid the specified wage, and regularly, might also receive cash bonuses for doing so. These performance bonuses could be paid to central-government implementing entities as well, just as CARE imposes a penalty for underfulfillment of specifications on the Ministry of Relief and Rehabilitation. The proposed measures would have the effect of raising the cost to project executors of not paying workers properly--in terms of the cash bonus or the project approval foregone.

The construction season for works projects should be altered so as to exclude the period of demand for labor after the commencement of spring rains in April. To the extent that the partial withholding of wages results from the fear of losing workers during this period, such a modification would reduce the withholding of payments or, at the least, the justification for it. The construction season could be advanced a few weeks from mid- to early January or late December, and terminated in April when the rains begin, instead of in June; or, there could be a two-phase construction season, before and after the spring peak, with acceptance by project committees of considerable labor turnover between the first phase and the second. Such turnover, though perhaps cumbersome for project supervision, is actually desirable from the point of view of employment-generation, since it

spreads scarce employment opportunities across more individuals. A
shorter construction season would require smaller projects, which would
lessen the need for and the desirability of using migrant labor and
labor contractors.

The possibility should be explored of depositing wage
payments directly in individual accounts for workers at local post offices
or bank branches, as has been done in a works programs of the Indian
state of Kerala. This would make more difficult the misappropriation
of wages by project committees, and the withholding of wage payments by
contractors to cover other costs. To deal with the latter problem, and
in the case of projects with non-labor cost components, wage payments
might be authorized and transferred in a way that they could not be used
to finance these other costs. Finally, in works projects where the
local community pays a part, the government might limit its contribution
to cover only wage costs, while the local community would pay for
materials and equipment. This is exactly the opposite of the current
practice, and would reverse the incentive of the present system for the
community to minimize the cash cost of its contribution by relying on
conscript or underpaid labor. (This last recommendation is the subject
of Section IV.)

If these recommended actions were effective, they would
probably result in some increase in project cost in the form of cash
outlays for bonuses or commissions and the deflection of graft from
worker wages to total allocations for wages or to non-wage cost
components. Though this might result in more underfulfillment of
specifications, such a deflection of misappropriation would also
represent a shift of the costs of financing graft from workers to those
who fund programs. Though underfulfillment of specifications is
undesirable, then, it is also a less regressive form of financing the
graft costs of works projects.

III – Earthworks Without Structures

Because of the overwhelming role of relief agencies and
employment-generating objectives in the rural works programs of
Bangladesh, many earthworks have been built without their structures--
embankments without bridges or culverts, and canals without drains or
sluice gates. The economic losses of this way of building infrastructure
are obvious: the facility does not yield all its intended benefits and,
in the case of missing culverts and drains, the absence of the structure
causes damage to the embankment and to surrounding agricultural
production.

The earthworks-only experience in Bangladesh suggests that there are also certain advantages in this piecemeal form of construction. Even in an asset-creating program, that is, there may be good reason to de-couple the task of earthwork construction from that of appurtenant structures. This will be particularly relevant in an environment where (1) technical and monitoring capabilities are scarce, (2) graft is a problem, and (3) local execution and employment generation are important program objectives.

Building earthworks separately from their structures is a much less complicated task, technically and organizationally, than building the two together. As carried out in Bangladesh, earthwork is entirely labor-intensive, requiring no equipment or materials except for the headbaskets and hoes usually supplied by workers. The equipment and materials required for structures complicate the supply logistics and management of the earthworks task considerably. The greater simplicity of the earthworks task, then, has facilitated its execution by unsophisticated local bodies, and its management by relief organizations with lean technical and monitoring staffs.

Another aspect of earthwork construction without structures is that the incomplete facility often spontaneously elicits private local contributions from surrounding communities to complete it-- financing that would not be forthcoming if the complete facility were undertaken from scratch. Communities, that is, will put bamboo and timber bridges into embankments without them and they will tunnel under embankments without culverts. Though the response to missing drainage is damaging to the embankment, which will ultimately cave in over the tunnelings, both reponses illustrate the willingness of local communities to invest their own resources in the completion of infrastructure facilities. Recent grants and loans for such missing structures by donor agencies show that donors are also willing to supply the missing pieces, after it has become clear that the earthworks are in place and are missing a vital part.

Given a significantly larger number of unbridged spans than funds available to bridge them,[1] the community-supplied bridges can indicate to central planners which spans are most profitable to bridge first. Local decisions about where to put structures and how to do them

---

[1] The construction activity of the WFP half of the Food-for-Work program will alone result in 1,000 missing bridges and culverts per annum for the next several years.

can therefore result in a more economically desirable mix of projects. Local choices of technique and design can also be more economically efficient and, at the same time, more compatible with the employment-generating objectives of rural works programs. For communities that raise their own funds, that is, the scarcity of capital is a more compelling constraint on project design than it is for central-government technicians choosing project designs in a capital-city ministry. Decisionmaking by such technicians is influenced equally by the professional prestige and familiarity of certain design choices, and the supervisory effiency of concentrating projects in one place-- e.g., spending a budget for appurtenant bridges and culverts on one or two embankments in the same area, as CARE has done, so as to minimize expenditures of scarce monitoring and supervision resources and problems of materials and equipment supply.

Local choices, being more technically rustic, can diminish problems of supervision and supply becuase the cruder techniques rely more on locally available skills and materials. Since most equipment and materials used by contractors are imported, and subject to major delays in arrival at the project site, the use of techniques reliant on local skills and materials can reduce significantly the economic cost of structures projects. The more rustic local approach, then, may do better than "rational planning" at counteracting a certain tendency for cost inflation to occur in structures projects when choices about their design are made by technicians in central-government ministries.

Recommendations

Because earthworks will continue to be produced without their structures for some time in Bangladesh, the proposed works program should exploit some of the advantages of de-coupling the two tasks. Community willingness to respond to missing bridges and culverts with funds and organization should be encouraged by providing technical and financial support for such responses--and, in the case of missing culverts, to facilitate a response that is not damaging to the facility. A central-government matching fund should be set up to elicit these community rrsponses, as discussed in Section IV.

Technical assistance should be provided to communities in a way that increases their ability to make good use of skills and materials already in the community. Such an approach, it should be noted, might result in less a standardization of design than is usually proposed for such programs. Brick bridges merit particular attention, because rustic brick manufacture is widely dispersed throughout Bangladesh, and the use of brick as a substitute for stone and concrete in construction is common. Brick bridges, in turn, can be half as costly as the reinforced concrete bridges preferred by central-government implementing agencies in Bangladesh.

With respect to programs that continue to rely on complete central-government funding for missing structures, two criteria for project selection could be introduced. One would give preference to missing culverts over missing bridges: the absence of culverts in an embankment gives rise to greater economic costs than that of bridges—including the fact that the community's response to the missing culvert is damaging to the embankment, whereas the makeshift bridge enhances it. Priority should also be given, in the selection of appurtenant bridges for central-government financing, to those spans that already have makeshift bridges supplied by the community. This selection criterion is a convenient proxy for choosing the spans for which the economic returns to bridging are the greatest. This will simplify considerably the identification of desirable bridge projects and the justification of their benefits, though it will not result in the concentration of project sites that minimizes supervisory resources.

IV – Financing Local Works Initiatives

The Ministry of Local Government should modify and expand its "local-participation" program so as to assist local bodies (unions) with matching funds to finance the installation of missing structures in earthwork projects. Such a program would (1) offer unions a flat allocation of government matching funds, which could be used for any project without approval and subject only to the criteria listed here; (2) limit matching-fund financing to appurtenant-structure projects only; (3) be available only to unions, the smallest administrative unit in Bangladesh; (4) limit the central-government contribution to labor costs only, while the local contribution would cover equipment and materials; (5) reward good performance in project execution and payment of labor with (a) a larger matching contribution from the central government for next year's projects, and (b) commissions paid to project executors; (6) be executed through the existing system of project committees, without use of contractors.

Providing flat allocations to unions, without requiring approval by government field officers or ministries, would remove some of the disincentives to economic project selection that now exist—i.e., ambiguous selection criteria or the bypassing of such criteria through political pressures or bribery. Local resources previously invested in bribes to get the project approved, moreover, would now go to the project itself. The resulting project choices may come closer to those intended by "rational planning" than choices resulting from the present filtering-up system, and its incentive to maximize the number and variety of proposed projects, in the blind hope that a few will strike someone's fancy. The severing of project choice from official approval would also be consistent with the government's interest in transferring power over project selection in rural works programs from technicians to local bodies.

Projects financeable under the matching fund would be limited to appurtenant structures because (1) this would result in project choices that were by definition asset-creating or -preserving, without having to impose formal criteria on the selection process; (2) this limitation would severely circumscribe the area in which rural elites could manipulate project selection and location so as to benefit only a few of them; (3) earthworks without their structures have already proven to be a powerful magnet in drawing financing and organizing out of communities; and (4) in comparison to earthworks, structures in Bangladesh have a high non-labor cost component (60%-70%), which makes it possible for the central government to cover all labor costs and still leave a substantial amount of non-labor costs to the community.

For the central government to cover all labor costs, leaving equipment and materials costs to the community, is to reverse the traditional pattern of financing for "self-help" schemes, whereby the community "contribution" takes the form of unpaid labor. Keeping the community contribution away from labor costs, is one of the only ways of preventing the drafting of conscript labor, and the resulting regressive pattern of financing that is typical of such projects. The financing of labor costs by the central government would also encourage appropriate technical choices to the extent that the community tries to maximize the government contribution (labor) and minimize its own (equipment, materials). Since the present system of central-government responsibility for design decisions and financing of equipment and materials costs carries a tendency toward overdesign, the incentive to minimize equipment and materials costs should result in less costly projects. Finally, the limitation of the community's contribution to equipment and materials will create some natural checks on graft. Under the present system, the rural elites lose nothing of their own as a result of graft-caused faulty project execution, if the local contribution has been in the form of unpaid labor. Graft under the proposed scheme, in contrast, would compromise resources invested in the project by the elites themselves.

The limitation of the proposed matching fund to unions, the smallest administrative unit in Bangladesh, is meant to put interunion rivalry to work for project selection and execution—instead of this rivalry being disruptive, as under the present system, which seeks to promote "integrated" planning and design of projects by groups of unions (the thanas). Unions would be allowed to continue behaving in an "unintegrated" way under the proposed mechanism, which would stimulate them to compete with each other to get scarce project funds and execute projects well. Appurtenant structures, as opposed to earthworks, are more suited to this "unintegrated" approach, since they are less likely than earthworks to involve more than one union.

The use of contractors would be discouraged under the proposed scheme, as in the Rural Works Program of the 1960s. According to Bank research, the use of contractors in rural works programs is associated with various tendencies that the proposed program is trying to avoid: higher costs, lesser labor intensity, more graft, and less efficient project selection. The use of local bodies rather than contractors would also tend to decrease that part of structures costs that results from delays in the delivery of equipment and materials because (1) local execution and local financing of equipment and materials will result in projects that use less equipment and materials from outside the area; (2) local execution will not be characterized by the juggling of equipment and materials back and forth between various projects in construction, as occurs with contractors; (3) the construction season, the busiest for contractors, is the slow time for agricultural production and hence for local elites, who will have more time available to work on the breaking of bottlenecks in supply deliveries; and (4) local bodies may be more interested than contractors in resolving delay problems—particularly in the case of drainage structures, where the lack of drainage during and after the monsoons can inflict heavy damages on agricultural production.

Rewards to local bodies for good performance would be based on measures of (1) the rapidity with which projects are executed, (2) the extent to which specifications are met, and (3) "wage" performance, a combination of the extent to which laborers are paid the specified wage, and the frequency and regularity of wage payments. These rewards would act as incentives to execute projects well and would impose costs on graft-takers, since graft-taking could result in foregone rewards. This system may be more effective than formal sanctions in dealing with graft, because it is immediate and because it is politically easier to mete out rewards rather than punishments.

The proposed scheme is consistent with the ongoing interest in the Bangladesh government in exacting contributions from the local beneficiaries of works projects. The matching fund would elicit such contributions in a way that is less regressive than current custom,

without encumbering the process with the introduction of a new tax.
The proposed scheme, finally, is capable of raising funds for
decentralized works programs at a time when the central-government
budget for such programs is not likely to increase--because of the
greater bureaucratic power of the government ministries in charge of
more capital-intensive and centralized contruction programs.

NEW DIRECTIONS RURAL ROADS

by
Judith Tendler

A.I.D. Program Evaluation
Discussion Paper No. 2

The Studies Division

Office of Evaluation

Bureau for Program and Policy Coordination

U.S. Agency for International Development

March 1979

Summary and Recommendations

The search for New-Directions impacts of road projects
has focused on labor-based methods of construction. In recent
years, the donor world has supported considerable research
investigating the competitiveness of labor-based
techniques of roadbuilding as opposed to equipment-based ones.
Donors have also started to finance labor-based road construction,
mostly pilot projects. After years of tutelage in equipment-based
construction, recipient governments or their highway departments
are often reluctant to adopt labor-based techniques. Equipment-
intensive projects are in many ways "neater" than labor-based
ones: there is only one large contract to let and monitor, the
pace of work is easier to plan, and the exact nature of the task and
the expenditures required to do it are more easily predicted and
described in a bid document.

Ironically, the appeal of equipment-based construction
is in some ways greater to donor organizations than to recipient
countries—notwithstanding the genuine concern of the donors for
getting away from equipment-based techniques. Under current AID
procedures, equipment-based projects take less staff time than
would labor-based projects—at least for an initial period of
transition to such techniques. AID procedures contribute,

inadvertently, to the greater attraction of equipment-based
construction; for example, AID loans do not provide operating capital
to contractors for the large and frequent wage expenditures
necessary under labor-intensive construction. Also, AID often
supplies equipment to the same road-construction agencies with
which it has labor-intensive projects, thereby increasing even more
the lure and the relative cheapness of equipment-based techniques.

Given the reluctance to adopt labor-based techniques,
AID training and persuasion will not be enough to induce the
transition to such techniques. Similarly, the power of cost-benefit
analysis to show that labor-based techniques can be competitive
with equipment-based ones, even at market prices, will also not
be sufficient. In order to facilitate the adoption of labor-
based construction, AID should pursue a strategy that seeks
to lessen the relative costs of such techniques. This can be done
partly by refraining from actions that decrease the real costs of
equipment-based construction, and partly by seeking out institutional
environments in the recipient country where labor-based
construction is more desired, more familiar, and more functional.
In these latter environments, correspondingly, equipment-based
construction will be less attractive, less available, and less
professionally respectable.

AID should avoid financing labor-based projects in
agencies receiving parallel AID or other donor funding for
equipment-based construction programs. The resulting easy availability
of equipment makes the introduction and acceptance of labor-based
techniques into these agencies more difficult than it normally
would be. Though this suggestion may seem an obvious one,
many donor attempts to initiate labor-based programs take place
exactly in these kinds of agencies--i.e., highway departments
receiving simultaneous injections of equipment and funds for
equipment-based construction, often together in the same loan with
the labor-intensive project. To stay away from such highway
departments, one might think, would result in proscribing AID
financing for many of the world's highway departments, thereby severely
limiting AID's possibilities for financing labor-based projects.
But the suggestion actually points the way to placing such projects
in government agencies outside the highway departments--for example,
regional development authorities or integrated development programs.
Such agencies are somewhat removed from the influence of fleets of
construction equipment and of engineers trained in equipment-based
techniques. In addition, labor-based construction is likely to
be more in the interest of these agencies than of highway departments.
The principal objectives of such agencies, that is, often include

employment of the rural poor, local organization for community
construction projects, and construction of rural roads as opposed
to arterials. This contrasts with highway departments, for whom
construction in itself is most important--particularly of arterial
roads. For the professionals of the highway departments, moreover,
only certain design standards are considered technically acceptable;
these standards are often incompatible, or more costly to execute,
with labor-based techniques. Unfortunately, the rural roads
found in AID's rural-development projects have so far been neglected
as institutional opportunities for labor-based construction.

Another way to place labor-based programs away from
the undermining influence of equipment-based techniques is to seek
more decentralized decisionmaking settings and financing, if
possible, for such projects. Regional development authorities are
also an example of an entity more decentralized than a highway
department. Decentralizing road-construction decisionmaking not
only takes decisions away from where the equipment is. Roadbuilding
decisions at more local levels will also produce a higher ratio of
unpaved to paved roads and a higher ratio of maintenance to
construction efforts. The decisions will be characterized by a
higher affinity for labor-based construction, if only
because such techniques are more in use at local levels. Projects

at such levels, then, involve more of a continuation of existing techniques than a weaning away of roadbuilders from other, desired techniques. The difficulties that donors are having in winning over recipient governments to labor-based roadbuilding, then, may be more a result of the fact that donors are not working at the level of design and implementation where labor-based techniques are more accepted.

Decentralization of roadbuilding can elicit local financial contributions to road construction and maintenance in a way that centralized decisionmaking does not. Decentralization, moreover, is more likely to result in a piecemeal approach to road construction. Such a division of traditionally lumpy roadbuilding investments into smaller parts--strung out through time and built with more rustic materials and techniques--is in keeping with the relative capital scarcities and labor abundances of recipient countries.

The approaches to labor-based projects suggested here can be beneficial for the rural poor not only because of the employment they generate. They can also result in more rural roads and maintenance per dollar spent on road construction, and a more balanced development of rural and arterial roads in any particular region. In the search for New-Directions impacts of rural roads, the impact of such alternative patterns of road-system growth has been somewhat neglected--because of the exclusive focus on labor-based construction techniques.

Project on Managing Decentralization, Institute of International Studies, University of California, Berkeley, California 94720 USA

New Light on Rural Electrification:

The Evidence from Bolivia

Background paper for an evaluation sponsored by the Bureau of Program and Policy Coordination of the U.S. Agency for International Development

by

Judith Tendler

September 9, 1980

*The research reported herein was performed pursuant to Cooperative Agreement #AID/DSAN-CA-0199 between the University of California and the United States Agency for International Development. The opinions expressed herein are those of the author and should not be construed as representing the opinion or policy of the Project on Managing Decentralization, the Institute of International Studies, the University of California or any agency of the United States Government.

Introduction, Summary and Conclusions*

In 1973 and 1974, AID lent US$24.5 million to Bolivia for a US$29.5 million program to create seven rural electric systems in six of Bolivia's nine departments. The new systems would be added onto those of already-existing municipal utilities in the departmental capitals (with the exception of La Paz department, where the two completely new systems were to be exclusively rural). The new rural power was expected to serve 48,000 consumers in the first year after construction and almost double that number ten years later, when the systems would be working at full capacity. The new rural consumers would account for 25% of the consumers and 10% of the consumption and revenues of the expanded systems, the rest representing urban consumption (except for the two La Paz systems). The expanded urban-rural systems would not be interconnected with each other, and would buy their bulk power as they had done in the past, from hydroelectric or gas thermal plants owned by the government power enterprise, ENDE. ENDE would be the executing agency for the loan with full responsibility for all phases of implementation.

At the time of this evaluation, three of the systems had been completed and in operation for one or two years (Santa Cruz, Cochabamba and Chuquisaca); two more were partially energized (Tarija and Potosí), and the two La Paz systems were just being energized. The number of connections made by the time of project completion was close to that anticipated--except for the La Paz system, where various problems and delays resulted in about 30%-40% less connections than planned. Given the number of consumers connected at the time of the evaluation, or projected for connection by the time of project completion some months hence, unit investment costs were US$400-$900 per household connection, depending on the system.

The new rural electric systems, of course, were newer than one would have liked in order to do an evaluation of project impact and in order to separate out startup problems and hopes from longer-term phenomena. Partly for this reason, considerable time was spent checking impressions in certain towns that had had electric power for several years prior to the project. Impressions were also checked against the reports coming in from other evaluations of AID's rural electrification projects. Because of the brief post-project history, then, the findings on impact presented below may well be overturned by subsequent years of experience with the new systems.

Installing seven rural electric systems and connecting them up to 81,000 consumers over ten years was meant to serve three broad

---

*
The Bolivian peso was devalued from 20 to 25 pesos to the U.S. dollar at the end of November 1979. All current cost figures in this report were converted to U.S. dollars at the 25-peso rate (mainly, current electric-power rates and costs of household connections); and all pre-1980 costs were converted at 20 pesos (mainly, project costs and household-connection costs under the project).

and interrelated objectives: improvement in the condition of the rural poor, stimulation of economic growth in the countryside through the use of power for production, and creation of viable electric utilities. These three objectives are the subject of my report.

The distributional consequences of electrification were of central importance to this evaluation effort not only because the Bolivia project was expected to bring significant benefits to the rural poor. In addition, and contrarily, recent evaluations have suggested that rural infrastructure projects are not particularly suited to reaching the rural poor. Because the electric systems and the roads are available to everybody, and because the rich are often more in a position than the poor to take advantage of them, the new facilities often turn out to benefit the rich more than the poor. Though this latter view of rural electrification, as well as the New-Directions' concern for targeting projects on the poor, postdates the conceptualization of the Bolivia project, the project still provides an excellent opportunity to collect evidence on this important question.

Much of the support for rural electrification arises from the belief that the provision of adequate and cheap electric power to rural areas will "release" productive potential lying dormant there. This new production, it is also expected, will help to decentralize the pattern of economic growth typical of countries like Bolivia, where production and infrastructural capacity are concentrated in and around large cities, with attendant problems of urban congestion and large settlements of the poor. Many of the new rural producers, it is also assumed, will be "small" and therefore poor--or poorer, at least, than the urban industrial users of electric power. These assumptions about the interaction between rural electrification and growth were reflected in the justifications for the Bolivia project.

Finally, it was central to the realization of the above two objectives that viable electric utilities be in place after the completion of construction. Viable organizations would be necessary not only to run the new systems, with their capacity to handle at least ten years' worth of demand growth, but also so that demand for new connections could be vigorously met. In this latter sense, electrification projects are quite different from some other projects because what the electrification entity does after construction will be crucial to the realization of the economic and financial benefits of the project. Though post-construction operations are typically neglected in the design of many infrastructure projects, the implications of neglecting this phase are more serious for electrification. If roads are left unmaintained by an inadequate highway department, for example, this will not prevent their being used in the years immediately following construction, or their economic benefits from being realized. With electrification, as will be seen, the case is quite different.

Rural electrification and the rural poor

Contrary to the new wisdom about rural electrification, the Bolivia project showed that certain qualities of electrification projects, if handled properly, actually suit them for having a uniquely favorable impact on the rural poor. In certain ways, the technology of rural electrification makes it easier to benefit the poor than with projects in health, agricultural credit and agricultural inputs—the projects currently thought of as more suited than rural infrastructure for targeting on the poor.

One of the major problems of projects that are considered appropriate for targeting on the poor is that the subsidized services—the health clinics, the subsidized credit, the subsidized inputs—often end up in the hands of the rich. Rural electrification does not have this problem, because of the highly arbitrary way of determining who gets access to the service—namely, those houses that happen to be within reach of the distribution lines. The poor get connected, then, simply because they live mixed in with the better off in the rural communities, because they are more numerous, and because it is in the utility's interest to connect as many houses as possible under the net. This gives little opportunity for the rich to shoulder out the poor.

The city subsidizes the countryside. The Bolivia project also demonstrated another potential of rural electrification for benefiting the rural poor: through the rate charged for electricity, some types of consumers can be made to subsidize other types, and consumers of power in general can be made to subsidize non-consumers—all with very little political visibility. Grid-system electrification facilitates this use of the power rate for distributive ends because it tends to centralize and unify-rate-setting policies. In the case of the Bolivia project, AID and the Bolivian power sector agreed to a rate policy whereby rural consumers were charged the same kilowatthour rate as urban consumers in the same system, despite the fact that the costs of providing rural power were, as is typical, three to four times higher than urban power. (This is because the unit costs of power increase substantially as population density decreases.) The subsidy to rural power users by urban users represented an unusual reversal of the more common bias in the other direction—i.e., the food-price and exchange-rate policies that result in the much-criticized subsidization of the city by the countryside. To the extent that the poor were more represented among rural as opposed to urban consumers, the subsidy also amounted to a transfer of funds from the rich to the poor.

The subsidization of the country by the city through the uniform power rate, though of favorable distributional significance, was somewhat misplaced in terms of where the greatest payoff from subsidization is to be found. The financial implications of the urban-rural subsidy for the utilities, moreover, may ultimately undermine the subsidy's positive distributional impacts: that the urban-based Bolivian utilities were required to charge the same rate for their rural service as for their considerably less costly urban service gave them a financial incentive to pay greater attention to the urban part of their service--and thus to give preference to urban requests for new connections. The subsidization of poor consumers of household electricity through the power rate may also have been misplaced in that the Bolivian poor were more than willing and able to pay their monthly light bills (minimum monthly charges under the project systems varied between US$.90 and $2.00). Those without electric power were often paying three and four times that amount for candles and kerosene; household electricity costs, moreover, represented a small portion of total household expenditures of poor families, so that subsidization of the rural poor through the power rate might not have had a significant impact on their incomes.[1] A greater impact might be had on the access of the poor to electricity through subsidization of the capital rather than running costs of household electricity. This was also done in the Bolivia project.

The hookup costs of the simplest household connections (one or two lightbulbs) in the AID-financed systems are far beyond the reach of the Bolivian poor--about US$120, including the cost of the internal house wiring. The AID project included credit for these capital costs, reducing the down payment and subsequent monthly installments to about US$2.50-$5.00, or 2%-5% of the total capital costs. But unlike the subsidized power rate, this connection credit ran out when construction was completed, and in some cases before that. Since the loading up of rural

---

[1] Expenditures for cooking with kerosene, wood and dung were considerably greater than those for lighting. Cooking with electricity is almost non-existent in Bolivia, partly because of the availability of cheap bottled gas, and partly because electric stoves are approximately three to four times as costly as gas stoves.

distribution systems takes ten to twenty years, and since the poor tend to apply for connections last, this termination of connection funding limited the distributional impact of the project significantly.

A last note of caution about using the electric-power rate for reversing the rural-urban bias of third-world economic policies. Adding new rural systems to existing urban ones makes it politically more difficult to raise power rates than would be the case in an exclusively rural system. Protests over increases in electric power are not the problem in rural areas that they are in cities; rural consumers are used to spending more money for traditional sources of energy, or to paying high rates for the autogenerated power systems that often precede grid electrification. Because of the political difficulty of raising urban rates in Bolivia as well as other countries, therefore, a unified urban-rural rate is already a low one, from the point of view of the financial viability of the utilities. When a rural area is brought together in a grid with an urban system, therefore, the advantage that rural areas have in being able to charge more adequate rates is lost. The urban-rural subsidy may thus lead to the financial inability of utilities to add the new consumers for which the rural system was built.

The social uses of electric power. The Bolivia case illustrated another distributive potential of rural electrification, through the development of certain other public services that can use power--health, education, potable water, street lighting. The impact of these public services on the poor is potentially greater than that of electricity for household use because these other services reach those households without electricity, among which the poor are more than proportionately represented. In a few instances, the Bolivia systems financed street lighting and potable water through the rate charged to household consumers of electricity; in this way, consumers were paying the costs of water and public lighting for non-consumers, as well as for themselves. One attraction of using the electric-power rate for this form of distributive "taxation" is that it is not politically conspicuous--in comparison to progressive taxes and other redistributive policy instruments.

Though the justification for the Bolivia project placed great emphasis on the benefits to result from the social uses of power--health services, potable water, night classes--these uses usually did not materialize. A partial exception was potable water, where several diesel-powered systems were converted to electric power with the advent of project power. The expected social services did not appear partly because electricity was not necessary to their functioning, or because other missing inputs represented more of an impediment. In mountainous countries like Bolivia, many village water systems can function on gravity alone and do not need electric power. Refrigerators in health clinics were problematic usually because of the lack of spare parts for power-using equipment. Where health and night education services were not operating, this had mainly to do with the lack of programs in these areas rather than with a lack of power. The coming of electricity in most of these cases, then, made no difference.

The only strong potential linkage between electrification and social services seemed to be that of potable water, in cases where gravity flow was not available. A disadvantage of forging this linkage in an electrification project is that it requires complicating the project with a separate program in a separate agency. At the same time, the relatively simple management demands of village water systems mean that the installation part of the water program might be entrusted to the electric utility itself as part of the construction task. Forcing the linkage between electrification and potable water in this way would not only heighten the distributional impact of the electrification project; it would also hitch the cause of a significant social investment to the state electric-power sector, which is usually among the most powerful in the public sector. Except in a few instances, the Bolivia project did not take advantage of the potential of rural electrification for introducing social services and financing them progressively.

Electrification and economic growth

Given the prevailing assumptions about the importance of cheap and adequate power supply for the growth of rural production, it was striking to find that productive uses of the new supply of electric power were negligible in the three systems already fully functioning. Irrigation, which had been singled out in particular in quantifying project benefits (accounting for 10%-30% of benefit flows), also seemed unlikely to materialize to any significant degree.

Central to AID's design standards, and to its justification for introducing central-system rural electrification, was that the new systems would provide 24-hour service, as opposed to the nighttime-only service characteristic of the smaller isolated utilities usually found in rural areas. Nighttime service was said to be insufficient for the productive uses of power that central-system projects would facilitate.

Thus the paltry response of Bolivian rural producers to the new power, despite its excellent quality and low prices, requires some explanation. Most of the reasons for this outcome fall into two categories—project design, and the economics of production and of electric-power use in the electrified areas. I will take up the latter topic first.

The economics of rural production and power use. The use of electric power for production was not occurring in the electrified areas because it was not particularly profitable, for the following reasons: (1) power-based equipment was not competitive with labor-based techniques of production; (2) the seasonal production patterns of agro-processing operations made central-system power uneconomic, as compared to user-owned generators; (3) opportunities for profitable production in the electrified areas were limited; and (4) in the case of irrigation, project designers had not looked into the question of whether irrigation was economically worthwhile, nor was the system designed to pass through irrigable areas (with two exceptions) or to accommodate potential users.

That all the above factors were operating was attested to by the many producers who were using electric power only to extend the work day into the night, with electric light, while continuing to use manual techniques; by the many small agro-processors who preferred to continue using their own diesel motors because with the new public power supply they would have to pay minimum monthly charges for power whether or not they used it, and by the paucity of power-using production in some towns that had had 24-hour service for several years prior to the project. In the communities receiving power for the first time, moreover, there was little previous production based on user-owned power-generating equipment. The only exception was the Santa Cruz system, where substantial economic growth had occurred prior to the AID project. Not coincidentally, Santa Cruz was also the only system where productive use of power after the AID project was significant.

That the Bolivia project did not bear out the assumption that new, cheap and 24-hour power would be sufficient to elicit previously "repressed" production is not surprising. The literature on central-system rural electrification suggests that it becomes economic only after a certain stage of economic growth, and thus is not a precursor of growth. This particular stage occurs when previous economic growth, accompanied by the acquisition of user-owned power units, has demonstrated that profitable opportunities for production and for the use of central-system power actually do exist. This prior stage had not occurred in the Bolivian case, except for the Santa Cruz system.

The expectation that rural electrification would contribute to more decentralized economic growth and a reversal of rural-urban migration flows also seemed not to be borne out by this particular project. The Bolivia project involved the expansion into the countryside of the urban systems of five departmental capitals. This meant that the new rural transmission lines extended out from the city along the major road arteries, connecting up towns and communities along the way. This approach to electrification had various implications for decentralized growth. Most obviously, because of their location near Bolivia's major cities, the new distribution systems would no doubt enhance rather than offer alternatives to the infrastructural endowment of the greater urban areas. This seemed particularly the case in Santa Cruz, where almost half of the household connections went to the poor suburban areas of the city of Santa Cruz.

The placement of transmission and distribution lines along arterial roads leading out from cities is, of course, the most logical way to build such an urban-based system. At the same time, however, this form of expansion may also have contributed to the lack of profitable production opportunities in the rural electrified communities. Highways that connect rural communities to urban centers will lower transport costs drastically and, in may cases, remove the competitive edge that small producers hold over cheap mass-produced goods from the cities or abroad. The urban-based expansion of rural systems in Bolivia, in sum, may have contributed more to urban than to rural growth--or, at the least, may have had no contrary impact at all on centralizing growth patterns.

Making it possible to produce with power. When small rural producers did have some interest in using the new rural power, that interest was in many cases not realized for reasons more within the control of project designers than those discussed above. Two types of potential productive users, it seemed, were not being connected up: those without capital for the high connection costs, and those who had capital and were somewhat beyond the reach of existing lines, but who were willing to pay the costs of the additional lines and/or transformers necessary to service their place of production. For the small rural producers without capital for connecting up to the system, the project offered no credit--though such credit was provided for household connections, as mentioned above. For the opposite type of producer--proffering his own capital to finance the additional costs of his connection to the system--neither the project designers nor the utilities seemed alert to the possibility for gaining additional capital and revenues in this way. Though rural electrification was supposed to break the "bottleneck" to the growth of rural production, then, the project missed the opportunity to accommodate a significant potential for such growth.

The small and unsophisticated rural producer envisioned in project justifications experienced various other impediments to connecting up to the system--impediments that could be partly removed through project design. Most important, small rural producers did not have the access to credit and technical assistance that larger and urban-based producers did--not only for the capital costs of the power connection but, more important, for the purchase of appropriate electric motors. In many of the electrified communities, small producers had acquired inappropriate motors; or they did not know that it would be possible for them to use the system's power without considerable investment; or they did not know where the appropriate motors could be acquired. The utilities had no program for responding to the inquiries of such users; only one or two staff members spent any share of their time in the electrified areas.

Whether or not rural producers had the capital to purchase the power connection and the electric motors turned out be be considerably more significant than the price of power in their decision to connect up to the system. All producers, whether small or large, seemed to base their decisions to use public power on the capital cost of the connection and the electric motors, rather than on the expected cost of monthly power bills. The availability of "cheap" electric power, in other words, did not have much significance for locational and production decisions. In those cases where rural electrification might actually have had the potential for "releasing" economic growth, in sum, this potential might have been realized more by reducing the costs of the conversion and connection, and of obtaining information about it, than by offering cheap central-system power. Such a capital-cost subsidy, of course, would not have the adverse consequences on the financial viability of the utilities that the rate subsidy does.

That the Bolivia project included arrangements to finance household but not productive connections reflected a certain lack of interest in productive use by AID and Bolivian project designers themselves. AID's rural electrification projects in general have followed the U.S., household-oriented model of rural electrification. The Bolivian government, in turn, saw rural electrification as having a primarily social purpose--i.e., of placing light in as many poor rural households as possible--an objective that is attested to by the large share of connections that reached truly poor households. The fact that the electric utilities were primarily urban systems also contributed to the lack of interest in productive use and its promotion; the utilities could count on their urban load for productive uses, since the urban load represented an overwhelming share of consumption and revenues anyway (about 90%).

The lack of interest by Bolivia project's designers in productive use also reflects the inherent nature of electrification projects which, like other infrastructure projects, are focused almost exclusively on the large and demanding task of construction; they tend to neglect what has to happen after construction is completed, a subject that will be discussed further below.

So far, in conclusion, various ways of trying to make the productive uses of power materialize have been suggested. An alternative approach to the lack of productive use would be to simply abandon the hope of linking electrification to economic growth, rather than trying to make it come true. Trying to force the linkage between electrification and production may not only bring limited results; it also requires a greater organizational complexity that may burden excessively the already fragile institutions entrusted with such projects. Or, a bigger distributional payoff might occur, for a given complication of the project, from forcing the linkage to potable water rather than to production.

Designing for low-productive use and high social objectives

It is perfectly reasonable to ask what was wrong with the lack of productive use if, indeed, household consumption was what project designers and policymakers cared about most and if that goal was realized. The answer is, in part, that productive users in grid systems, by consuming power during the otherwise unused daytime hours, bring down the unit cost of electric power to a more reasonable level. A 24-hour central-system facility like that installed in Bolivia, in other words, makes more economic sense when there is significant use of capacity during a good number of hours of the day--in contrast to the predominantly four-hour nighttime consumption for lighting that occurred.

The rest of the answer to the question posed above lies in the answer to another question: given the implicit goal of bringing rural electrification to as many households as possible, how did the Bolivia project do? For an investment of US$29.5 million, the project reached between 12% and 22% of the households in the electrified cantons (equivalent to U.S. counties), representing only about 7% of Bolivia's rural families. As seen above, the project reached fewer households than was possible partly because of the investment that went into providing unnecessarily high-quality service. In addition, grid systems have economies of scale that do not start to operate at the small size of communities characteristic of those electrified under the Bolivia project--about 85% of the electrified communities had less than 200 families.

There were less costly alternatives to grid-system power that might have brought many more households into the system for the same investment--for example, independent systems supplying individual towns with diesel or microhydro generating units. Yet one of the principal justifications AID used for the Bolivia project, as well as for other electrification projects, was that it replaced the "inadequate" service of such systems, which provided power "only" at night. This brings the argument full circle: the allegedly "inadequate" independent systems, that is, might have been considerably more appropriate than a grid-system if the goal of the Bolivia project was to provide light to as many poor rural households as possible.

The question of cost is no more important than that of whether a decentralized approach, and its many small independent utilities, would have been as institutionally effective as the small number of centralized urban utilities of the Bolivia project--especially after construction. Experience with local public services in small rural towns in some countries suggests that whereas concern for cost might lead to one choice--the decentralized approach--the concern for post-construction continuity and effectiveness might lead to the more costly, centralized choice. Unfortunately, the time constraints of this evaluation did not permit a more adequate investigation of this question through an evaluation of the many small independent utilities in Bolivia financed outside the AID project.

If one agreed from the start that a central-system electrification project were being designed for household use, technical specifications could be such as to result in considerably lower unit costs. For example, standards for the quality of service--the maximum acceptable number and length of power cuts and of variations in voltage--could be considerably lower than those followed in the Bolivia project; this is because the main economic justification for the large additional investment in high-quality service is that power cuts and variations in voltage would result in significant losses of production, which is not the case when electricity is used mainly for lighting and only at night.

With an explicitly social purpose, a rural electrification project would also have to be designed so as to maximize the number of household connections. The Bolivia project was designed for an average monthly household consumption that was considerably larger than could be expected--namely, 30-35 kwh per month immediately after project completion and 50-70 kwh by the tenth year, as opposed to the more typical 10-20 kwh actually registered in the first years after completion. The result was that whereas the number of consumers was roughly the same as projected, the amount of power sold was considerably less--by 36%, for example, in the Cochabamba system. Fewer consumers were connected than was possible or socially desirable, in sum, while at the same time the utilities were without funds to make up for, by adding new consumers, the shortfall in average consumption.

In assessing the impact of the Bolivia project as a mainly social project, finally, it is important to compare its cost to other social projects valued highly by the rural poor: health, potable water, education. In making future decisions as to how to best benefit the rural poor, AID should seek to determine how rural-electrification costs--US$400-$900 per family in the Bolivia case--compare to the costs and post-construction effectiveness of similar investments in these other sectors.

There is one important argument in favor of the use of grid-system electrification for social purposes--as opposed to making social investments in other sectors or to using more economic approaches than grid systems to rural lighting. Large-scale electrification projects generate considerable political support--from contractors, consultants, engineering professionals, equipment-supply firms, utilities, donors and, most important, political leaders. Investments in other social sectors, or in less capital-intensive and less centralized approaches to rural electrification, are usually less in the interests of these particular groups and therefore receive less support. This is one reason why rural electrification projects are so prevalent, despite the fact that many of them are not economic or appropriate; one sees less expenditure and extravagence in rural potable water or health, for example, where the groups listed above have less to gain. If the grid approach to rural electrification is rejected for other sectors or for less centralized technologies, in other words, the poor may simply end up with considerably less investment going their way.

Creating viable electric utilities

The attempt to create viable electric utilities seemed to be undercut in some ways by the very design of the project itself. The result could be seen in a post-construction "letdown" by the utilities. One or two years after construction, they were not able to keep up with the requests for new house connections and line extensions.

Grid-system projects put capacity into place that is meant to serve between ten and twenty years of demand growth. For this reason, aggressiveness in making new connections is crucial to the utility's earning of an adequate return, as well as to realizing the project's economic and social benefits. The high unit costs and excess capacity of rural electrification projects in the years immediately following construction mean that the marginal costs of adding new consumers are extremely low; bringing in new consumers during this period is essential to lowering these high average costs of rural electric power and, hence, to assuring financial viability for the utility. Actually, the importance of loading up the system and making sure the utilities are fit to do so is one of the rare cases where distributional objectives coincide with economic and financial ones: the inability to load up the system limits the distributional impact of the project, especially because the poor tend to connect later rather than in the first wave of connections undertaken during the construction period.

The reasons for the lack of vigor by the Bolivian utilities in bringing more consumers into the grid fall into four categories: (1) there was no concern for this post-construction phase in the design of the project; (2) technical specifications were set without concern for their burden on operating costs after construction; (3) unrealistic assumptions were made about the ability and the willingness of the utilities and the power sector to seek rate increases that would finance expansion; and (4) a major alternative source of financing for line extensions and new hookups was neglected--i.e., the willingness of many productive and household consumers to themselves pay at least a part of the utility's cost of extending the lines or putting in transformers for them.

Overdesign: its origins and consequences. A lack of concern for costs in project design has burdened the Bolivian utilities with higher operating and amortization costs than necessary, as well as system capacity for twenty years rather than the ten projected. The overdesign of the system grew out of a project-design environment where cost constraints were not present. This happened for various reasons. AID and the design consultants, for one, insisted on technical standards used by the United States Rural Electrification Administration. The international design consultants typically used for such projects, moreover, have everything to lose from using the more appropriate, less internationally familiar standards: if something goes wrong, they are more likely to be held accountable for the design standards than when international standards have been used, in which case failings can be more readily attributed to others--e.g., manufacturers of construction materials, construction contractors, etc.

Another reason for overdesign is that design consultants on rural electrification projects are given a task that does not elicit cost consciousness: instead of being asked how one would design a system for a given cost that would serve a specified and unusually large (for U.S. standards) number of consumers, they are given only the cost or the number of consumers as constraints, or are allowed to use their own experience as guides for determining how many consumers can be served for a given cost. Finally, the project-design process leads to overdesign because, in making technical choices, it does not sufficiently involve and pay attention to those persons who will have to bear the higher administrative costs and complications resulting from overdesign; project design, that is, is dominated by design engineers, rather than those involved in utility operation and responsible for financial performance.

Mixing city rates into rural systems. When rural-electrification systems are added onto urban systems, as in the Bolivia project, it is unrealistic to expect that utilities will be able to charge rates compatible with a vigorous expansion policy--loan agreement commitments notwithstanding. The political problems of raising rates for urban public services are a well-known feature of the political economy of third-world countries. It is not only that policymakers fear the political repercussions of raising the price of urban services used by the poor. In addition, they are often deliberately pursuing a policy of keeping down the price of urban "wage goods" like food and public services; this is one reason for the bias against the countryside in the form of food-price controls. The pursuit of electric power rates that are high enough to finance a vigorous loading up of the system, then, will usually conflict with another common, and more politically compelling, policy objective. In countries that are more politically open or have a tradition of being politically sensitive to working-class demands, the problem of allowing electric-power rates to keep pace with inflation will be more acute.

The tendency of rates to lag behind inflation, contributing to the difficulty that the Bolivian utilities had in loading up the system after construction, was also caused by the fact that the utilities and the power policymakers themselves did not pursue adequate rates as vigorously as they might have. This happened because: (1) the long grace period under the AID loan (ten years) provided a time of freedom from amortization which, though financially desirable, also gave the utilities a false sense of relief from concern about rates; and (2) even before project construction had terminated, AID and the Inter-American Development Bank entered into discussions with Bolivian power officials about large follow-on loans for rural electrification; this also created a sense that there was no need to worry about rates as a source of funds for future expansion.

Willing and neglected financiers. The Bolivian utilities, finally, were not alerted by the project to the possibilities for mobilizing the kind of financing that private utilities have long resorted to when confronted with similar situations of high demand for new connections and inadequate revenues to meet that demand; a "forced" financing from the consumers desiring connection. Households and producers with sufficient capital are often willing to pay or finance the additional costs necessary to connect them up to the system--costs that the utility would normally bear. This practice, which had also been used in the city of La Paz, has not always been looked upon positively, because of its association with large foreign utilities in third-world countries and their alleged attempt to get the most revenue out of their system while putting in the least funds of their own. The circumstances in the Bolivian public power sector, however, are similar in some ways to those of the private utilities; because of inadequate rates, the public utilities will also have little of their own funds to put into expansion in the future.

There are other reasons for taking advantage of the opportunity for consumer financing of the loading up of rural electrification systems. Resort to this source of financing represents a charging of close to the full value of a service to its users, in a situation where charging that value through the rate is politically impossible. The willingness of individuals and firms to put up these funds, moreover, represents a rare opportunity to "tax" the users of public infrastructure investments according to their willingness and ability to pay, as revealed by the large extra investment they are willing to make to get the connection. Accepting the financing of these better-off applicants for connections also addresses the concern that the better-off benefit disproportionately from public investments in rural infrastructure. Finally and most important, this way of accommodating some of the unattended requests for connections is a way of keeping the utility out of its post-construction financial doldrums, by bringing in capital and subsequent revenues from power use at a greater pace than can otherwise occur.

The problems noted in this section have serious implications for the financial viability of the Bolivian electrification project, and for its potential distributional impact. In contrast to many such problems and to the investment made in the facility itself, these problems require little funding for their resolution. They would require technical assistance and some budgetary support to the utilities during the immediate post-project years--as well as costless changes, such as attentiveness to the technical choices in project design that minimize operating costs, or involvement of the operational staff of utilities in this design.

Conclusion: bringing out the social objective

The Bolivia electrification project has shown that the ability of electrification to touch the lives of the rural poor may be greater than was thought. The rural poor themselves placed great value on receiving household light, often ranking it as important a "purely" social investment as potable water, health care, and education. The coming of electric light to their towns gave the poor a sense of optimism about the future, and made them much happier about the quality of their life at night. Bolivian policymakers and power managers, moreover, wanted an electrification project with a mainly social goal--to put light into as many poor rural households as possible.

What was wrong with the Bolivian project was that the strong social objective did not sufficiently guide the technical design of the project. Though the Bolivians and AID were comfortable with an exclusively social objective, the project was also designed to meet a production objective that was unrealistic. There was little evidence in the towns to receive electric power that opportunities for use by small producers existed; where such opportunities did exist, the project did nothing to help them be realized. Two other aspects of the project worked against its ability to fulfill the social objective: overdesign, and the assumption that any alternative to central-system electrification was inadequate. Together, all of these factors worked toward minimizing rather than maximizing the number of rural households reached by the project.

If project designers had been able to follow their social preferences openly, it would have been easier for them to come up with a more technically appropriate and financially viable project. Admitting to purely social objectives, of course, would have been difficult. Rural electrification projects were supposed to have "hard" economic justifications--how else could one justify such heavy investment?--and engineers were more familiar and comfortable with capital-intensive and centralized design, whether or not it was appropriate or made for financial viability.

The Bolivia project has taught us, in sum, that the pursuit of social objectives partially clothed in other guises can do ill to electrification projects: it leaves the project without its anticipated economic returns, creates an operation of questionable financial viability and, most important, undercuts the realization of the social objective itself.

FITTING THE FOUNDATION STYLE:

THE CASE OF RURAL CREDIT

Judith Tendler
October 1981

The Inter-American Foundation

I - The Foundation and Evaluation

To evaluate the Foundation's rural credit projects, or to raise the questions that should be central to such an evaluation, is also to ask how the Foundation goes about its work, and what it does best. The Foundation has a distinct style, quite different from other donors, to which staff allegiance is strong; it has developed a comparative advantage in certain types of projects and project-design processes. Any evaluator of the Foundation's projects must always keep in mind a set of questions related to that style, in addition to the normal concerns about the operation of the project itself.

What are the types of projects that build on the Foundation's comparative advantage, or are compatible with that unique style? What are the project types that do not fare well under the Foundation style— projects that need, for example, a kind of support or monitoring that the Foundation cannot or does not believe in delivering? When the Foundation chooses to finance this latter type of project, one of two unhappy outcomes may occur: the project and its organization may go badly, or the Foundation may have to change its style, against its better judgment, in order to make the project go well. A similar appreciation for the Foundation's style must underlie the evaluation methodology it chooses. How can evaluation be done, that is, in a way that maintains the Foundation's comparative advantage and respects its way of dealing with grantees—rather than playing havoc with those ways in the attempt to do "respectable" evaluation work?

The following discussion raises questions in three areas: (1) rural credit projects or project components; (2) rural credit projects vs. other types of projects; and (3) evaluation methodology. Since the questions raised in all three areas relate to a considerable extent to the Foundation's own perception of its mission and its strength, I start with my understanding of this perception.

The Foundation style

The Foundation seems to follow three canons of behavior: it grants funds primarily to nongovernmental organizations, it wants to support organizations in which the poor participate in decisionmaking and, most unusual, it believes strongly in a donor-grantee relationship with little intervention from the donor. This last tenet, along with the small annual volume of Foundation grants (about $23 million in 1980), makes the Foundation less akin to other donor organizations, with their much larger level of operations, than to other foundations. Yet in trying to improve the quality of its processes of project selection and evaluation, the Foundation tends to compare itself (unfavorably) to the other donors, rather than to the more kindred other foundations. The "better" and more comprehensive evaluation tactics of the other donors, after all, are partly a function of their much higher levels of lending and, more important, of a lack of compunction about intervening heavily in the project design and implementation process.

The Foundation's stand against intervention grows out of the belief that donor intervention and control are not conducive to the growth of a healthy and self-sufficient organization. If intervention stifles the

108

kinds of organizational growth that the Foundation wants to nurture, then
the project design and evaluation methodologies that go along with
intervention will also stifle that growth--or, at least, will not combine
very well with it. The dilemma for the Foundation, then, is to improve
its methodologies not by emulating those of the more interventionist
donors--of which it is so critical--but by improving upon its own
noninterventionist approach.

The interventionist style of most donors, it should be pointed out,
brings to the donor a certain control over project outcomes--or, at
least, an illusion of control. This means that the intervening donor
considers itself more responsible for how a project turns out. It can
claim responsibility for project success, and it will worry over possible
project failure--either trying to make it not happen, or covering it up.
Because intervention makes one feel more responsible for project outcomes, this can lead to more intervention--more attempts to gain control
over the outcome, or at least, over the way the outcome gets written up.
These attempts to gain more control, and the acutely felt accountability
that causes them, all contribute to the difficulty that the intervening
donors have in being flexible during the course of project evolution --in
letting a project take a different path, for example, than that on which
it first started. The Foundation, in contrast to these other donors, has
been less subject to unfavorable outside scrutiny--for reasons discussed
below--and therefore has been able to afford the luxury of being less
interventionist with its grantees than these other donors; it has not had
to worry so much as the others about mistakes made by its grantees in the
course of their growth. This particular aspect of its style is not

109

only a function of its preferences, therefore, but of an environment that allowed the pursuit of those preferences.

The interventionist donor style is most successful in projects where control over project outcomes can actually be achieved, where participation of project beneficiaries is not important, and where formulae according to which the project will unfold can be laid out beforehand. Infrastructure projects approximate most this project ideal. The interventionist style is less successful, however, in areas where control over outcomes cannot be achieved, and where flexibility during implementation is necessary; in these types of projects, the interventionist style and its accountability behaviors cause donors to act as if they can control outcomes that they simply cannot. In these cases, the interventionist style can take on pathological forms--preventing, that is, the very outcomes that the project is meant to achieve (e.g., institution building, participation, adoption of new practices). It is with these latter, less controllable projects that the Foundation's comparative advantage lies since, in contrast to the intervening donors, it has made a point of not taking control.

The Foundation's doctrine of minimized intervention has two implications for its attempts to improve its project-evaluating processes. First, it should try to identify types of projects that are less vulnerable than others to a lack of donor presence or, put more positively, types of projects that do best when left alone by donors. Second, the Foundation must gain a systematic understanding of its failures and successes so that it knows which types of projects and project environments to choose the next time around. After all, the

110

moment of choice and, previous to that, of encouraging would-be
applicants, are moments at which it exercises considerable control.

As a result of these differences between the Foundation and other
donors, its sense of responsibility is quite different from that of the
others. Failures can be attributed to a bad Foundation decision, or to a
"lemon" project, but not to a lack of close monitoring--a commonly heard
explanation for failure of the projects of the intervening donors. In
this sense, the Foundation is more free and, at the same time, more
constrained than the intervening donors. On the one hand, its non-
intervening credo means that it has less responsibility for the way its
projects evolve--for their successful aspects as well as their
inadequacies. This means that it can be more relaxed and flexible,
precisely the qualities that are needed for certain types of projects.
On the other hand, the Foundation has even more responsibility than the
other donors to make the right decision in the first place--to be very
knowledgeable about what works and what doesn't among its own projects.

People vs. tasks

How does the Foundation now go about making its decisions about
projects? Like many other foundations and unlike other donors, it
devotes most of its time and reflections to making judgments about the
people involved in the organizations requesting support--are they honest,
are they dynamic and, most important to the Foundation, are they
committed to helping poor people? This process will sometimes receive
more thought and attention than the contents of the project itself--rural
credit vs. agricultural marketing, the purchase of agricultural inputs

vs. the supply of consumer goods, etc. Here and elsewhere in the report, I will therefore refer to certain aspects of Foundation decisionmaking as "people-oriented," "people-centered," "people-related," etc. My understanding of a "people-oriented" style is one that judges a project by the organization that proposes it--more than by the type of project being proposed or by the formula for carrying out that project type. Judgments about the organization, in turn, are made more in terms of the people who manage it and the way they serve or involve the poor, than in terms of certain "technical" features of the organization itself.[1]

What does the people-oriented kind of decisionmaking process involve? It means "hanging around" with the applicant, being on the scene to see how the poor are treated by an applicant organization, finding out the opinions of others on the scene whose commitment is known. This means that if the Foundation's process of judging projects is to yield good decisions, certain skills are essential--mainly a high degree of fluency and familiarity with the project environment. These are precisely the skills in which Foundation staff excel--language fluency, knowledge about the history and politics of the project's environment, and a keen taste for being around the people and

_____

[1]I use the term "people" for lack of a more accurate, shorthand way of referring to this characteristic--and even though the term causes problems for Foundation staff, because it harks back to a time when they feel they relied too much on the ability of a charismatic leader to make a project successful. When I say "people-oriented," I am including the organization as well; I do not instead say "organization-oriented" because it implies additional criteria that the larger donors, I feel, have sometimes placed excessive reliance on--bookkeeping procedures, organization charts, "modern" organizational procedures, etc. For purposes of the discussion in this paper, I feel that the contrast to the other donors is more relevant than the maturing in the Foundation's way of thinking about charismatic leaders.

the culture where the project is taking place. These skills and sensitivities are also those that other donors have been faulted for not having--and that other donors have tried at great pains and with mixed results to inculcate in their staffs. To the Foundation staff, they seem to come easily.

The Foundation, of course, has deliberately looked for these skills in recruiting new staff members. Just as important, however, its people-oriented style of operating has constituted a reward to staff for the continued development and use of these skills. The more technocratic orientations of other donors, in turn, have represented rewards to the mastery of standard techniques of analysis and the management skills required to produce and monitor many large projects. Correspondingly, these organizations have done better with these more technical skills and the kind of subject-related rather than people-related analysis that goes along with them.

People-judging talents in choosing projects are not accorded the legitimacy in the donor-assistance world that technical skills are. This results in part from the prevailing concept of development as a technical task rather than as also influenced and constrained by events of a political and institutional nature.[1] Whether right or wrong, the

---

[1]That this technical conception of development continues to predominate after so many years of experience with development projects is not only a result of inadequate understanding about how development occurs. It is also a result of the difficulties of incorporating criteria of a political and institutional nature into the decisionmaking of large organizations engaged in financing large projects--and of arriving at a consensus on what these criteria should be. Because the Foundation is so small in relation to other donors, it has been able to maintain a nonspecialist, generalist, and remarkably homogeneous staff in terms of skills and commitment. (Of a total staff of 63, approximately 30 evaluate grant proposals.) Hence, it is able to incorporate less quantifiable criteria into decisionmaking without ever having to make explicit what those criteria are.

"technical" concept of development has been a fairly workable approach to certain types of projects, mainly infrastructure; but it has turned out to be inadequate for decisionmaking about projects that have high recurrent expenditures in relation to capital expenditures, a characteristic of many projects which attempt to redistribute resources to the poor. Other donors have come to understand that in many of these latter types of projects, outcomes have been more dependent on the degree of commitment of the agencies executing the projects than on the technical features of the projects. Because the Foundation's funding has always been oriented toward the poor--in contrast to the change in this direction by the other donors in the early and mid-1970s--the Foundation has had more years of experience in gauging that type of commitment and has become good at it.

The Foundation, then, has a different way of thinking about projects than the other donors: it first chooses persons or institutions for their commitment, and then lets the type of project fall into place, as desired by the applicant. The other donors, in contrast, search for places where they can do certain types of projects--agricultural credit, agricultural extension, potable water, rural health--and then try to hook these types of projects up to the government agencies that are where such project types "belong." The Foundation, in short, determines who the "desirable" people and organizations are, while other donors determine whether the technical components of a project make economic and financial sense--disregarding, somewhat, who the people are.

Clearly, a considerable amount of people-judging is also done by the other donors. Indeed, the other donors have sometimes been criticized for relying too much on a certain person in charge of a project-executing agency--judging that person to be dynamic and charismatic enough to overcome the constraints of the project environment. This people-judging process of the other donors, however, is still subordinate to their emphasis on project type. Though reliable people are also sought out by the other donors, this is for the purpose of carrying out already-conceived notions of projects; people or institutions deemed to be dynamic and trustworthy are rarely allowed to carry out the activity that they think is best for their organization. This contrasts with the Foundation, which proceeds as if it believes that reliable people and organizations can be counted on, if supported, to improve conditions for the poor. What these people choose to do--rural credit or people's theater--is secondary.

To compare the people-centered vs. project-centered approaches to development assistance is not to say that one is better than the other, but, to point out the extent to which the Foundation is doing something very different from the other donors. It has developed comparative advantage in an area where the other donors are quite lacking. At the same time, it is lacking in the technical skills that are being developed by the other donors in response to their conception of development as a technical task. The Foundation may find it difficult to improve its project design and evaluation skills simply by acquiring the technical expertise of the other donors, or by doing evaluation that looks like what the others do and is as "respectable." If the Foundation attempts to become more technically respectable, it runs the risk of losing its own comparative advantage and extending itself into an area where it has a distinct comparative disadvantage.

115

All this is not to say that there is no room for improvement or no ground for criticism of the Foundation's way of doing things. It means, rather, that the models for needed improvement cannot necessarily be sought at the other donors. These models will have to be found within the Foundation itself, and by looking at organizations that have similar ways of making decisions--whether or not they are working on development or in third-world countries.

It is ironic that Foundation staff have a certain sense of inferiority about the fact that their technical expertise falls short of that possessed by other donors. Though Foundation staff have become more sophisticated in recent years about technical aspects of project analysis, many still feel that they could bring about the necessary improvements in their project evaluation procedures by acquiring some of that expertise possessed by the other donors. This sense of inadequacy can also be interpreted as a faltering of belief by Foundation staff in their own people-centered approach, as a desire to become more like those of whose methods they disapprove. It is a testimony to the strength of technical approaches to problems in our culture that this fiercely people-centered staff would consider themselves inadequate by the very standards with which they so heartily disagree.

The Foundation's failings, then, do not lie in its lack of skills possessed by the other donors, but in its lack of a better understanding of how to take full advantage of its own particular approach and expertise--including an understanding of the areas in which its style works well, and the areas in which its style is less compatible with its objectives of helping the poor. In the course of gaining such an understanding, the Foundation may find it necessary to acquire more knowledge of a technical nature about its projects. But this is quite different from saying that Foundation staff should themselves become more "technical."

The dilemma of improved evaluation

What would be so threatening for the Foundation if it were to adopt a more "rigorous" technical style? For one, the Foundation is quite distinct from the large donors in that it is not internally rent with quandaries about equity and efficiency, and the extent to which the pursuit of equity compromises growth. Demonstrated and significant increases in output are considered desirable but are certainly not required for Foundation projects, not even in a "cosmetic" sense. Staff do not bend over backwards searching for or elaborating economic arguments to show that their project does not compromise efficiency or growth in the course of pursuing equity--a very major concern of, and constraint on, the larger donors in their attempts to analyze and justify their reorientation to the poor. Foundation staff are unabashedly and refreshingly comfortable with projected results that are pure equity. This approach, of course, means that some projects may end up having insignificant impacts on the incomes of poor people during the project's life. But it is the Foundation's credo that increased incomes will result only from a certain project process--participatory or committed organizations working on problems defined as urgent by the beneficiaries themselves. This contrasts with the view implicit in the operations of other donors, according to which favorable outcomes result from certain project types, involving certain combinations of inputs. The Foundation needs to learn more about the circumstances under which its particular view of the world actually turns out to be accurate. It needs to learn what types of participatory organizations and circumstances are particularly conducive to favorable impacts on poor people's lives.

The Foundation is free of the problems of fitting equity-oriented projects into efficiency justifications because it has declared its interests to be elsewhere and is small enough that it is not subjected to outside demands for performance on output-increasing grounds. The absence of staff divisiveness in the Foundation about the relative importance of social, cultural, and economic objectives also results from the generalist nature of the staff. Except for administrative tasks of the four regional directors, all project staff have approximately the same function: they seek out, decide upon, and monitor projects in the country for which they are responsible. To the extent that they specialize, it is in a country more than in a discipline or skill. Unlike disciplinary specialities, moreover, they can change their specialty after a period of time--from responsibility for one country, that is, to responsibility for another. In the larger donor organizations--where specialization by field (engineers, economists, financial analysts, educationists, etc.) and tasks (operations, programs, evaluation, research) is an inevitable outcome of sheer size--conflict and ambivalence among staff about the extent to which some objectives should be given priority over others is not unusual. The various sides of the conflict often correspond to the various task or field specializations.

The Foundation, in sum, is remarkably free of some of the tension, confusion, and factionalism that characterize the other donors and their larger, more diversified organizations. Clearly, the smallness of the organization and its more limited mandate--i.e., support for primarily nongovern- mental organizations--help make it easier for the Foundation to pursue its credo and to operate with as undiversified a staff as it does. The lack of specialization also contributes to the low level of conflict among staff about what the organization is up to.

What does all this have to do with introducing more technical rigor into the organization, and with improving techniques of project evaluation? Technical rigor can be brought to organizations in one of two ways: (1) by bringing persons specialized in certain tasks or fields onto an organization's staff, permanently or temporarily through consultancies, or (2) by requiring that each member of the unspecialized staff acquire some "technical" skills. As pointed out above, Foundation staff already possess a set of skills that are hard to come by in donor organizations--mainly, language and country fluency, and a heightened understanding of the interaction of economic and political events. It would not only be difficult to keep up these skills while at the same time acquiring a set of new ones; but the new technical skills in themselves often carry value implications that in some ways run against the grain of people-centered decisionmaking and strong commitment to the poor. To introduce technical skills into the organization through specialization among the staff also presents some risk--that of introducing divisiveness into the Foundation, along specialist lines, over the nature of its task.

119

Perhaps there are other approaches to improving the Foundation's project evaluation skills that would build on its comparative advantage, rather than going against it. One such approach, as suggested above in another context, is to try to identify those projects that fit the Foundation style best--i.e., those projects that suffer least from the Foundation's inability to do high-powered "technical" analysis and monitoring of projects. Viewed in this light, rural credit might be an example of a project that does not fit the Foundation style well-- because of the dependence of project outcomes on the building up of a successful business organization. More will be said on this point later.

WORLD BANK STAFF WORKING PAPERS
Number 532

Rural Projects through Urban Eyes

An Interpretation of The World Bank's New-Style Rural Development Projects

Judith Tendler

The World Bank
Washington, D.C., U.S.A.

SUMMARY AND CONCLUSIONS

i.   The current attempts of the World Bank to address problems of poverty
in the third world have taken the form, mainly, of certain kinds of projects
directed at the poor of rural, as distinct from urban, areas. These "new-
style" rural projects of the 1970s have resulted from a growing consensus that
trickle-down approaches to poverty do not work or, at the least, that they do
not work fast enough. Poverty and maldistribution of income, it has come to be
believed, will not automatically give way—as implied by the development strategies of the 1950s and 1960s—in the course of economic growth. This evolution
in thinking about the development process has brought with it a corresponding
change in the kinds of projects favored and designed by the Bank. Whereas it
had been previously assumed that the poor would benefit along with everyone
else from roads, hydroelectric plants, ports, and irrigation projects, it is
now believed by many that poverty can be alleviated only if some development
projects are "targeted" directly on the poor. The idea of seeking out the poor
directly through projects shares considerable similarity with the earlier and
urban "War on Poverty" of the United States, as does the use of the language of
war to describe these efforts.

ii.   How did the change from a trickle-down strategy to one of direct
engagement with the rural poor manifest itself in the design and selection of
projects by the Bank? Briefly, the change took three forms. (1) Infra-struc-
ture projects, central to the trickle-down approach, were relegated to an
inferior position because the distribution of their benefits was thought to be
skewed toward the rich. (2) In contrast to infrastructure projects, agricultural projects were considered suitable for targeting on the rural poor;
projects built around agricultural credit, extension, and input supply, it
seemed, could be more easily converted into "targeted" projects, simply by
specifying a ceiling on the income level of the beneficiary. (3) Finally,
projects were changed to fit the new concern for the poor by adding "new"
sectors like health, nutrition and potable water to the agricultural production
projects. Though it would not necessarily be easy to exclude the nonpoor from
the services provided by these "equity components," investments of this nature
were still considered to have a greater potential for improving the income of
the poor than, say, investments in roads and electrification. The equity
sectors had received relatively little attention under the previous develop-
ment-assistance strategy because investments in them had been consideredas not
contributing to a nation's exports or output.

iii.   The new attempts to alleviate rural poverty through projects have met
with a certain disappointment—somewhat similar in its prematurity to the negative pronouncements made about the U.S. poverty program. Unlike the U.S. case,
fortunately, the current criticism of rural development projects has not been
so sweeping as to cause these attempts to be abandoned—at least so far.
Disappointment over the rural projects covers three areas: (1) they have
reached the poor much less than was hoped; (2) they have taken longer to
design, negotiate and execute than was expected; (3) they have had difficulty
in building and leaving behind institutions that are able to function on their
own and actually deliver services to the poor.

122

iv.   Current explanations of the problems of the new rural projects fall into three broad and overlapping categories. (1) Technologies are said to be inappropriate, such as agricultural production packages that encourage the substitution of equipment for labor, or new crop varieties and planting practices that are not adopted because they do not pay off for poor farmers. (2) Organizational designs are said to be unsuitable for the task at hand—e.g., top-heavy and overcentralized organizations for projects that should be administratively decentralized, or inadequate incentives for field staffs to do their work. (3) The last category of explanations is the focus of this study, and involves considerations of political economy. It covers the political actions and reactions of groups affected by a project—included and excluded beneficiaries, participating and non-participating agencies, supplier and other private interest groups, local and central government elites, and other political actors with something to gain or lose from the project.

v.   Actions or no action by the groups named above are singularly important to the implementation of the new rural projects, for three reasons. If successful, such projects will redistribute public-sector services and subsidies to the poor, and are therefore likely to arouse the opposition of the groups who think they have something to lose from this process. To a considerable extent, moreover, the new rural projects represent a move of the central government into previously "unoccupied" rural territory; the projects are therefore replete with implications for the balance of power between central and local elites, implications that will be played out in the implementation of the project.

vi.   The support of projects by strong interest groups, finally, has been central to the successful execution of all projects, whether redistributive or not. This is one of the most important lessons to be learned from the Bank's experience with the infrastructure projects of the past, whose execution has been tenaciously supported by engineering design firms, equipment suppliers, construction contractors and, most important, political leaders. Supportive groups can also take the form of beneficiary organizations or strong agencies, as well as the private groups such as those behind infrastructure projects.

vii.   Political-economy variables and their influence on development projects have received little attention, partly because project successes and failures have seemed to be satisfactorily explained by more obvious factors closer to the project itself—the quality of supervision and technical assistance, the presence of a committed project director, the availability of qualified construction contractors. In addition, "political" influence on project implementation has usually been assumed to be bad; it is frequently cited as causing corruption, misallocation of resources, or appropriation of project services by undeserving groups. Little attention has been paid to the positive effect that supportive and powerful political interests can have on projects— the most salient example being the infrastructure projects noted above. As long as political-economy influences were seen as only bad—rather than with a variable potential for bad or good—there was reason to try to exclude them from the world of projects and, by extension, not to consider them as a systematic feature, good or bad, in determining how projects turned out.

123

viii.   The political-economy approach suggests, in sum, that there must have been a high degree of political commitment or interest-group support behind past projects that were successful. This study attempts to understand better the mechanisms that link such support, or lack of it, to implementation.

III

ix.   When analyzed in political-economy terms, the new rural projects turn out to be wanting in two important dimensions: they do not attract supportive and powerful interest groups and, what is worse, they may actually provoke the displeasure of some of these groups—usually local elites. The absence of interest-group support, combined with opposition from some groups, goes a long way in explaining some of the problems of the new rural projects.

x.   The political economy of the new rural projects is better understood by comparing them to urban projects for the poor, where the concept of "targeting" on the poor originated. Urban projects for the poor—the focus of the U.S. poverty program and of the Bank's urban development program—are distinct from rural projects in two significant ways. The urban poor, for one, live densely and separated from the urban rich. This makes it easier to target projects on them, simply by locating the projects in poor neighborhoods. The rural poor, in contrast, live mixed in with the rich; one cannot reach them simply by locating a project in a certain place. A particularly significant aspect of this distinction is that infrastructure projects, while eminently suited for targeting on the urban poor, have been declared unsuitable for reaching the rural poor, as noted above. Whereas urban infrastructure projects can be confined to poor city neighborhoods, that is, there are no such exclusive concentrations of the poor in the countryside. Yet infrastructure projects are those that attract political support the most, no matter who the beneficiaries are.

xi.   The second main distinction between urban and rural projects for the poor is that urban projects involve mainly the physical quality of life of the poor—health, housing, streets, sewerage, light, water. Rural projects, in contrast, focus on the production activities of the rural poor in agriculture—credit, inputs, planting practices. Rural projects therefore invade the domain of the elites as landlords and employers of the rural poor—whereas urban projects do not. Indeed, to the extent that urban projects make for a healthier work force, they are to the benefit of the urban elites who are employers and producers. Because rural projects focus on the poor as agricultural producers rather than on their physical quality of life, moreover, these projects also invade the domain of rural elites in that they introduce competing clients for the subsidized goods and services already enjoyed by these elites as agricultural producers. Urban projects for the poor, in contrast, in no way threaten the access of urban-based producers to government services and subsidies.

xii.   As currently conceived, in sum, rural projects for the poor turn out to be more politically radical than urban projects—even though, by concentrating on increasing the agricultural production of small farmers ratherthan on purely social objectives, they do not seem so. At the same time, the rural projects are particularly bereft of interest-group support: the new beneficiaries, being poor, are not very powerful; and infrastructure, which is very rich in interest-group support, is not available for targeting in the countryside.

xiii.   The political-economy problems of rural projects for the poor are not inevitable or insuperable. In part, they result from a borrowing of the concept of targeting from its more successful application in urban poverty projects and in war--and a grafting of that concept onto the agricultural production projects of the past. The grafting procedure did not bring out the best, from the point of view of interest-group support, in the environment of the new rural projects.

IV

xiv.   If the problem of rural projects is that they have almost no interest group support and, at the same time, bring out the opposition of local elites, then perhaps their design can be modified with the purpose of decreasing opposition, or eliciting more interest on the part of powerful groups. Some of the advantages of urban projects, in other words, might be simulated in the rural projects--namely, the lack of strong disharmony between urban projects for the poor and urban elite interests, the physical separation of the poor from those elites who might otherwise appropriate project benefits and, a related feature, the appropriateness for urban targeting of infrastructure projects, with their coterie of powerful interest groups.

xv.   The urban comparison suggests three ways in which one might improve the chances for rural projects to reach the poor: (1) by simulating the "targetability" of the urban poor--i.e., their physical concentration and isolation from the nonpoor; (2) by changing project designs in a way that causes less umbrage to the elites; and (3) by compensating for the lack of powerful and supportive interest groups behind project implementation.

xvi.   There are certain ways in which the "targetability" of the urban poor might be simulated in rural projects. One would be to locate projects in areas where the rural poor are concentrated--that is, where there are less of the elites or, at least, of those elites who would have the most to lose from a project benefiting small cultivators. Projects might do better in those areas, for example, with unimodal rather than bimodal landholding distributions. Another place to find concentrations of the poor is in frontier areas of spontaneous colonization where, for lack of infrastructure and services, large landowners have not yet arrived. Such projects would be analagous in concept to urban "sites and services" projects. A final example of isolating the rural poor from the nonpoor for purposes of project design would be to limit a project's activities to those in which the rich have no interest--e.g., low-status crops--or to provide services in a way that is costly, inconvenient or uncomfortable for the rich to take advantage of.

xvii.   Less opposition might be elicited from rural elites if projects represented less of an invasion of their territory as producers, employers and landlords. One way to achieve this, ironically, would be for projects to concentrate more, on the social sectors--health, potable water, education--in

125

contrast to agricultural production. Social-sector projects represent less of an invasion of the domain of the elites than do production projects for the poor; their benefits, moreover, may be less readily appropriable by elites. Such a change, of course, would tend to take the new rural projects away from the output-oriented focus that is their hallmark and the source of much of their support--both within the Bank and from ministries of finance and planning.

xviii.   Another approach to reducing elite opposition to rural projects would be to take the social-sector components out of the production projects alto- gether, and make them into separate projects. In this way, the social compo- nents would at least not be adversely affected by the opposition that the pro- duction components arouse. Another advantage of such a move away from multi- component projects would be a reduction of the inter-agency coordination that such projects require, which places an unnecessarily heavy burden on project implementation.

xix.   Another way of reducing opposition to the new rural projects is to give the elites something of the project--in deliberate violation of the concept that such projects must benefit only the poor. Considerable caution would have to be exercised in buying off the opposition of elites in this way: the piece of the project given to them should be located far from the component meant for the poor. Otherwise, the attempted cooptation of the elites will simply put them in the position of eventually taking a much larger share of the project than was meant for them. In an agricultural credit project for the poor, for example, one might place a livestock-research component for the elites, administered by a different agency and not requiring coordination with the agency executing the component for the poor. A large-farmer credit line in a small-farmer credit project and administered out of the same bank, in con- trast, would defeat the purpose. The latter approach, by the way, is the one usually taken when elite unhappiness about being excluded from an impending project is given in to.

xx.   Making up for the lack of powerful groups behind project implementa- tion is the most challenging of the political-economy problems. One approach is to provide a certain isolation to the agency or agency department executing the project. If the agency already services large-farmer clients, it will feel highly divided about taking on the poorer group. A separate agency or agency unit, in contrast, does not internalize within the executing agency the class conflict between employer and employee, peasant and landowner, small producer and large producer. The separateness of a project-executing agency or agency unit can provide an environment in which the agency itself becomes an important support group for the project--as happened with some of the urban poverty projects in the United States. This approach, it should be noted, may involve placing certain tasks in agencies where they do not normally belong; the credit-and-extension projects that were most successful in reaching the poor in Northeast Brazil, for example, were those run out of the nutrition agency which, unlike the extension agency, had no competing and previous clientele among the elites.

xxi.   Another approach to generating support groups in the new rural
project's environment is to imitate those interest-group configurations that
have been important in the promotion of past agricultural projects--i.e.,
interest groups among the beneficiaries themselves. The new rural projects
might bring incipient groups among the poor into project design and monitoring
in a limited way. Note that the argument here is somewhat distinct from that
which is made in favor of popular participation in projects: the role for
groups of the poor in project design or monitoring proposed here is meant to
legitimize and strengthen such groups so that they will later make demands,
when the project starts to fall off course, that benefits not be diverted to
others or that funding not be delayed. Project design, in other words, should
encourage the growth of groups that will pressure from outside the project,
whether or not they actually participate in it. Needless to say, a role for
groups of poor beneficiaries would also improve the quality of project implementation by providing feedback from those whose participation is necessary to
make projects work well--as, for example, in the case of adoption of new agricultural practices, inputs and varieties.

xxii.   Finally, the grave dearth of supportive and powerful interest groups
in the environment of the new rural projects suggests that infrastructure
projects be given another look to see if, in some instances, they might be made
more suitable for targeting on the rural poor. Though the new rural projects
often include infrastructural components, these components are usually not conceived of in terms of how their impact on the poor might be increased. In some
instances, then, certain locational and design choices might be made that would
sharpen the focus of rural infrastructure projects on the poor.

Turning Private Voluntary Organizations Into Development Agencies
Questions for Evaluation .

by

Judith Tendler

A.I.D. Program Evaluation Discussion Paper No. 12

Office of Program and Management Support
Bureau of Food and Voluntary Assistance

and

Office of Evaluation
Bureau for Program and Policy Coordination

U.S. Agency for International Development

April 1982

Suggestions to Evaluators

The following set of suggestions for evaluators is meant to help them get at the issues raised in this paper. Many of them are obvious, but have been included because the evaluations done so far have usually not yet yielded this kind of information. Some of the suggestions are repeated from the text of the paper; others follow directly from arguments in the text. The questions are divided into five categories, even though many do not fit neatly in one category or another; some of the questions in certain categories are elaborations of questions raised in previous categories.

Participation, benefit distribution, innovation, cost

1.   Locate the participants and the beneficiaries of the PVO activity in the income distribution of the community, approximately by thirds. Elaborate on how the benefits and results of the PVO activity are distributed among dwellers in the area. (Further questions elaborated below.)

2.   Learn the history of community decisions and acts that took place up to and during the PVO activity. Find out to what extent existing community groups were included in project decisionmaking, and to what extent the poorest groups participated--the landless, women, ethnic or social outcast groups, temporary (vs. permanent) workers, land tenants (vs. owners), small (vs. large) owners, etc. (Further questions below.)

3.   Did indigenous organizations exist prior to the project? Among the poorest too? How were they included in project decisionmaking? If not, why?

4.   Find out what innovations or experimentation have resulted from the PVO's presence. What have been the changes in course, if any, and what were the results of these changes?

5.   Estimate the cost of the activity, separating out person-hours and their costs from other contributions; use this information to make estimates of cost per beneficiary, per-input, or per-output; compare these estimates to those for public-sector projects of a similar nature.

6.   If decisionmaking is not particularly participatory, are there ways of making it more so? Does project history show that decision-making is more participatory now than it was originally? How was this accomplished?

7.   Are there certain project tasks or activities that are not
as suited to participatory decisionmaking as others? That is, does
participation result in less effective project outcomes in some
cases? What are the tasks that seem better suited? less well suited?
Why?

8.   When decisionmaking is in the hands of local elites and
therefore non-representative, do the excluded groups nevertheless
benefit? In situations of elite control are there some activities
where excluded groups benefit regardless of elite control, and other
activities for which elite control results in mainly elite beneficiaries?

9.   Do some activities seem more appropriable by elites than
others--e.g. fertilizer supply vs. health-clinic services?

10.   Does the project exclude elites from decisionmaking or benefits
in any way? If so, how were they bypassed? Some examples are activities
in which the elites have no interest, low-status activities, class-based
organizations from which elites are naturally excluded--like women's
organizations, tenants' unions, labor unions, etc.

11.   What aspects of the project, if any, seem to be reaching the
poorest stratum of the population? Why are these activities, as distinct
from the others, able to reach the poorest? What is the nature of the
relation between the PVO and the poorest in these particular activities--
participatory, "enlightened" top-down?

12.   By reading country-specific studies on income distribution,
and by talking with local people, find out how to identify the poorest
groups--e.g., lowest caste. casual laborers, women, etc. Seek them or
their representatives out to ascertain how they are being affected by
the project.

13.   Watch for examples of, or opportunities for, targeting on the
poor by type of activity--e.g., low-status activities and goods,
absence of elite interest in participation in the activity, class-
based organizations, etc. Are these opportunities being exploited,
and if not, how might they be?

14.   To gauge the degree of representativeness of local participation
in the project, find out about the history of some important issues and
how they were resolved. One evaluation, for example, chronicles the
history of some suggestions made by a group of coop members to its
board, and how and why those suggestions were overriden.

15.   With respect to project activities involving women, determine to what extent they augment women's income-earning capacities and other forms of power, and to what extent they reinforce women's traditional role as homemaker. If the latter is the case, make suggestions as to what changes in project design would be appropriate.

16.   Where there is a community contribution to projects, ascertain its distributional burden. For example, voluntary labor might fall disproportionately on the poor while contributions in cash or kind might fall disproportionately on the rich.

Impact

17.   ' Give some idea of the importance of the project in the region or country--percent of the population affected, percent of project expenditures in relation to total government expenditures in the sector, percent of the goods provided in the country or by the public sector (e.g., health clinics, fertilizers, seeds, credit, schools, standpipes, trained specialists, etc.). To save time, use the national or regional-level figures for comparison that can usually be found together in national five-year plans, annual economic reports, or economic surveys carried out by the World Bank.

18.   Much of the impact of these projects will be discovered through institutional history rather than data. This requires being alert to the history of the project in the community and the area--what was accomplished, what chain reactions were set off (in prices, in private-sector behavior, in town politics, in public sector responses). It is not necessary to catalogue what has happened in all these areas; rather, in asking questions and listening to histories, one should be sensitive to the possibilities of finding impact in one of these ways. Don't ask people what the impact was; ask, rather, "what happened" and then ask, "what happened next?"

19.   If benefits have gone mainly to elites, try to determine which category the case belongs to: (1) the poor are also benefited, through a trickle-down or spread effect (describe this indirect mechanism); (2) the poor are harmed (as in the case of subsidies for large livestock, resulting in the eviction of cropping tenants); and (3) the poor are not affected one way or another.

Training and extension

Many projects involve teaching people new ways of doing things--nutrition education, agricultural extension, vocational training, etc. A series of questions should be asked about these teaching projects.

20.   . Are the "new ways" appropriate, in light of the current literature on or experience with this sector?

21.   What was the extent of adoption of the new ways among those who received assistance or training?

22.   What was the difference between adopters and non-adopters, or participants and non-participants, in terms of income, occupation, . sex, and landholding status?

23.   What was the extent of adoption among non-participants, through the demonstration effect? This question relates closely to impact, since training can have a considerably larger impact if the non-participants copy what the participants are doing--i.e., if there are "spread" effects.

24.   If there was "spread" from adopters to non-adopters, or participants to non-participants, find out what the mechanism of the spread was.

25.   Is there a natural barrier to spread, such as requirements like capital, location along a good road, landownership (vs. land tenancy or landlessness), privileged access to inputs or credit?

26.   Are certain aspects of training or extension more apt to be picked up by non-participants than others? E.g., seeds that one can grow on one's own and then pass along to neighbors--in contrast to hybrid seeds that have to be bought each year, or other agricultural innovations that require close supervision by extensionists or capital and other inputs not accessible to many.

27.   When people adopt the new ways, what is the result for their lives and their incomes? Sophisticated data are not necessary; ask the people what difference the new practice made in their lives; don't ask only the project staff.

28.   Of those participants who did not adopt the new ways, find out why. Were their income constraints? Irrelevance to their lives or

production activities? Inappropriateness of the recommendations? Try to avoid traditional explanations of non-adoption that point to "ignorance" or "lack of understanding" on the part of the participant.

The public sector

Adoption and amplification by the public sector of PVO ideas, approaches, and programs is an area of large potential impact of PVO projects. The interactions of public-sector entities with PVO activities—and the reflections of public-sector managers and technicians about these activities—are therefore a very important area of observation. Public-sector response is also important for determining whether the PVO is playing an innovative or "precursor" role.

29.   What has the public sector been doing in this particular activity or sector, if anything? How does the PVO activity differ from what the public sector is doing? Try to explain the difference.

30.   Thinking about the PVO-government relationship can be organized into one or more of the following categories: (1) complementarity, (2) filling unoccupied territory, (3) replication or diffusion, (4) government takeover, (5) competition or substitution, and (6) brokerage. Place the project in the relevant category, and try to elaborate on the relationship and its effect on the project, its relevance to project goals (e.g., projects designed to provide technical assistance or new inputs may instead be providing brokerage between the poor and government institutions).

31.   If the project involves interdependence with a public-sector entity, find out in what ways the cooperation is working well, and in what areas badly. Suggest an explanation for the variation in the experience. Be sure to get at least as much information on the question from public-sector persons as from the PVO. Does it seem that certain activities are more conducive to successful cooperation than others? Why?

32.   In the cases of interdependence, is there a division of labor between PVO and government that works particularly well? Does the PVO seem to have a particular comparative advantage in one area and the government in another?

33.   In the cases of public-sector interactions, pay attention to the commitment of the public-sector entity to serving and working with this particular client group. Is it high or low? Pay particular attention to field staff, and their interactions with the client group.

34.   Interviews with relevant public-sector managers and technicians are also important even when the project has little relation to the public sector. Find out whether these persons have found the PVO to be doing something interesting, to be a problem, to be relevant, etc.

35.   Interpret PVO complaints about governments with care, and learn both sides of the story.

36.   Try to distinguish between what is good for the PVO organization, and what is good for project impact. If a PVO project is successful, the government may want to copy it; if the PVO is so successful that it is becoming too important in a particular sector, the government may feel that this is politically undesirable. Governments, that is, may sometimes make things difficult for PVOs, or crowd them out, because PVOs have been so successful that the government wants to take over. From an impact point of view, many such cases may be characterized as successes, even though they may represent problems or failure from the PVO's point of view.

37.   In cases where there are successful transitions from PVOs to governments, try to understand what made the PVO able to manage the transition. Has the government tried to take advantage of the PVO experience, or has it instead discredited it. Why?

38.   At a more general level, be alert to the effect of national economic policies and political environments on the PVO project. Do certain economic policies overwhelm the effects of the political environment--for good or for bad--or vice versa?

Success and failure, achievements and problems

39.   The evaluator should treat any successes with a sense of awe. Do not be content to say that something worked well, but venture an explanation as to why it worked. Explain what is happening in the project against a background of what is predictable and what is a surprise.

40.   Be alert to the possibility that certain project components or tasks may work well consistently across different project sites and countries while certain others consistently do poorly. Try to explain the reasons for the pattern.

41.   Approach the pattern of problems and achievements through time, in addition to gaining an understanding of the current moment

134

in time. Ask questions about the history of the project--false starts, changes of course, unanticipated events. Ask PVO staff and community participants what they do differently now than they did before, and why.

42. Don't hold organizations to their stated objectives, especially if they seem to be doing well in other areas. First look open-endedly at what the organization has accomplished, regardless of its objectives; then compare the reality and the objectives. Does the reality shed any light on the objectives?

43. Be on the alert for unanticipated success. Such achievements may be obscured by the fact that the project failed in its stated objectives.

44. In trying to explain success and failure, try to go beyond explanations having to do with the quality of the program leader. Some types of projects are more apt to attract good leaders than others; some types of projects do well even with mediocre leadership. Think about whether the project type itself has contributed to program out-comes, in other words, and explain what it is about this project type or task that makes it more amenable to success (or failure).

45. Related to the above suggestion is the fact that certain problems experienced by projects are recurrent and therefore not a surprise--e.g., faulty maintenance, lack of coordination between agencies, lack of funds for operating costs, schools without teachers, health clinics without doctors. Be aware of what these recurrent problems are in the type of project under observation. If the problems are occurring, spend relatively little time in exploring and explaining why they occur--since they are to be expected. Instead, look for cases where the expected problems are not occurring, and then try to explain why they did not appear.

46. The discussion of problems or problem projects should be set in a broader context of why this particular problem might or might not be characteristic of this particular type of project or project setting. Attention should be focused, in other words, not only on what the PVO did that went wrong, or on what went wrong in the circumstances surrounding this particular project.

47. When looking at projects involving construction, keep in mind the following: (a) post-construction problems are the rule rather than the exception, and they should be known about beforehand and watched for; and (b) successful transitions from construction to operation deserve special attention, and an attempt should be made to understand what brought the transition about.

135

48.   A companion to the above suggestion is that certain types
of successes are more frequent than others--e.g., community cooperation
in the construction of facilities. Achievements in these latter areas
come as less of a surprise, and therefore require less elaboration
than achievements in areas where success is less common.

49.   Successes are sometimes facilitated by the sequence by which
certain events or activities take place, rather than by a certain
constellation of factors at any one time. Be aware of these sequences
of project development through time, and think about whether they are
associated with achievements or problems.

50.   Be alert to the possibility that some achievements are made
by project organizations that look disorderly or in other ways deficient
as organizations. Don't let the disorderliness of the organization
obscure its achievements. Be alert to the possibility, moreover, that
certain achievements will have been made because of the disorderliness
of the organization, and not despite it. Judge the PVO not only on its
completeness as an organization, in other words, but by the quality of
its project. The project may be good, though the organization looks
bad. Try to explain this.

Fieldwork style and other suggestions

51.   Consider the unit of observation to be the community or the
area where the project takes place, and not the PVO.

52.   Do not rely heavily on project input and output data as the
main source for what the project has accomplished. If the project has
carried out a series of training courses, for example, attend the courses,
talk to the participants, go to their homes. If the project has promoted
kitchen gardens, go and look at the gardens and talk to their owners.

53.   Make an assessment of the competence of project staff, in terms of
their training, experience, language ability, and commitment.

54.   Pay just as much attention to junior and field staff as to managers.
Junior field staff of projects are often neglected in interviewing. Yet they
often have more contact with and understanding of beneficiaries than persons in
managerial positions. They also will often have good ideas about how the
project might be improved, what the source of its problems are, and the
nature of the project's impact on households and on the region. Their ideas
and perceptions are often unexpressed because of hierarchical patterns and deference

to authority in office meetings. Try to talk with these persons, therefore, away from the office. The best opportunity for this is to take jeep trips with these persons to visit faraway beneficiaries or project sites. Much can also be learned about project staff and their style with beneficiaries by doing some interviewing of beneficiaries with project staff accompanying or participating.

55.   Ask project managers and staff what information they would find useful from an evaluation. What are the questions, perplexities, and contradictions they face that make it difficult for them to proceed as they would like?

56.   Be careful not to accept the assumptions behind project design as truths--e.g., that vocational training per se accomplishes its purpose of increased opportunities for employment. Similarly, do not accept achievement of project outputs as *prima facie* evidence of achievement of project objectives--e.g. number of participants trained should not be accepted as a proxy for achievement of the employment objective. Do not assume that agricultural extension automatically leads to increased production and therefore is good in itself; do not assume that nutrition training automatically leads to changed habits; do not assume, when habits *do* change, that the changed habit automatically leads to better-nourished and more healthy families; do not assume that vocational training automatically leads to employment. Do not use project outputs, in sum, as a proxy for indicating the achievement of project objectives.

57.   Much of what is to be learned about the project will come from interviews and not documents--in the community, and not in the project office. Since interviews take so much time, evening hours should be taken advantage of. They represent an opportunity for learning about the project by "hanging around" in the communities where the project takes place, eating and drinking with local people or local staff.

58.   Interviews with community members who participate or benefit from a project are just as important as interviews with project staff. Similarly, interviews with community members who do not participate or benefit from the project are equally important as those with participants or beneficiaries.

59.   In assessing project outputs and achievements, pay less attention to what people and organizations say they intend to do than to what has actually happened. Information about intentions is not helpful for judging an organization because the intentions may or may not come true.

60.   Make a special effort to talk to ex-clients or ex-participants of a project. They will have a longer experience, a more reflective

view, and a different perspective. Ex-staff members or managers, moreover, will often feel free to talk more openly, and will have had more time and distance to be reflective about their experience.

61.   Do not give up on assessing impact because there is not enough time to do an adequate quantitative assessment, or because the time and the data do not allow establishing causality between the project and what has happened. As a proxy, ask beneficiaries and community members how their lives are different as a result of the project. This will give some indicators of impact, or at least of clues to pursue.

62.   Be sure to know the state of the art in the sector you are evaluating. Use this knowledge to comment on the extent to which the project is innovative, is following the latest wisdom on the subject, or is using approaches that the current wisdom has proven to be inappropriate.

What to Think About Cooperatives:
A Guide From Bolivia

Judith Tendler
in collaboratiion with
Kevin Healy and Carol Michaels O'Laughlin

The Inter-American Foundation

139

Overview

I visited four peasant cooperative associations in Bolivia and came away perplexed. On the one hand, the four groups--which are described below--were decidedly successful in certain ways. On the other hand, they lacked some of the basic qualities considered vital to this kind of success. In fact, they had various traits and problems that we usually associate with failure. My puzzlement over this strange combination of success and inadequacy, and my struggle to reconcile the two sides of the picture I saw, were the inspiration for most of what is written here.

A word, first, about the nature of the success I witnessed, before describing the seeming mismatch between success and inadequacy. The most obvious achievement of the Bolivian groups is that they still exist, almost ten years after their creation. Though they have not yet suffered the ending of outside donor funding, their survival and active life are something of a record, when compared to many other endeavors to organize rural cooperatives in Latin America. A second category of achievements of the Bolivian groups is the benefits they provided to peasant-farmer members and, in many cases, nonmembers: (1) better prices, greater reliability, and honest weights resulting from cooperative purchasing and marketing of their crops, using coop-owned trucks; (2) better prices, honest measures and weights, and unadulterated products available at coop stores supplying consumer staples and agricultural inputs (the price differential tended to diminish after awhile, in marketing as well as retailing, either because coop prices drifted back toward prevailing prices or because private merchants adjusted their prices downwards to meet the coop competition); (3) savings in transport and other expenditures for farmers who previously had to travel some distance to buy consumer staples and inputs, and now could buy them nearby; (4) transport savings to producers resulting from the establishment of coop processing facilities (rice mills, cacao-processing plant) where before there were none; (5) availability of credit to those who previously had no access to banks; and (6) new opportunities for employment and apprenticeship in coop service operations, of which agroprocessing created the most jobs.

In addition to these benefits, two of the coop associations provided benefits to whole communities through community infrastructure projects undertaken in their early years--schools, potable water, irrigation, road grading. Another association initiated a campaign to combat cacao blight, which could have a significant impact on grower incomes. And the agricultural equipment-rental service of one association allowed peasant farmers to make the move from shifting to stable agriculture, and from rice-growing to cane-growing, with corresponding increases in income. Many of the benefits named here were reaped by nonmembers as well as members.

These direct benefits of coop activity tended to diminish as the groups struggled with the problems of running a business. Perhaps more enduring than the direct benefits were some less tangible results. In each region, the coop association represented one of the few institutions voicing the economic interests of peasant farmers. As organized groups, with one or another successful business ventures to show for themselves, the associations were able to (1) make effective claims on public-sector goods and services available previously only to larger farmers (official lines of subsidized credit, agricultural research and extension services, favorable tariff treatment for imported equipment, etc.); (2) gain entry to private-sector industry associations (of rice-millers, rice cooperatives, grape growers, grape distilleries), from which the coop associations gained valuable information about prices and marketing, and in which they could wield some influence on the side of peasant interests; and (3) set an example of how banks and public-sector agencies could relate to peasant groups, creating some confidence in these powerful institutions about the possibility of working with such

142

groups and giving both sides experience with what such a relationship could be like. Again, these benefits were available to members and nonmembers alike.

Viewed against this picture of benefits, the inadequacies of the coop associations are striking. The most impressive inadequacy was in the area of management and administration. Prices charged for merchandise and services were sometimes too low to cover costs, credit collection was casual, inventory and sales records were often not kept, coop leaders were frequently the largest borrowers from coop credit funds, and acts of malfeasance were common.

The second surprising inadequacy of the coop associations had to do with membership growth. Membership seemed to stop growing at an early stage, even when the associations were expanding their services and income-earning activities. Each association had an average of 20 member coops with 17 members apiece, for a total of only 350 members. At most, coop membership reached only 25% of the families in a community, and a much smaller share of the population of the area served by the association of coops. Given that each association group had received roughly US$350,000 from the Inter-American Foundation, the small size of membership could be taken to mean an average investment of US$1,000 per member family--in addition to significant investment in the form of member and other donor contributions, and IAF staff expenditures. Measured against the low-cost model of

development assistance aspired to by the IAF, these costs would appear
to be disappointingly high--an appearance that turns out to be
modified significantly when we take nonmember benefits into account.

The final shortcoming of the four Bolivian groups had to do
with leadership. Leadership and management positions usually rotated
among the same few persons, who were from among the better-off members
of the community. Though entrenched and better-off leaders are not
necessarily incompatible with success, they are usually thought of as
leading to trouble--misappropriation of coop goods and services,
programs that benefit only a select few, and the corrupt behavior that
flourishes in an environment where there are no "democratic" pressures
to be accountable.

It is obvious why the first inadequacy I list, weak
management, would be cause for surprise. We are used to seeing this
problem singled out, after all, as the cause of coop failure. It is
not so obvious why we are bothered when coops have small and declining
memberships, little participation, and entrenched leaderships. What
does this matter, if they succeed in generating some significant
benefits? The problem, of course, lies partly in our vision of coops
as participatory and democratic. If they turn out to do some good, it
is hard for us to believe that they are low on participation. In
reaction to this contradiction, we tend to see more participation and
less control by entrenched leaders than actually exist or, more

skeptically, we suspect that significant benefits for the poor have really not been achieved. Also when we find that our favorite qualities are lacking in coops, we tend to prescribe or fund remedies for catching up--more training in cooperativism, more rotation of leadership, more drives to expand membership.

Coops with entrenched leaderships, small and declining memberships, and weak participation also cause us concern because of the faith that we, as donors, have placed in them. We see coop groups like the Bolivian ones as more desirable and genuine approaches to the alleviation of rural poverty than many programs of the public sector--particularly in countries with weak and hierarchical institutions serving the countryside, or with repressive regimes that are unsympathetic to a more proportional distribution of public-sector goods and services. If the membership of even the successful peasant federations is so paltry after so many years of our support, then how can we maintain our faith in these groups as a hopeful alternative to the deficient public sector?

Finally, we are uncomfortable about an entrenched and better-off leadership because we think it leads to an elite-biased distribution of coop benefits. This kind of distribution, after all, is what has disappointed us so many times about the programs of the public sector. If coops are to have an impact on the rural poor, in other words, we expect to see them larger and growing, more democratic

145

and participatory, and with a leadership that rotates more vigorously and reaches more broadly into the community.

My search for ways to see the inadequacies of the Bolivian groups as more in harmony with their achievements led to four kinds of explanations: (1) the inadequacies turned out to be not as problematic as they are usually thought to be--or, resolving the problems was not always a prerequisite for doing well; (2) some of the problems were the side effects of improvements in management; (3) some of the inadequacies were more troublesome when they occurred in combination with certain crops, social structures, and tasks; and (4) certain tasks were distinctly more vulnerable to management inadequacies than others. All this is not to say that the shortcomings of the Bolivian groups are not to be taken seriously. Rather, the causal link between problems and failure--and between "prerequisites" and success--turned out to be looser than we are used to thinking it to be.

Conclusion

I have made various suggestions about how donors might improve the way they make decisions about coops and other projects that seek to improve the conditions of the rural poor. These suggestions, if followed, do not necessarily require a cooperative as their instrument. Sometimes, as we will see, the coops are a good form in which to undertake the pursuit of our goals, though the form will not always fit our image of what a good coop should be. Sometimes, moreover, we will want to conduct the pursuit of our goals through coops for a limited time only, after which the coop may tend to stagnate, decline or limit its benefits. At this point we may want to facilitate a transfer of the activity from the coop to the state (or to another entity), or at least support some interaction between the two. To do this would be to support a sequence of institutional development of which coops are an early stage. This means that our support of coops may not be worth its while unless the subsequent steps in the sequence also take place.

Finally, our experience with coops can teach us a great deal about decentralized community or regional initiatives. Sometimes, non-cooperative forms of these endeavors will be an even better approach to the task. Normally, we tend to ignore or reject these

147

other-institutional forms because they do not have the "good" qualities we associate with coops--they may be controlled by elites, they may be weak on management, they may involve only a few people. But since our study has shown that coops themselves often have these same "failings"--even when they yield substantial benefits--then we need not be so restrictive in our search for alternatives. At the same time, we will have to pay careful attention to the structural factors that contribute to the good results, a central theme in this study.

Unfortunately, I have not come up with a better description, or term, for what "coops" actually are when they are doing the good things that the Bolivian groups were doing. Though this kind of naming would help us recognize the kinds of groups we want to support, it would also be inconsistent with the findings of my analysis. What determined the various accomplishments of the Bolivian groups, that is, was not only their organizational form. It was also a combination of structural factors--the sequence in which activities were undertaken, the social structure of the communities, the varying characteristics of the principal crops grown, and the traits of the various activities undertaken by the coops. Since these combinations are different for every group, the same organizational form can easily give rise to different results--some satisfying to us, and some not.

1 - Introduction

I wrote this study in the course of puzzling over some striking
contradictions. On the one hand, the four Bolivian peasant groups I
visited were decidedly successful in certain ways or for certain
periods of time--in contrast to many other coop ventures.[1] The groups
had become a presence in the region where they operated, providing
peasant farmers with control over certain markets, and yielding them
benefits. On the other hand, the four groups were deficient in the
basic qualities considered vital to this kind of success. In fact,
they had various traits and problems that we usually associate with
failure.

The seeming mismatch between the coops' accomplishments and
their qualities can be divided into three areas. First, their memberships were small, did not grow and, in some cases, had even declined.
Second, leadership and management positions circulated among a few
better-off members of the community. Third, coop administration was
weak, or had been for a long time after the IAF-financed activities
were started: accounting was poor, prices charged for merchandise
and services were often too low to cover costs, credit collection
was casual, inventory and sales records were often non-existent, coop
leaders and managers were frequently the largest borrowers out of
credit funds, and episodes of taking from the till were plentiful.

---

[1]A description of each group can be found in the Summary and Conclusions.

It is obvious why the last category, weak management, would give us cause for surprise. Immediately previous to my study trip, for example, an AID-sponsored evaluation of coops in Bolivia found the groups to be largely unsuccessful, precisely because of the management weaknesses we cited above—as well as shortcomings in membership size and control by an entrenched and better-off leadership, our first and second categories above (Devres 1982). If these management inadequacies caused failure in the AID-financed program, then how do we explain the partial success of the IAF-funded groups, with their similar weaknesses?

It is not so obvious why we find it problematic that coops have small and declining memberships, little participation, and entrenched leaderships. What does this matter, after all, if they succeeded in generating some significant benefits? The problem, of course, lies partly in our vision of coops as participatory and democratic. If they turn out to do some good, it is hard for us to believe that they are low on these qualities. In reaction to this contradiction, we tend to see more participation and less control by entrenched leaders than actually exist or, more skeptically, we suspect that significant benefits for the poor have really not been achieved. When we find that our favorite qualities are lacking in the recipients of our funding, we tend to prescribe remedies for catching up—more training in cooperativism, more rotation of leadership, more drives to expand membership.

Coops with entrenched leaderships and small memberships are a problem for us also because of the faith that we, as donors, have placed in them. We see coop groups like the Bolivian ones as more desirable and genuine approaches to the alleviation of rural poverty than many programs of the public sector--particularly in countries with weak and hierarchical institutions serving the countryside, or with repressive regimes that are unsympathetic to calls for a fairer distribution of public-sector goods and services. If the membership of even the successful peasant federations is so paltry after so many years of our support, then how can we maintain our faith in these groups as a hopeful alternative to a deficient public sector? Finally, we are uncomfortable about an entrenched and better-off leadership because we think it leads to an elite-biased distribution of coop benefits--which is what disappointed us so about the programs of the public sector. If coops are to have an impact on the rural poor, in sum, then we expect to see them larger and growing, more democratic and participatory, and with a leadership that rotates more vigorously and reaches more broadly into the community.

The organization of this study reflects my attempt to put together these seemingly contradictory findings in a more harmonious way--though I stray from the contradiction problem throughout the paper, covering various topics of little direct relation to it. First, I attempt to explain why membership was low and declining, whether this reflected a natural dynamic, and whether there might be a positive side to this phenomenon. Second, I search for an explanation for the successes of the studied groups at certain activities, and for the benefits they generated, despite their small memberships and their classic weaknesses in management. Third, I try to separate out the expansion of membership from the expansion of income-generating activities and services. This leads to a mapping of some of the paths to expansion, as well as the barriers along the way, as revealed in each coop's story. And fourth, I explore the relationship between control by the better-off and the distribution of benefits. The result of all these attempts is to come up with some suggestions for the IAF, based on the Bolivian experience, on how to make decisions about coops and any other projects that seek to improve the conditions of the rural poor.

My suggestions, if followed, do not necessarily require a cooperative as their instrument. Sometimes, as we will see, the coops are a good form in which to undertake the pursuit of our goals, though the form will not always fit our image of what a good coop should be. Sometimes, moreover, we will want to conduct the pursuit of our goals through coops for a limited time only, after which the coop tends to stagnate, decline or limit its benefits. At this point we may want to facilitate a transfer of the activity from the coop to the state (or to another entity), or at least support some interaction between the two. To do this would be to support a sequence of institutional development of which coops are an early stage. This means that our support of coops may not be worth its while unless the subsequent steps in the sequence also take place.

Finally, we will find that our experience with coops has taught us a great deal about decentralized community or regional initiatives. Sometimes, non-cooperative forms of these endeavors will be an even better approach to our task. Normally, we tend to ignore or reject these other institutional forms because they do not have the "good" qualities we associate with coops--they may be controlled by elites, they may be weak on management, they may involve only a few people. But since our study has shown that coops themselves often have these same "failings"--even when they yield substantial benefits--then we need not be so restrictive in our search for alternatives. At the same time, we will have to pay careful attention to the structural factors that contribute to the good results, a central theme of this study.

Unfortunately, I have not come up with a better description, or term, for what "coops" actually are when they are doing the good things that the Bolivian groups were. Though this kind of naming would help us recognize the kinds of groups we want to support, it would also be inconsistent with the findings of the analysis that follows. What determined the various accomplishments of the Bolivian groups, that is, was not only their organizational form, but a combination of structural factors--the sequence in which activities were undertaken, the social structure of the communities, the varying characteristics of the principal crops grown, and the traits of the various activities undertaken by the coops. Since these combinations are different for every group, the same organizational form can easily give rise to different results--some satisfying to us, and some not.

11 - Conclusion

We have seen that coops, if successful, can turn into the very monsters that they are supposed to slay. They may preach the rhetoric of participation and community mindedness, while in truth catering to a small and better-off portion of the population they say they represent. Whether these coops will also engage in activities with high spillover benefits, therefore, will often depend on the characteristics of the task, and the socio-economic environment, and not necessarily on a concern for social impact. Donors can take some of the randomness out of this process by choosing to support the activities that tend to have these more desired impacts.

Identifying the "good" activities and the coops that do them, as seen above, will not be enough. Though the good qualities may seem to inhere in an activity, they will often be present only at certain stages of a coop's history, and only in certain social and economic environments. Donors will therefore have to be alert to changes in the benefit distribution of the activities they finance, and be careful not to accept uncritically the dramatic historic symbolism associated with the starting moments of these activities. Donors should also stand ready to encourage the taking on of tasks which, though "good," may not have been appropriate or feasible at earlier stages of coop history.

It is easy to overlook the opportunities for coops to move into activities with greater social impact because the critics start to get vocal about "capitalistic" and "elitist" behavior, and the supporters get disheartened. In the fray, no one notices that the "capitalistic" operations have set the stage for the new, high spillover activities; and that coop rhetoric about exploitation has become so familiar that the better-off leaders of a coop may be quite interested in undertaking a beneficent activity that helps their image; and that the donor, finally, can have tremendous influence at certain moments by expressing a preference for one activity over another.

Some readers may question the wisdom of encouraging coops to move in directions that make them less like coops. In various ways, however, I have shown how the studied groups already strayed markedly from the principles of cooperativism—particularly with respect to their entrenched leaderships, the dependence on outside financing as opposed to internally-generated capital, the merging of manager and elected director, the contracting of coop directors and other members as paid employees, the lack of patronage refunds, and the tolerance for mismanagement and graft. Thus the achievements that we witnessed in the studied groups were themselves not the result of a faithful application of cooperative principles. If the changes proposed above were to cause coops to diverge from cooperative principles, then, this should not worry us. We should be disturbed only if the groups we finance do not provide the kinds of benefits and benefit distributions we are looking for.

It is important to remember, in thinking about these questions, why donors chose to support coopsratives in the first place: coops could sometimes do a better job than the state and its large development projects, it was felt, in improving the conditions of the rural poor. In various instances, the studied groups in Bolivia did seem to be the only institutions of significance working with peasant farmers. Since the state was doing almost nothing at all--at least in the Alto Beni--then it was perhaps not that difficult for the coops to fulfill our criterion of "doing more than the state." Whatever the case, our benchmark for judging this performance was the public sector, its goals, and its performance (or lack thereof) in meeting these goals. To the extent that we considered the studied groups successful, it was because they were moving in the direction of these goals, and not because they were particularly faithful examples of cooperativism.

If the studied groups were not cooperatives, then what were they? There is no handy name for what they are, which is probably one reason why they get called cooperatives, and why we tend to measure their performance in terms of cooperativism--or as deviations from it. It has been the task of this paper to try to come up with

a more realistic description of what they are when, indeed, they

are achieving our expectations.

WHAT EVER HAPPENED TO POVERTY ALLEVIATION?

Judith Tendler

A Report Prepared for the Mid-decade Review
of the Ford Foundation's Programs on
Livelihood, Employment, and Income Generation

March 1987

Executive summary

Of the Foundation's programs in Livelihood, Employment, and Income Generation (LEIG), six stand out: their beneficiaries number in the thousands, they have grown into competent organizations, and they have had an influence on policies that affect large numbers of poor people. Though five of the six programs are carried out by nongovernment organizations (NGOs), one is part of a public-sector enterprise. The NGOs, moreover, are quite different from the typical NGO in this field: three are trade unions, one is registered as a bank, and the other is a private consulting firm. Despite the difference between these programs and their environments, they share a surprisingly consistent set of traits--traits that are absent from a large number of the LEIG programs funded by the Foundation and other donors. While the six programs do not represent the full breadth of the Foundation's grantees, the findings about the traits they share help us to gain a better understanding of programming in the LEIG field.

The common traits are: (1) a narrow focus on a particular trade or sector, at least at the beginning, (2) or a narrow focus on one activity, particularly credit, in an unusually "minimalist" form, (3) organizational leadership well linked to powerful institutions, and (4) an urban setting, or at least an urban beginning with its economies of agglomeration and the closeness it allows to important centers of power.

The economic activities of the clients supported by the better-performing organizations also shared common traits which, in turn, were different from the activities often promoted under LEIG programs: (1) clients were already producing what they were receiving assistance for or, if new activities were introduced, these new activities were well known in the region and easily mastered; (2) the grouping of clients for purposes of assistance did not require collective production or, if it did, managerial and work requirements of the ongoing collective operation were minimal; (3) assisted activities did not face competition from large-scale capital-intensive industries; (4) the assisting organizations did not need to support marketing activities because sales markets were securely in place; (5) supplies of basic inputs were assured; (6) many of the supported products or services had high social value in economic and distributional terms, such as garbage-collection services and the provision of irrigation water; and (7) powerful consumers often played an important role in bringing about support for the assisted producers.

These findings should be of use to the Foundation in designing future LEIG programs and advising grantee organizations. At the same time, however, the fact that so few of the LEIG grantees reached a significant number of the poor, and that the better-performing NGOs were so different from most, suggests that the search for effective LEIG programs must be more selective, on the one hand, and broadened beyond the NGO sector, on the other.

The nongovernment sector, where much of the Foundation's LEIG program is concentrated, has a certain structural inability to expand or to have its experiments replicated. This is why the impact of NGO projects is usually quite limited, a disturbing finding for donors interested in having an impact on poverty. The constraints on NGO expansion and replication by others have to do with the fact that: (1) NGO strength and effectiveness often derive from smallness and social homogeneity, which get lost when NGOs try to expand; (2) NGOs see each other and the public sector as competitors for scarce donor funding, rather than as cooperators in a quest to alleviate poverty, which makes it inherently difficult for them to cooperate with each other or imitate each other's successes; (3) foreign funding accounts for a large share of NGO funding in some countries, which places the NGO sector somewhat at odds with the state, thereby blocking the path to replication of NGO experiments by the public sector; (4) though NGO projects may have small budgets in comparison to the public sector, their costs per beneficiary are often high, which means that even their successful projects are not necessarily feasible as models for serving larger populations; and (5) NGOs themselves often do not strive to serve large numbers of clients, nor are they under pressure to do so, which means they are often content to accomplish programs that work well in a handful of communities.

For various reasons, our better-performing NGOs were free of the above-listed constraints, or they operated in an environment that forced them to be different from the pattern traced above. Part of the task of choosing effective LEIG programs, then, involves watching for NGOs that have the traits that facilitated expansion, one of which is the ability and willingness to link up to the public sector. The Foundation's efforts to improve its LEIG programming might therefore focus on those NGOs with links to the public sector, or with the capacity and the will to develop them.

Though narrowing the Foundation's requirements for supporting NGOs might increase the probability of greater impacts, it would also make the Foundation's task more difficult by limiting the already scarce supply of NGO programs from which to choose. A complementary strategy is to broaden the supply of opportunities by opening up the search to include the public sector, whose policies and programs have major impacts on employment and poverty. The Foundation itself is accustomed to working more with the public sector in its programs in agriculture, water, and forestry; the Delhi office has in particular tried to broaden its LEIG programming to the public sector. If experiments carried out in the public sector work well, then the institutional infrastructure to expand them is already in place, as well as the political pressure to do so.

Opportunities for experimentation with LEIG programs in the public sector are greater today than one might think, and are in some ways greater than they were in the 1970s when, ironically, poverty alleviation was in style. This is because (1) the harsh austerity programs of the 1980s have made third-world leaders more politically vulnerable than usual, creating a more receptive political environment for targetted programs, or at least for political gestures toward the poor; (2) the current economic conservatism of economists and policy advisors, with its emphasis on "getting the prices right," is sympathetic to policy reforms favoring informal-sector producers; (3) the current balance-of-payments and debt problems of third-world countries, leading to restraints on imports, have made it possible for some informal-sector producers to flourish; (4) the current sympathy for decentralization has created a more enabling environment for local-level experimentation in the public sector; and (5) public-sector actors, humbled by the disappointing experience with state-sponsored poverty-alleviating initiatives of the 1970s, have become more receptive to modest approaches, and to learning from the NGO experience.

Finally, government policy and programs have had major impacts on employment over the last forty years of development assistance--not only through policies on exchange rates, credit subsidies, and agricultural development, but through the ways that powerful ministries spend funds and set standards for the construction of buildings, roads, and waterworks. We know a lot about the adverse effects of government action on the poor, which means that we also have learned a lot about what it takes to turn some of these programs to their advantage. But the rush of academic and policy interest to issues of debt and macroeconomic policy has left a vacuum in this area, and a dearth of support for public-sector actors who want to do something, have an idea of how to do it, and can mobilize considerable resources. This kind of experimentation is difficult for governments to undertake, even when funding is not a problem, because of the political problems involved in favoring certain geographic areas over others.

LEIG programs have difficulty achieving impact partly because they are plagued, more than others, with the syndrome of "reinventing the wheel." NGOs claim they are pioneering with a new approach when, indeed, they are not; project proposers allege that past efforts have not worked when, indeed, there is not enough of a record to know whether or not this is true; NGOs claim they "do better than the public sector" at poverty alleviation when, indeed, there is little evidence to support this claim. The LEIG sector, in other words, suffers from a lack of comparative knowledge about what has worked and what has not, in the public as well as the nongovernment domain.

The reasons for the lack of a comparative record on LEIG initiatives have to do with: (1) the "premature" abandonment by the development field of the state-sponsored poverty alleviation programs of the 1970s--much like what occurred in this country with respect to the 1960s War on Poverty--and hence of the efforts to evaluate these programs and modify them accordingly; (2) the change in focus of the field of development economics from institutions to prices and markets, resulting in a decline of interest in, and funding for, comparative evaluation studies of poverty-alleviating initiatives in both the government and nongovernment spheres; (3) the increased macroeconomic problems of third-world countries, starting in the mid-1970s, which replaced the research interest in poverty alleviation with issues of debt, austerity, and macroeconomic policy; (4) a mood of disappointment and disparagement about poverty alleviation among the researchers who did carry out evaluation studies, which resulted in an abundant chronicling of failures and what caused them, but very little understanding of the more successful efforts and their ingredients. If the Foundation's programs are to strive toward impact, then they will also have to create a record of what has worked and what has not. To do this involves not only the funding of comparative evaluation studies, but also restoring academic prestige, and therefore power, to this particular subject matter.

If the Foundation were to broaden its LEIG initiatives to include the public sector, it could distinguish its programming from that of other donors and move closer to its comparative advantage: (1) though the need for experimentation with programs capable of reaching large numbers of the poor is recognized by large donors, they cannot support it themselves because of the pressure on them to transfer large amounts of resources in relatively short periods of time; (2) most small donors in the LEIG area, unlike the Foundation, work only in the nongovernment sector and do not have the public-sector contacts that the Foundation has; (3) few donors who work in the public sector are as well connected as the Foundation to the nongovernment sector as well, which puts the Foundation in the unique position of linking the NGO experience to the public sector; (4) among donors, the Foundation is unusual in spanning the research sector as well as that of government and nongovernment, which means that it can play an important role in funding the badly needed comparative studies on LEIG initiatives and, just as important, in making sure the results of these studies are used to guide programming by governments and NGOs.

New Lessons from Old Projects

The Workings of Rural Development in Northeast Brazil

Judith Tendler

Operations Evaluation Department
The World Bank
Washington, D.C.

Executive Summary

In 1974, as part of a wider program targeted at poverty reduction in general, the Bank announced a bold new approach to reducing rural poverty and stimulating agricultural growth. Born out of dissatisfaction with the inability of past development efforts to reduce rural poverty and inequality, the "new style" rural development (RD) projects differed from, and supplemented, previous interventions in two ways. They targeted the poor directly with agricultural production services and subsidies. And they provided certain regions with a complete array of development investments, ranging from roads to agricultural credit to health—regions chosen for their agricultural potential and high concentration of small farmers. By 1986, twelve years later and after US$19.1 billion (current) of Bank commitments to RD worldwide, of which US$6.3 billion has been for "new style" area development projects, the new approach had fallen into disfavor. Myriad problems had plagued the implementation of the projects, and serious questions had been raised about their effectiveness at reducing poverty and increasing agricultural productivity. These concerns, outlined below, were laid out in a major review of the RD experience carried out by OED in 1987.

Though targeted rural development deserved much of the criticism it received, some of these projects—or parts of them—performed well. Though the exceptions in themselves do not justify bringing back this form of RD, they raise the question as to how some projects could have worked well with a design and in an environment now considered not conducive to good performance. More constructively, if certain projects or activities could stand the test of such adverse circumstances, they certainly must have some lessons to offer about improving the design of programs today. Though the Bank has largely abandoned the "new style" RD approach, it continues to devote major policy attention and resources to the same sectors, individually or in pairs, that were all linked together in the RD projects—agricultural research, agricultural extension, rural finance, irrigation, farm-to-market roads, drinking water, health, education.

Because past evaluations of the RD experience have been more illuminating about the causes of failure than about the causes of success—as the above-noted OED review itself pointed out—they have thrown more light on what *not* to do than on what *to* do. This study seeks to do the opposite. It identifies patterns that ran across a variety of instances of better performance in a set of 23 RD projects in Northeast Brazil—one of the Bank's most comprehensive RD programs. The study asks what lessons these patterns of good performance reveal about project design and, more generally, about the role of the public sector in rural development.[1] As the reader will see, the answers to this question do not add up to a case in favor of or against "integrated rural development," but are of relevance to a wide variety of projects and sectors in which the Bank operates today. As discussed in note 1, the Government of Brazil has been concerned that readers should not take this study as being in any way a substitute for an evaluation of the RD portfolio as a whole.

Various problems have afflicted certain types of the Bank's rural development projects worldwide, including those of the Northeast:(1) too many components and excessive complexity, (2) the lack of productivity-increasing technical packages for small farmers, (3) the absence of beneficiary participation in project design and implementation, and (4) a policy environment that penalized agriculture. The Northeast projects suffered, in addition, from (1) chronic delays in the transfer of Brazilian counterpart funds to the project units and executing agencies, and (2) the high and increasing rates of inflation (up to triple digits), and hence fiscal crisis, experienced by Brazil in the 1980s. This study asks why certain projects or agencies were sometimes free of these problems, or how they were able to perform well despite the presence of such adversity.

The Northeast Projects

Between 1975 and 1987, the Brazilian government committed US$3.3 billion to 22 integrated rural development projects in the ten states of Northeast Brazil[2] and a region-wide land-tenure project—of which the Bank financed 42 percent or US$1.4 billion. A "first generation" of these projects included roughly a dozen components—ranging from agricultural credit and extension through feeder roads and electrification to health and education, though any one project would not include all of them. The staples of each project were credit (23 percent), feeder roads (20 percent), land-related activities (16 percent), and agricultural extension (14 percent)—accounting for 72 percent of appraised costs. In an attempt to reduce the complexity of the projects and focus more exclusively on agricultural production, a second generation of projects eliminated health, education, and roads—as well as some smaller components. Credit (30 percent), extension (24 percent), and a new community-participation component (16 percent) accounted for 70 percent of expenditures projected at appraisal; associated land-related activities were unified in a separate regionwide land-tenure project (an additional 16 percent).[3]

Typical project organization involved the Bank and several levels of the Brazilian government—the federal government ministries, the Northeast regional development authority, semi-official banks, and the state-level project units and executing agencies. The project-coordinating units, set up in state departments of planning or agriculture, were in charge of designing the annual programs and supervising their implementation, but had neither executing responsibilities nor the formal power to grant funds or withhold them from the executing agencies—a subject treated in Chapter 2; an exception was the community-participation component (APCR)[4] in the second-generation projects, described momentarily, in which the project units shared formal implementation responsibilities with rural labor unions, extension services, and/or some farmer cooperatives. Municipal governments, though often represented on ad hoc councils that vetted the APCR sub-projects, had no formal place in the projects as such, but sometimes ended up making important contributions that were not anticipated (Chapters 2 and 3).

The community-participation component, at US$222 million, represented one of the most significant attempts of the Bank to make the implementation of its RD projects more participatory. The APCR fund, with the assistance of an average of 36 community agents and supervisory staff per state, makes grants of up to US$10,000 to associations formed in communities of less than 5,000 inhabitants: (1) 65 percent for community-owned ventures like grain-milling facilities, seed banks, input-supply stores, and storage facilities, (2) 25 percent for small works projects (road repair,

community laundries, public toilets), and (3) 15 percent for institution-building in community organizations, used mainly by the rural labor federations for training.

Good Performance (Chapter 2)

Defining "success" or, more accurately, "better performance," turned out to be more difficult than originally expected. Early in the review, the cases of better performance *seemed* to be falling into three categories: (1) whole *projects* (Tabuleiros Sul in Sergipe, Ibiapaba in Ceará), (2) *components* (roads, electrification, drinking water, health, and education *versus* agricultural credit, research, and extension), and (3) *agencies* (the project unit in Sergipe). Because of the widespread dissatisfaction expressed by many with agricultural credit, research, and extension, moreover, several cases of successful disseminations of improved varieties to small farmers were also identified—in order to explore why performance had been so different in these cases (Chapter 5).

The three categories of projects, components, and agencies did not hold up for long. (1) The better-performing agencies did not always stay that way (and mediocre agencies sometimes performed surprisingly well); (2) good performance was often bracketed in time by the term of office of a particularly supportive and demanding governor (for example, 1982—86 in Sergipe, and 1987—89 in Bahia, Maranhão, and Pernambuco)—a subject treated in Chapter 2; (3) the high ratings given by many to infrastructure, health, and education sometimes said more about things *other than* impact or agency performance—for example, the relative conspicuousness of the results (new roads *versus* productivity-increasing seed varieties), or the relative easiness of the task (installing rural water systems versus agricultural extension); or the fact that the project unit or other agencies had taken the tasks away from the infrastructure agencies because they had been performing *inadequately*—the subject of Chapter 2; and (4) though many observers rated health and education high on impact, these components got consistently low grades for agency performance in supervision reports.

To sum up, there were no projects, components, or agencies that could be said to have performed consistently well throughout the whole period under review, or consistently better than the others. People talked about *episodes* of good performance that had come and gone, as distinct from consistently "good" agencies, components, or projects. Trying to make sense of these puzzling ebbs and flows of performance led to the discovery that good performance often had less to do with the *inherent capabilities* of an agency itself than with a set of other factors—namely, (1) the ease and difficulty of tasks, (2) the presence of outside pressures, (3) built-in incentives to perform, and (4) the involvement of keenly interested actors and organizations at the local level. When one of these variables changed significantly, performance went from good to bad, or vice versa. Since project design and supervision tend to concentrate on improving the inherent capacity of agencies, this finding might seem to make the task of institution building even more difficult. But it is often no more difficult to influence these variables than it is to improve, from the inside, the quality of what agencies do—sometimes it is even easier.

A few caveats on what this study does *not* do. As explained in note 1, the study does not discuss macro policy issues like overvaluation of exchange rates and other policies affecting agricultural exports, or subsidization of agricultural credit and other inputs. Second, it does not attempt to judge the strategy of the Brazilian government or the Bank for alleviating poverty in the Northeast. Third, it is not an evaluation of the Northeast projects, nor of integrated rural development in general.

Reinventing the Projects (Chapter 2)

The better-performing activities departed consistently from their original design in five ways. (1) They were often implemented in *less time* than that allowed for at appraisal—the installation of wells and standpipes in rural communities; campaigns to widely distribute improved varieties of seed and rootstock and, in some cases, the acquisition of land for redistribution. This happened against a general background of *delays* in execution, which had actually caused the Bank to lengthen the execution period from five years in the first-generation projects to more than eight years in the second generation. The longer execution periods, though seemingly more appropriate for such difficult tasks of institution building, actually *deprived* the projects of certain pressures and incentives that were very much present in the environment of the good performers.

(2) The better-performing projects ended up being a much *narrower* version of what was envisioned at appraisal, with one or two components elevated to center stage. Particular favorites were rural water, community participation, and land-distribution activities. This "reinvention" could take place because (a) a supportive governor would choose one of the project's components as his "signature" activity; (b) project managers gravitated toward their *own* favorite components; (c) shortfalls and delays in the transfer of counterpart funds—though a major problem throughout implementation—scrambled budgets enough to give project managers liberty to remold the projects to their liking and reduce them to more manageable proportions.

(3) The relative *ease* (or difficulty) of the tasks that the projects assigned to agencies influenced their ability to perform well. Water agencies found rural water supply to be easier than irrigation, for example, because water was less "analysis-intensive" and less dependent on outsiders beyond one's control—namely, other agencies and users. This explains why the design and installation of rural-water systems typically went better than irrigation, as well as why Sergipe's new rural water agency performed well in rural water and poorly, subsequently, in irrigation. Also, the goals and standards of the projects themselves made tasks more difficult or unsatisfying to some agencies—namely, the redirecting of public-sector services toward the poor, the desire to rely on less capital-using technologies for infrastructure and, partly a reflection of the latter, the concern about reducing unit costs and reaching larger numbers of people.

(4) When performance was good, project management had been subject to clearly identifiable outside "demand" *pressures* to get things done, reach significant numbers of people, reduce costs, or be accountable in other ways. These pressures came not only from beneficiaries, but from governors, other state agencies, development banks, municipal governments, nongovernment organizations, the World Bank. The arrival of such pressures on the scene helps explain why mediocre agencies sometimes produced surprising bursts of good performance; the lack or withdrawal of such pressures also helps explain why agencies already deemed strong suddenly performed poorly.

(5) Better-performing agencies routinely "took over" tasks from the agencies meant to carry them out. First, the excellent public managers who were attracted to the project-coordinating units did not want to "merely" coordinate the work of other agencies, but wanted to "carry things out" themselves. Second, managers took over tasks out of frustration with footdragging or shoddy work by the designated executing agency; "takeover" gave them the control they desired over the pace, quality, and cost of project execution, and made their work less vulnerable to uncertainty and ill will. Third, powerful and supportive governors, impatient with "the lack of results" from the established agencies, sometimes helped give project managers the excuse and the wherewithal to take over from the other agencies.

How could agencies in an institutionally "underdeveloped" environment and with no experience at a task have simply taken over from the established agencies and done a reasonable job? First, they sometimes broke project rules and contracted out the work to public agencies other than the designated ones, or to private firms or nongovernment organizations; they succeeded best at getting other agencies to perform, in other words, *not* when they were "coordinating" these agencies but when they had the power to contract or force the agencies to do what was required. Second, when a project unit or other agency lavished its attention and scarce funding on the components it could manage better, this reduced the complexity and difficulty of the projects for them. Third, the takeover agencies *liked* the tasks that the established agencies disliked; this gave them and their staff the advantage of high motivation, which often turned out to be more important to good performance than long experience with an activity. Fourth, because public-sector professionals flowed back and forth between agencies, the takeover agencies could draw on the expertise of *all* professionals in the public sector—getting a specialist seconded to them, often from the taken-over agency itself. Indeed, creating a pool of such expertise in the public sector of the Northeast may be one of the most important contributions of the Northeast projects—not fully appreciated precisely because it is an externality and therefore not captured in the evaluation of any particular "unstable" agency.

The takeover phenomenon, and its association with better performance, throws some light on the issue of working with established agencies versus creating new ones. Learning from past experience, the Bank and the Brazilians decided to work through *established* agencies in the Northeast projects—creating from scratch only a "modest" project-coordinating unit, which had no executive functions. But the takeover stories often showed good performance coming also from agencies *not* established or specialized in a particular activity, and *not* originally meant to carry out the component—as well as from dynamic managers *not* wanting to play "modest" coordinating roles. The importance of takeover also helps explain why there was so much dissatisfaction with agricultural extension, research, and credit: these components were simply more difficult to take over than the others. Finally, takeover was not always associated with good performance, and established agencies designated at appraisal did not always perform poorly. Rather, takeover and good performance were associated with each other in enough cases to draw one's attention and to require an explanation.

Mobilizing Additional Finance (Chapter 3)

Better-performing projects, or pieces of them, frequently elicited the mobilization of additional resources above and beyond what was expected at appraisal—by governors, agency managers, state secretaries, mayors, banks, or beneficiaries themselves. These resource-mobilizing initiatives merit close attention because they occurred at a time of extreme fiscal austerity in Brazil, when it was difficult enough to get the Brazilian government to come up with counterpart funding for the projects, let alone with unanticipated *additional* funding. Three examples of this resource mobilization follow.

(1) A state loan fund for works projects in municipalities resulted in a kind of informal municipal betterment levy in the form of land, materials, and fencing. (2) A Bank imposed ceiling on per-hectare costs for tubewell and riverine irrigation led to the unanticipated donation of land for small-scale irrigation by municipalities and by private

farmers in an innovative cost-sharing arrangement. (3) A healthy spread between the return paid by rural banks on deposits and what they earned on lending led to aggressive mobilization of deposits by rural banks *and* increased lending to small farmers. Interestingly, none of the incentives of these cases to mobilize additional resources were intentional, but there is no reason why they could not be.

A considerable part of these additional resources came through municipal governments. Yet they had no formal role in the Northeast projects because they are typically seen as bankrupt, clientelistic, and the technically inadequate, which is often true. In each category of examples, some cases involved the Northeast projects, some involved other projects intermingled with the Northeast projects, and a few did not involve these projects at all, though the design features and place of implementation were quite similar. The way in which the municipalities were drawn into resource mobilization, moreover, transformed them into a source of healthy outside pressure on *state* agencies to behave accountably, get things carried out on time, keep costs down, and use less sophisticated and capital-intensive standards. Bank staff had tried, often to no avail, to accomplish the same thing.

Bank concern about resource mobilization has concentrated almost exclusively on securing the commitment of counterpart funding *before* projects begin, and in cajoling federal and state governments to come up with the promised funding during implementation. The additional resources mobilized in these cases were *not* committed beforehand: they resulted from a structure of incentives that made it worthwhile for institutions and individuals to contribute *after* things got going—and in a way that did not add to inflation or the fiscal deficit. Bank-sponsored and other research, moreover, has demonstrated that the mobilization of rural savings is critical for the development of strong *rural financial institutions* which, in turn, are critical for agricultural development itself. But the Bank's agricultural and rural development projects have not linked the provision of credit to the mobilization of deposits, a linking that could also help to solve the problem of excessively subsidized interest rates.

The Question of Land (Chapter 4)

Some important lessons about land emerge from putting together (1) the above-noted cases of additional resource mobilization in land, (2) some aspects of agrarian reform and settlement in Bahia, Ceará, and Maranhão, and (3) a successful experience with cooperative land purchase and settlement in Sergipe. There was some variation across these cases in the characteristics of land tenure and the availability of land for expropriation or purchase. Nevertheless, some common themes ran across these disparate cases which pointed to an approach to land settlement that was cheaper, quicker, more decentralized, more reliant on settler participation, less adversarial than expropriation, and more economically viable.

First, land markets worked better for small farmers when local organizations (coops, labor unions, local government) and beneficiaries participated in the search for land, the decision to acquire it, and the settling of its price. Second, this more decentralized approach introduced some checks against collusion between large landowners and the state. Third, many cases of successful land transfer (and of successful agricultural development) took place at the edge of "internal frontiers" in *already settled* regions, where the market promised clear returns from the intensification of agriculture in small farmer crops—tomatoes in Ibiapaba, oranges in Sergipe, irrigated vegetables in the Irecê region of Bahia. This particular feature stands in contrast to the customary view that the increase in land values accompanying development and the intensification of land use makes land-transfer actions *less* possible. Fourth, opportunities for transfer in the more settled regions occurred in "patches" rather than the large blocks customarily envisioned by planners for settlement projects. Fifth, dedicated project managers were highly motivated to make land markets and other mechanisms work in a way that would "produce" land parcels at low cost or none at all, because (1) expropriation of parcels under 500 hectares was not allowed by the law, leaving purchase or acquisition by donation as the only option available for acquiring smaller parcels, and (2) more project funding was available for infrastructure investments and agricultural services than for land acquisition (by expropriation *or* purchase). Sixth, small-scale private irrigation associated with high-value agricultural production was a notable feature of several of the cases reviewed.

The lessons of these cases suggest greater possibilities for land transfer to landless farmers than those conveyed in the *World Development Report, 1990* on poverty. They also have particular relevance for that report's new focus on "rural infrastructure" as a means to bring about equity-oriented rural development. In the most successful cases described above, that is, project agencies strictly linked the provision of roads and irrigation to the process of acquiring land and transferring it to small farmers. The Ibiapaba project was an exception: the project provided roads and electrification without securing the distribution of land, contributing to the inequality of landholdings becoming worse than it was before the project.

Research, Extension, and Agricultural Development (Chapter 5)

During the episodes of successful dissemination of improved varieties, the *nature of the task and the environment* faced by the executing agencies was strikingly different from what they were doing during other times. The chronic inability of research and extension to collaborate disappeared; or coordination between extension and research turned out *not* to be necessary for adaptation and dissemination to occur. Many of these episodes originated in "campaigns" against crop disease and pests—the boll weevil in the cotton-producing states, orange disease in Sergipe, and banana-root fungus in Paraíba—and transformed the work environment of research and extension in the following ways:

(1) Attention was riveted on a *single crop*, or a *single problem* with that crop. (2) Results were clearly *measurable*, penalties for poor performance were high, and performance was judged in terms of *outputs* (for example, reduced levels of pest incidence, number of diseased plants eradicated). (3) Powerful "demanders" were frequently on the scene, loudly clamoring for results—governors, directors of other agencies, mayors, farmer associations, and high-level officials who worried about the serious impact of possible crop loss on state tax revenues and on the region's agricultural economy. (4) The task had a *clear beginning and end*, usually within the four-year period of a governor's mandate and sometimes even within a one-year crop cycle—well within the five-to-eight year life, in other words, of the RD projects. (5) The intense public-sector effort mobilized around the crop in a particular region, and for a limited period of time, guaranteed the smooth *supply of the improved inputs* that was so problematic in more routine times; reducing input-supply uncertainties, in turn, made adoption more attractive to small farmers. (6) The *agency* itself felt energized, and instilled with a sense of mission, by having such a concrete and dramatic problem to work on, with potentially large and foreseeable results. (7) Local *boosterism* played an important role in driving many of these stories of agricultural dissemination and, more broadly, of microregional development. Though this list of traits might seem unique to disease and pest campaigns, various other episodes of good performance by extension and research turned out to have at least some of these same characteristics.

The traits named above contrast sharply with those under which extension and research customarily work. Typically, (1) performance is measured in terms of *inputs*—number of farmers visited, number of courses given, number of demonstration plots—as opposed to outputs like adoption rates of improved varieties or yield increases; (2) agencies work on a *broad* agenda of crops and activities, and for *open-ended* periods of time, with no urgency behind the introduction of any particular improved variety or practice; (3) frequently, neither the private nor the public sector is able to provide the improved inputs smoothly, in a timely way, and at reasonable cost—thus reducing the returns to be had from their adoption. The disease campaigns and other episodes of better performance redefined the task of extension and research, in sum, in a way that made it possible to get good performance out of the same agencies that did not do well with a much broader agenda.

Conclusions and Recommendations

Projects performed better when (1) agencies had more control over the quality and pace of project execution, which they acquired partly by carrying out tasks that other agencies were supposed to—or by contracting these out and supervising them; (2) project tasks were particularly "easy," or new agencies and units could "cut their teeth" on easy first tasks, or the project was changed in a way that made difficult tasks easier; (3) incentives were such that additional financing from government or beneficiaries was elicited during the course of implementation, and in a way that made for better-quality projects; (4) agencies were subject to pressures from the outside to be accountable, particularly pressures from "demanders"; and (5) there was an unusually complementary combination of action by state and local government—the local involvement helping to reduce costs and delay, make state agencies more accountable, and elicit the greater use of local materials and labor.

Though the importance of *demand pressures* in inducing good performance is not a new finding, the Bank and other donors customarily take a "supply-side" approach to project design—dedicating themselves mainly to building up the capacity of particular agencies. Though the realm of demand might seem beyond the reach of project officers, the experience reviewed provides numerous examples of how agencies could be subjected to these kinds of demand pressures. Two particular suggestions are:

• "Good" governors and other elected leaders could be attracted to support projects more by breaking up planning-and-execution periods into four-year cycles that coincide with the election cycle. These leaders could be allowed to pick and choose from a "menu" of possible activities that the Bank would support—which is what many governors did anyway, in backing only the components they liked best and sometimes raising additional funding for them. There should be enough flexibility for one state to choose rural water and another small-farmer credit—just as the Sergipe governor and the Pernambuco governor, respectively, did. This contrasts with current project design, in which the many components and the long execution periods cause elected leaders to lose interest, or use project resources simply to meet short-term budget needs or pay off political debts.

• Executing agencies should be subjected to demand "shocks" by channeling a part of their funding through the "users" of their services—not just beneficiary groups, but other public agencies, development banks, municipal governments. Just as the takeover managers contracted out what they could not do themselves or get the executing agencies to do, the demanders would "contract" the supplier agencies for their services. Funding supplier agencies through users would also bring to the project environment the traits of the successful cases: narrowly specified tasks, measurable and conspicuous standards for performance, and clear penalties for not performing.

Activities should be chosen for funding and assigned to particular agencies partly in accordance with their relative *ease and difficulty*. Some examples of possible "easier" tasks—at least to start out—are campaigns to combat epidemics of crop disease and pests, installation of simple rural water systems, and some forms of land acquisition. Given the new interest in rural infrastructure, moreover, it must be recognized that established infrastructure agencies often do quite poorly at tasks assigned to them by Bank projects of this nature; other agencies, with less experience or specialized expertise, often do better. This suggests that such activities should sometimes be placed outside their traditional bureaucratic homes, perhaps only temporarily, in "inappropriate" agencies or even new units—*if* these units are more motivated by sympathy and outside pressures to do well.

With respect to the lessons to be drawn from the *takeover* experience in general, (1) a *single* agency should be given sole power over a project, whether the tasks are few or many, whether that agency is an established one or new, or whether it is an executing agency or a coordinating unit; and (2) that single agency should be given the political and financial wherewithal to carry out the project's tasks itself or contract them out—to other public agencies, private firms, or nongovernment organizations. The lesson of the takeover experience, in other words, is *not* that (1) the Bank should go back to creating new and powerful parastatals; *nor* (2) that project units (as opposed to other agencies) should necessarily be given the power to carry things out themselves; *nor* (3) that the number of tasks should simply be reduced—though that wouldn't be a bad start.

Based on the findings stated above, the operational conclusions for *research and extension* are fairly clear. (1) Projects should favor single-crop or other highly-focused interventions, with a clear beginning and end, and that tend to have results measurable in terms of *output*. Though the broad-palette type of support currently provided is more consistent with the recent emphasis on farming-*systems* research, it is also organizationally burdensome; this kind of support is more appropriate in projects dedicated to building up a *single* agency over a long period of time—like the Bank's successful support to Brazil's agricultural-research parastatal, EMBRAPA, over many years. (2) Projects should fund research and extension at least partly through "demanders" because they place a higher value on applied work and dissemination than research agencies do. (3) Projects should fund research centers to more widely disseminate one or two of their favorite successes.

More generally, the Bank should (1) take more of an "urban" approach to its rural projects—as in its "intermediate-cities" projects in Brazil and elsewhere—resorting to matching funds and other incentives as a way of (a) tapping into the resources and developmental entrepreneurship available at the local level, and (b) placing certain functions at a level where they work better; (2) pay more attention to linking small-farmer lending to the mobilization of rural savings, which may require projects focused exclusively on rural financial institutions and *not* therefore embedded in agricultural-development projects; and (3) act on the myriad possibilities for mediating the transfer of land to small farmers for productive agriculture in a more decentralized way, particularly in conjunction with the provision of roads and irrigation water.

Notes

1. In commenting on a draft of this report, the Secretariat for Regional Development of the Office of the President emphasized that this report does not follow the usual approach used by the World Bank in analyzing Bank-financed projects. As explained in the text this study is, intentionally, *not* an evaluation of the Northeast projects, but has viewed them with a particular question in mind and a concern for arriving at conclusions of general utility outside RD and outside the Bank. The Secretariat would have also liked to see a fuller treatment of various issues (the economic, political, social and cultural context of the region and the country; the relationship of the take-over discussion to issues of management and of the allocation of resources among components; the relationship of good performance to different social groups like landowners, squatters, sharecroppers, tenant farmers; the relationship of the single-crop successes to issues of market distribution, information on which project did well in terms of spending a lower percentage of project tasks on administration). We could not be more in agreement that these subjects merit a much fuller treatment, but were not able to do so because of constraints on time, financial resources, and length of the final report. We agree that these are issues of importance, and would endorse the need for further evaluation work, as the Secretariat suggests, on the joint World Bank and Government of Brazil projects in the Northeast. The Secretariat would also have liked to see an investigation of the components where interagency coordinating did *not* work well. We have not, indeed, analyzed poorly performing components in detail in this report, partly because we have done so more generally in other evaluation studies, particularly OED's 1988 report on (worldwide) experience with RD. More to the Secretariat's point, this report does describe what worked well in the context of the most frequent types of failures—for example, to deliver credit on time for planting, of extension and research to collaborate, of projects or components to be carried out on time. A number of OED audits have discussed the problems of individual projects. This work is no substitute for an evaluation of the portfolio of projects, or a study of Northeast Brazil, rather it uses the unusually large sample of related projects to provide pointers to the Bank and development economists generally on effective project design for delivery of assistance to the rural poor.

2. Alagôas, Bahia, Ceará, Maranhão, Paraíba, Pernambuco, Piauí, Rio Grande do Norte, Sergipe, and Minas Gerais. See note 3 in Chapter 1 for an explanation of why the non-Northeast State of Minas Gerais was included in these "Northeast" projects.

3. The Bank's Regional Office notes that the "second generation" of projects has been reformulated. The lessons distilled in this report have been drawn from the first and second generation projects, as originally implemented. The Region has also commented that "the implementation of the 'second generation' is only, at best, at the midpoint and has been very distorted by financing problems, conclusions reached drawing on experience from that generation are largely unrelated to the project design."

4. Apoio para Pequenas Comunidades Rurais (Support to Small Rural Communities).

Social Capital and the Public Sector:
The Blurred Boundaries Between Private and Public

Judith Tendler
Department of Urban Studies and Planning
Massachusetts Institute of Technology
Cambridge, Massachusetts 02139

11 April 1995

The formation of social capital in developing countries has been typically viewed as a phenomenon occurring <u>outside</u> the public sector--often in protest against state actions, or in spite of the state, or under the threat of repression by the state. While this perception is in many ways valid, several case studies of social capital formation or good governance have now emerged that show the state to have played a quite positive role in social capital formation (SCF) outside it. Similarly, when governments perform well, they are often able to do so because they themselves have previously contributed to the formation of social capital outside the public sector--linking up to already-existing associations of citizens, or actually encouraging and financing the formation of "independent" associations of citizens that ultimately demand better service from government or loudly protest bad treatment by government.

Despite this mounting case study evidence, we know more about the many ways in which government action has undermined social capital, rather than contributing to it. The explanation for this imbalance in our understanding of both social capital formation <u>and</u> good government relates to the strong perception that there is, or should be, a fairly clear line dividing the public from the private realms. It is the assumption of such a clear demarcation, after all, that makes it possible to talk about social capital formation (SCF) as if it took place only "outside" the public sector, and as if it involved organizations always completely "autonomous" from government.

There are good reasons for the relative neglect of the idea that SCF or good government could be the result of blurred boundaries between public and private. Normative concerns in the development field have played a strong role in concentrating attention on drawing a clean line between public and private. Namely, the concern about corruption in LDC governments, and about the use of "personalistic" rather than "rational" criteria in making decisions and allocating resources, have caused the "blurred" line to be classified as a problem, rather than as part of any possible happy outcome. Also contributing to this perception is the current interest in nongovernment organizations (NGOs)--as social-capital "heroes," or as "better" alternatives to government in delivering certain kinds of services. This literature emphasizes, naturally, the "differentness" of NGOs from government and, in particular, their "autonomy" from government.

Understanding how social capital formation and good government can sometimes be associated with the blurring of the line between public and private is a particularly difficult task: the same traits that accompany bad government or the undermining of social capital are often associated with good outcomes. Cooperatives formed by government are often coopted by them, or simply run by local elites and not accountable to their members; but any longitudinal study of truly representative cooperatives often finds much less democratic origins associated with government support. Governments often finance and control labor union movements; but many independent locals often emerge from this past, shed their corporatist beginnings, and become truly local organizations representing their membership.

It is difficult to disentangle these cases, and to understand the circumstances under which social capital is formed, and those under which it is undermined. As a first step toward understanding the subject, I first discuss the formation of social capital (SC) <u>inside</u> government and, second, the relation of government to social capital formation (SCF) <u>outside</u> it.

I - Social capital within the public sector

There are two major aspects of social capital in the public sector that have been relatively ignored, not only in research on social capital, but in research on government itself. They are (1) government workers and managers themselves, and (2) public-sector labor-unions.

(a) Government workers and managers

The literature of the industrialized countries has a rich vein of work on government bureaucracies as social organizations--their informal norms and networks, and how they influence the carrying out of an agency's work. The literature on government agencies as social organizations in developing countries (LDCs[1]), in contrast, has been dominated by the fascination with organizational "pathology"--Wade's study of corruption in irrigation in India being one of the finest examples in the genre.[2] The arrival on the scene in the 1970s of rent-

---

[1]Forgive my use of the politically incorrect acronym "LDCs," which I do in order to not create confusion between developing countries (DCs) and developed countries (DCs).

[2]Yes, Wade went on to do an excellent study of South Korean irrigation bureaucracy, the picture of social health in comparison. But these kinds of excellent comparisons are as rare as the "pathology-type" study is common.

seeking explanations of government behavior, and the larger rational-choice theories in which these explanations were embedded, simply enhanced this vision of government bureaucracy as "structurally" or "inherently" pathological--particularly in developing countries (LDCs).

As a result of these peculiarities of the development field, we have little understanding of the aspects of social organization of government agencies that explains why they function well when they do. There are few studies, for example, in the tradition of Michael Lipsky's or James Q. Wilson's studies of street-level bureaucracies and what makes them tick. There is no analogue for developing countries to our understanding of the camaraderie between policemen explained by Wilson, or of Lipsky's (and also Piven and Cloward's) discussions of professionals and their greater allegiance to "the profession" than to their agencies--e.g., social workers uniting with their clients against agency management in favor of reform. In fact, given all the evidence on how government bureaucrats in LDCs work against their clients' interests, the question of how positive SCF has been able to take place in the public sector becomes quite a mystery--one of the basic ingredients of a good research question.

The pathological view of government bureaucracy has also kept the development field from doing more research on the heterogeneity within bureaucracies--one of the keys to understanding how SCF takes place inside the public sector, or is influenced by the public sector. Even though the political-science literature has long left behind a view of the state as monolithic and unitary, the applied development literature nevertheless sounds as if it still sees the world that way. Because we don't know much about the different groups that co-exist within any particular public agency, that is, we do not know why one group sometimes gains ascendance over another, nor appreciate how important these rises (and declines) are to the SCF question:

175

advances in public-sector support for socially desirable actions, that is, often result from shifts in power between groups within agencies--as well in the powerful "protectors" these groups lean on outside their agencies. With respect to interventions in support of such advances, then, movement in the "right" direction is sometimes achieved simply by a tilting of the balance in favor of one group as vs. the other within a particular agency. I have seen this happen many times in my own fieldwork.

(b) Labor unions in the public sector

Public-sector unions are strangely absent in the literature on LDC governments, let alone in the SC literature--except as spoilers of reform. Yet these unions represent a much larger part of the workforce in the public sector than of private-sector workforces in LDCs--particularly today, after more than a decade of decline in strength of labor unions in the private sector worldwide. They are also stronger than they are in the public sectors of some industrialized countries. The subject is relevant not just because these associations of workers are an important form of social capital; they also play a major role in making or breaking the reforms needed to be undertaken by LDCs today.

An example of the importance of public-sector unions has to do with the fact that the development literature now gives major prominence to reforming and expanding health and education services as key to the reduction of poverty and inequality (one of the learnings from the East Asian success stories). The education and health sectors of LDCs are classic street-level bureaucracies, where public-sector unions are widespread and strong. At the same time, these unions often prevent governments from undertaking desired reforms--or at least are blamed by government and donors as the culprits in explaining reform failures or slow progress. Some of these complaints are genuine, some represent scapegoating. Regardless, however, the strength of public-sector unions should certainly give researchers all the more reason to be interested in how they function as social units--and to study, in particular, the cases--of which there are now must be a numerous minority (especially if one includes state-owned enterprises)--in which unions were brought into discussions on public-sector reform and played a <u>constructive</u>, and not only intransigent, role.[3]

Why such silence about such important actors? In the U.S., where labor unions have not fared well either, there is at least a current research interest on the role played by labor unions in some of the restructurings of best-practice large firms (e.g., by Richard Locke and Rose Batt at MIT). Why is there no such work in the development field? When the subject of worker participation in restructuring of large firms is in such vogue in the U.S. literature, why hasn't this interest in workers and their associations spilled over into the development field? Public-sector agencies, after all, are some of the largest service "firms" around in LDCs.

To ask a set of related questions, why--when there is a large literature in the European field on pacts between business, labor, and government--is labor missing from so many of the studies of the role of the state in the developing world--except, again, in a negative sense? Why are the researchers of the newly emerging and rich literature on "embeddedness" of successful states interested mainly in "business associations" and not "labor associations"? The fact that

---

[3]Examples are a case of state-enterprise union playing a constructive role in reform in Venezuela; and a case I heard about in West Africa where, in contrast to most experience, the public-sector union was warned in advance of an impending World-Bank structural adjustment program, and its "labor-shedding" components, and proposed an alternative plan that reduced costs and increased productivity just as much, but required less layoffs.

177

labor is weaker in LDCs, or that tripartite pacts between the three are less common, is not a

sufficient answer--at least for explaining why there is no research interest in public-sector unions.

One of the problems involved in bringing public-sector labor unions "in" to the research

on reform processes is that public-sector unions see one of the key tenets of the reform package

in vogue today as undercutting them--namely, decentralization. Decentralization presents the

same problem to LDC public-sector unions that it does in industry, although you won't see

anything about it in the development literature. But labor's intransigence with respect to

decentralization in the public sector represents not only a digging in of its heels against highly

desirable reforms. Agency managers and politicians I have talked to explicitly describe

decentralization as a strategy for "busting" public-sector unions--particularly in education and

health--in terms of clearing the way for desired reforms. This view, though not stated as such,

goes hand in hand with the popularity of decentralization today--which, of course, does not deny

the desirability of decentralization on many other grounds.[4]   Although I am quite familiar

with the problems that public-sector unions can create--I have frequently been on the other side

of the fence--I am not quite ready to abandon the concept that workers need representation in just

---

[4]Another intriguing example in this vein is the SC "winner," the Grameen Bank--used to
illustrate a point later below. Grameen employs thousands of field-level or front-line workers,
who have ultimately organized a strong union. Grameen has come down heavily in combating
the union--which has struggled for higher wages, citing public-sector wages for similar work as a
standard. In resisting the union's demands, Grameen appealed to an aggressive U.S. NGO lobby
to lobby the U.S. Congress and the Executive to put pressure on the Bangladeshi government,
which was at that time of the same political party as the labor union, to call off the union. From
the point of view of SCF, is it Grameen or the union that is "non-excluding?"

societies. We need to think about how such worker associationalism can further the cause of an equitable economic development, rather than only undermine it.

I am also puzzled by the absence of attention to labor unions at a time when the development field is now looking at "nongovernment associations" of every type--including choir groups, to use Putnam's favorite example--as such important manifestations of healthy and democratic societies, and as deserving of more of a voice in what government does. Nongovernment organizations (NGOs) also figure quite prominently in the discussions of the advantages of decentralization, in terms of what institutions government will decentralize to: the development field sees NGOs (along with local government) as closer to "the people" or "the poor" than government.

The view of public-sector unions as culprit rather than subject of study, or as worthy of inclusion in discussions about reform, is also consistent with the broader view of labor unions in LDCs as being "unimportant" because they are a "labor elite." The development-economics literature of the last decade or so blames LDC governments and labor unions--whether inside or outside the public sector--for causing one of the most important prices in the economy to be "wrong"--namely, the price of labor and, particularly, the minimum wage. These "artificially" high prices of labor cause management to substitute capital for labor, the argument goes, which explains the segmented labor markets of LDCs with their large informal sectors.

LDC labor unions are ignored as respectable social capital, finally, because of the corporatist origins of many of them. To the left, they are seen as "sellouts" to government;[5] to

_____

[5]In Portuguese, there is a special word for the sellout or kept union, which is the word for the sheepskin that is placed between a horse and its saddle.

the right and the center of today, they are yet another manifestation of big and bad government.

This has also contributed to leaving labor unions (and other forms of worker association) in the

shadows of the development field when people are asking questions about the formation of social

capital.

Whether or not these interpretations of the impacts of labor unions are accurate, the

unions have nevertheless been cast for all these reasons as hurting the cause of reducing

unemployment and poverty--as, in SC terms, an "excluding" form of social capital. But this

should be the basis for a set of research questions, rather than a foregone conclusion. This is

especially the case, given that the other forms of social capital so much in vogue today--

cooperatives, mother's clubs, local elders' councils--can be just as excluding as unions are

considered to be. Why have these other forms of SC been exempt from the concerns about

exclusion?[6]

The development-economics argument about labor unions as "excluding" better jobs and

wages for the majority of workers outside misses a distinct feature of the way labor elites behave

in labor-surplus countries (as well as not recognizing the extent to which this assertion is still

vigorously debated today in the economics profession in the U.S.). Precisely because they are

elites bobbing along in a sea of surplus labor, they are often forced or guided in certain

circumstances to be more inclusive, if only indirectly. The benefits of their struggles sometimes

spill over, wittingly or not, to the non-unionized. Take, for example, the labor unions organized

---

[6]It should be noted that a large evaluation literature of the 1970s was quite concerned with the "rampant" exclusion it found at the local level in the course of evaluating the implementation of large decentralized rural development projects. But those findings--which probably went too far in arguing the "harm" that elite-dominated local organizations do--seem to have been lost in the swing of the pendulum to the other extreme in the 1990s.

in the first half of the century among the thousands of workers on the banana plantations of

United and Standard Fruit in Central America--among the most sophisticated trade unions of the

region.[7] In at least one country, Honduras, this "labor elite" played a major role helping peasant

farmers in surrounding areas to organize a movement for agrarian reform. This organizing

assistance was quite successful, and led to a major agrarian reform in that country carried out by

a populist military government in the early 1970s. What prompted the "non-excluding"

behavior among the banana labor-elite was the fact that these unions had, by the 1970s, "done

everything" there was to do in terms of organizing their own workers and obtaining reasonable

wages and fringe benefits for them, and now had to look elsewhere if they wanted to grow--or,

simply, to continue experiencing the "kick" of organizing. The fact that these unions were

geographically embedded in an area with many landless agricultural workers, many of whom

were relatives and friends of the banana workers, helped; also of help is the fact that the banana

companies were at that time laying off their unionized workers, releasing workers highly

experienced in organizing into the surrounding countryside of landless peasants.[8] The story

illustrates a set of interesting research questions about the conditions under which LDC labor

elites are or are not incompatible with desirable SCF.

---

[7]One of the reasons they are so sophisticated is that they received lavish assistance in their organizing in the 1940s and 1950s from the American labor movement, as well as from management itself, in order to head off organizing by Communist unions.

[8]It is interesting to note in this connection that the Bolivian Social Emergency Fund--a World-Bank supported employment-creating works project meant to counteract unemployment caused by structural adjustment--explicitly excluded ex-tin miners from access to these jobs, out of fear of their skills in organizing. Separate funds were set aside for the miners, where they would not intermingle with the other workers. The Fund is seen as a major exercise in SCF, since it channeled some of funds through Bolivian NGOs. What does one say about the SC of the Bolivian tin miners in this story?

Another fruitful and under-researched line of questioning within this rubric relates to why and how some of the locals of national corporatist unions in Latin America have broken loose from their moorings and gone "independent," becoming true representatives of marginal groups, and others not. (This is also relevant to the decentralization issues discussed above.) Brazil's rural labor unions are a classic example of this, many of them having shown true leadership in pressing for social and economic reforms in their domains, while others have remained tied to their government apronstrings.

II - Public-sector influence on social capital formation outside

We know more about the ways public agencies "erode social capital," to use Peter Evans' words, than about the ways they contribute to it. This is partly because the literature on development and social capital has proceeded as if there were a very clear boundary between the government and everything outside it. In this same vein, social capital is seen as everything "outside" government. And to the extent that government influences this social capital "outside," the thinking goes, it usually "crowds" it out--just as public-sector expenditure has been traditionally portrayed in development economics as crowding private investment out. But just as Lance Taylor has shown that in several cases public investment has actually crowded private investment "in" rather than out, an analogous phenomenon can be seen in the case of social capital.

There are perfectly good reasons that the line between government and what's outside it have been drawn so clearly. The industrialized world's "project" of the last 40 years has been to

182

support the creation strong developmental states and, hence, strong government institutions.

Hence the concern about corruption in government, and the perceived need to "unblur" the line between private and public by building strong civil-service institutions with "rational" criteria for making decisions. That government has so many times destroyed social capital is yet one more reason, of more recent vintage, to draw the line clearly.

Finally, the social-capital "heroes" in the development field today are usually thought of as the "nongovernment organizations" (NGOs). They, and those who look to them as alternatives to government in the provision of certain services, have emphasized the "differentness" of NGOs from government and, in particular, their "autonomy" from government. All these developments have influenced the assumption, so eminently reasonable, that one can draw a very clear line between the public sector and everything outside it. Drawing the line so clearly, however, has at the same time obscured another side of the public sector that relates to the positive role it has played in social capital formation, alongside the negative. Examples follow.

One of the most striking things about nongovernment organizations in LDCs is the movement of the people who work for and manage them back and forth between the nongovernment and public sectors.[9] "Socially committed" NGO people flow to the government when they like it--i.e., when it is "being reformist"--and back to their NGOs when they don't like it, when it is repressive or conservative. As a result, NGOs as a group tend to flourish under repressive or otherwise unpopular regimes, and to become decimated under reformist regimes. The latter phenomenon happened, with much hand-wringing in the NGO sector, when Allende

[9]Hirschman actually wrote a book on this phenomenon in industrialized countries, but mainly with respect to the decisions of individuals to move back and forth, and mainly between the government and for-profit private sector.

took over in Chile, when the Sandinistas overthrew Somoza in Nicaragua, and when a civilian president was first elected in Brazil in 1984. Conversely, some of the top Sandinistas today head or populate NGOs in Nicaragua (and are obtaining financing from the same donors who funded the opponents of the Sandinistas when the latter were in power); and many of the NGO personae of the Pinochet period are visible in today's Alwyn government in Chile.

All this means that the line between government and NGOs is not as clear as many would draw it. It also means that the concept of government or NGOs as stable organizations, each of whose "capacity" can be built--in today's parlance of "institution-building"--in an upward linear trajectory over many years is, for certain purposes, not accurate. Not accurate, also, given that the literature characterizes the public sector and NGOs as different partly because of the "different" kinds of people that work there (NGO managers and workers as a more dedicated breed.)

In analyzing LDC governments, finally, the development literature points to high "turnover" of government managers and workers as one of the causes of poor performance--too many new people being hired after a change of government and too many competent old ones being let go or marginalized. But the ebb and flow between public and NGO sectors actually takes a greater toll on NGOs, simply because they are so much smaller, and therefore suffer considerably more from the loss of one good manager.

All this is not simply to arrive at the uninteresting conclusion that NGOs are no better than government, at least on any index of turnover. More important, rather, is that what is more "stable"--and worth trying to describe--is the pool of expertise and commitment that flows back and forth between the two sectors, and what the effects are on each sector of its circulation. With a clear view of this ebb and flow, it is difficult to think of "social capital" as being only outside government. A few examples follow.

The ebb and flow between public and NGO sectors results in substantial cross-fertilization between the two. When government technocrats or managers "flee" to NGOs, the latter get the specialist expertise for which they are known to be wanting--peopled as they are by less-trained generalists, partly because of their lower salaries. These "cross-overs" from government also provide NGOs with people who are well connected to the world of banks, donors, and public authorities--connections that NGOs need and often do not have. From NGOs, in turn, government gets people who have substantial experience in how things work "on the ground," who have had the luxury of experimenting with various approaches, and on a small-enough scale that they can develop some notions of cause and effect with respect to their interventions. Those who go from NGOs to government talk of how they are seduced by the possibility of applying what they've learned on a large scale.

One of the most interesting results of the ebb and flow is the density of informal networks that sometimes bridge the NGO-government divide--a density, by the way, which characterizes some of the successful programs I've evaluated.[10] Much cooperation and exchange of information passes over these networks. That the networks might exist seems perfectly plausible and, indeed, perhaps not that interesting; they are barely noted in the literature, however, because both sets of parties to the network have an interest in denying their existence. NGOs fiercely proclaim their differentness and "autonomy" from government as their "comparative advantage"-

---

[10]In a recent case study I supervised, my research assistant--an outstanding field worker--simply could not verify and explain clearly the extent to which a particular agency providing support to small or medium enterprises was actually in the public or NGO sector.

-particularly when competing for funding from donors--and government views NGOs as inconsequential, thorns in the side, not capable of reaching large numbers of people, and staffed and managed by those who "couldn't get a job in the public sector." Let me illustrate what some of the results of this ebb and flow look like.

When observing front-line workers in government service agencies interacting with their clients in Latin America, one sometimes cannot distinguish between--for example--the way extension agents talk to small farmers from the way Liberation priests talk to their parishioners in terms of what they have to do to sever their links of dependency on landowners. Another example I recently observed in Brazil: a reformist state government used this same kind of "liberationist" language in a public information campaign about preventive health meant not only to inform communities about proper health practices, but to urge them to be more demanding of their mayors in the ways in which municipal services were run. ("You have the right to expect more from your government, your babies don't have to die at the rate that they do..."). These kinds of uses of rhetoric, persuasion, and the media by government have been neglected because they are usually associated with manipulation and repression of social capital formation.

Because of the tendency to draw such a distinct line between government and what's outside it--and to characterize NGOs as good for SCF and government as bad or, at least, not in the picture--the literature misinterprets SCF success stories. The Grameen Bank is an instructive example--an oft-cited story of success "outside" government, and in a country where government is seen as a "basket case." The extensive literature on the Grameen case does not reveal that it had, from the beginning, a very important relationship with the Central Bank of Bangladesh. First, it had to continuously meet standards set by the Central Bank for all banks. Second, its first managers were <u>ceded</u> by the Central Bank to work in Grameen--those who went being a self-selected group of those most interested in Grameen's particular SC-forming mission. In certain ways, then, Grameen partook of the "human capital" of the very government it is touted as being "better than"; at the same time, it was clearly subjected to the discipline of ongoing demands for accountability from the regulators of that same government.[11] Most NGOs are not subjected to these kinds of demands for performance from their funders, who are often far away--and frequently worried more about pleasing <u>their</u> constituencies than demanding accountability from their grantees.

How does one describe the mix of connectedness to government and performance-eliciting separateness in this history of the Grameen Bank? What does this say about how we should re-think our approach to studying SCF? Although the explanation I give sounds perfectly reasonable, the NGO world--and some of the development literature itself--characterizes government attempts to regulate NGOs as "interference," as "politicized," as "hostile," as "controlling" or undermining an otherwise socially "pristine" formation of social capital. In many cases, this characterization is perfectly correct. But research has neglected the other possibility, because it does not fit a mindset that sees social capital as totally outside government and affected by it, if at all, only adversely. This translates into neglect of the obvious interesting

---

[11]One of the founders of one of the most successful community-development banks in the United States, the South Shore Bank of Chicago--often mentioned by President Clinton these days as a model of community banking--gave me a remarkably similar explanation for her own bank's success: from the start, they were subjected to periodic visits of green-visored auditors from the Federal Reserve Bank, who had absolutely no sympathy for or understanding of their "social" objectives, and would not tolerate "bad loans."

question: what are the circumstances under which control by and/or co-mingling with government helps or hinders the formation of social capital?

So far, I have talked about the blurring of distinctions between the government sector and the social capital outside it. In addition, and more simply, the development literature has not grappled with the role played by government in supporting the growth of what is usually seen as "autonomous," "grassroots," or "indigenous" social capital formation. Many successful manifestations of SCF--like agricultural cooperatives, ethnic-based associations, and even mother's clubs--turn out to have a strong government presence in their past (examples below)-- just as do the unsuccessful ones. No one tends to document this past support from government for SCF because it conflicts with the self-image of "autonomy," let alone the characterization of government as undermining of social capital. The support is easy to forget, or not notice, precisely because these groups are successful--i.e, have become more autonomous than they once were. Jonathan Fox's study of the support of "reformist" bureaucrats in Mexico for the organization of "indigenous" peasant organizations in Oaxaca is an excellent example of what I am talking about. (It also illustrates the significance for SCF of the shifts in power balances within agencies, and in their links to outside actors, in that the reformist bureaucrats "used" the "indigenous" associations they helped form and support with program funding to turn around and "pressure" the conservative bureaucrats in their own agency, who were less sympathetic to the program's attempts to shift services and subsidies to truly needful farmers. Fox calls what they did a "sandwich strategy"--the reformists and the NGOs being the two pieces of bread, and the resisting bureaucrats being the meat that was "surrounded" by them.) Ultimately, moreover, the indigenous associations bit the government arm that had fed them earlier, disagreeing on many occasions with what their reformist benefactors were proposing.

A variation on this story can be told of the cooperative small-firm associations created by the even more "overbearing" Sandinista government, some of which not only became successful and independent enough to bite the Sandinista arm--taking literally the democratic rhetoric drilled into them by the regime--but survived the transition to the post-Sandinista regime. Another variation on this example is those among the rural labor unions in Brazil that have become truly creative forces for social change in their communities, as noted above, despite the fact that they were originally spawned by the corporatist legislation of a repressive military government.

These stories raise a series of questions. Why do some of these "government-created" or government-nursed associations evolve into successful and/or truly independent groups, while others do not? Which kinds of interventions by government do better at leading to the formation of such groups? Which interventions are clearly beneficial, and which are hostile or undermining? Which kinds of interventions or supports from government tend to work in the interests of SCF, even when the groups do not become independent? Though these questions are obvious ones, they aren't being asked (1) because the field sees government actions as only smothering SCF (which it indeed often does); and (2) because community associations have a deeply-felt need to see and tell their histories as tales of independent action. Finally, the results of such research are messier than prevailing views: they will often show that the same intervention by government has led to both coopted or "excluding" groups, on the one hand, and independent, public-interest-serving groups on the other.

In: **Rethinking Development in East Asia and Latin America**, *edited by James W. McGuire, Papers prepared for a workshop sponsored by the Pacific Council on International Policy and the Center for International Studies, University of Southern California, 1997, pp. 109-122.*

Ceará vs. Kerala (with Latin America vs. East Asia in Mind): The Devil is in the Disaggregation

Judith Tendler

Department of Urban Studies and Planning
Massachusetts Institute of Technology
19 June 1997

Memo for the workshop,
"Rethinking Development in East Asia and Latin America," sponsored by the Pacific Council on International Policy, University of Southern California, Los Angeles, 11-12 April 1997

This memo was written in response to a set of questions for the workshop posed by Jim McGuire--namely,

> To what extent and for what reasons has the [Brazilian] state of Ceará in Brazil developed more successfully since 1985 than other states in Brazil? What similarities and differences exist between the development experiences of Ceará and the Indian state of Kerala? Under what circumstances might cross-state [or cross-province] comparisons yield even more reliable and useful development lessons than cross-national or cross-regional comparisons?

McGuire set these questions against a larger set of contrasts and issues posed with respect to the workshop topic of rethinking the interpretations of the development experience in East Asia and Latin America, and its relevance to the thinking about human development. To sum it up crudely, McGuire's rendition of the now-familiar current thinking about the East-Asia/Latin-America contrast (henceforth EA vs. LA) portrays East Asian successes in poverty-reducing and employment-creating growth as a result of "autonomous" and labor-repressing governance, among other things. This is customarily contrasted to what the memo describes as Latin America's "public provisioning," which was considered to be ineffective because of a "populist welfarism" that misdirected benefits to the middle class. East Asia invested in health and primary education more effectively than Latin America, in this story, and in early asset redistribution through widespread agrarian reforms.

I first thought the comparison of Kerala to Ceará was a strange one. They seemed to have nothing in common except for the fact (not irrelevant) that they were both states rather than countries. The EA/LA comparisons of the workshop and the current development literature are usually made in terms of national, not subnational, units. Also making comparability difficult, though Kerala and Ceará are both state governments, Kerala's population is more than four times that of Ceará's--29 million vs. 6.7 million. In addition, Kerala's rural areas (as well as those of the rest of South Asia *and* East Asia) are much more densely populated than those of Ceará (and the rest of Latin America), with its (Ceará's) low 43 persons per square km.[1] One untrivial aspect of high population density is that it substantially reduces the difficulties and unit costs of delivering public services to poor people.[2] To make matters even less comparable, Kerala is in South Asia rather than the East Asia of the workshop's EA/LA contrast. And I know much less about Kerala than I do about Ceará.[3]

Upon further thought, I found that the Ceará/Kerala comparison turned out to quite useful for raising questions about the EA/LA comparison--which frames so much of the development discourse today--questions that might challenge researchers to move beyond it. First, Kerala represented a case of "welfarism" and public provisioning that, in contrast to the stylized

191

portrayal of Latin America, was associated with *effective* public provisioning and *good* governance. This raises questions as to why public provisioning worked in Kerala and not Latin America, and whether public provisioning generically is, indeed, the culprit in the Latin America story. Second, in that East Asia did not engage in public provisioning, according to the workshop memo, this suggests that places like Kerala and others that public provisioned successfully should be able to provide more insight than the East Asia comparison about the conditions under which such policies can actually work effectively.

I project the following Ceará-Kerala contrast against the backdrop of the broader issues laid out in McGuire's memo.

Kerala

I present less detail on the Kerala case, partly because the case is of longer duration and, partly for this reason, is better known in the development field (thanks, in the Western world, to the works particularly of Amartya Sen and, more recently, Patrick Heller, among others). I also know less of Kerala and South Asia and, like the workshop paper, am using it more as a foil for the EA/LA comparison.[4] The summary evidence of Kerala's success in expanding human capabilities relates to low infant-mortality rates (17 per 1,000 vs. 50 in India and 44 in today's Ceará); high life expectancy (71 vs. 60 in India); high adult literacy (91% vs. 50% in India and 56% in today's Ceará)--and, summing it all up, a Human Development Index that is almost 70% higher than that of India's (0.65 vs. 0.38).[5]

Less known, as discussed later below, is how Kerala was able to achieve this remarkable feat of public provisioning in terms of public administration and governance--let alone over a sustained period of time. Also less commented upon, but important to the Kerala story, is the long history of intense civic associationalism associated with demand-making on government, broad political mobilization (the Communist Party of that state), and the interplay of these forces with state government in the development of a broad program of public provisioning. Civic associationalism cut across ethnic, religious, and caste groups through various social movements (and, latterly, the Communist Party) and their demands for reform and accountability. It is a story that civic-associationalism buffs would love, though many of Kerala's associations were more inclusive and cross-cutting than singing clubs. This particular feature is consistent with research on the strengths of "cross-cutting cleavages" and also of "weak" ties.[6] Yet Kerala, as discussed further below, is strangely absent from the current literature on civic associationalism and governance.[7]

Ceará

Ceará is a state of 6.7 million inhabitants belonging, along with nine other states, to Brazil's Northeast region--a poor, semi-arid region, with a per-capita income half that of all-Brazil, and with roughly a third to a half of its population living below a line of absolute poverty. Half of its population lives in urban areas (lower than most of the rest of Brazil and Latin America), and roughly one third of the labor force works in agriculture, whose share in state output has declined from roughly 25% to 13% over the last decade--partly because of the structural transformation, and partly due to an attack on its principal crop and export, cotton, by the boll weevil.

Two indicators of Ceará's performance are the most widely cited as a sign of that state government's performance since it took over in 1987. One relates to economic growth--the "enlargement of private incomes," to use the workshop memo's terms; and the other relates to one indicator of the workshop's "survival-related capabilities"--the rapid decline in infant deaths per 1,000 births (the Infant Mortality Rate [IMR]).   During the 1987-1993 period-- encompassing part of "the lost decade," a time of stagnation and fiscal crisis for all-Brazil-- Ceará's economy grew at a rate four times that of Brazil and five times that of the Northeast region. While Brazil grew at only 0.87% per annum during this period, and the Northeast *declined* at 0.04%, Ceará grew at 3.4%.[8] During that same period, infant mortality fell by roughly 36%--from 100 per 1,000 to 65 or, depending on the indicators you prefer, from 77 to 44. During that same period, the Northeast IMR declined by only half that much (18%) and all-Brazil declined by only 22%.[9] If one takes the second of the two estimates for Ceará's current IMR (44 per 1,000), this comes close to that of all-Brazil (42)--impressive for a state with a per-capita income only 42% of that of Brazil--and is well below the IMR of the rest of Northeast (with the NE IMR at 65, Ceará's is 32% less).[10] Of significance to this decline in the IMR, the rate of vaccination coverage of infants and children for measles and polio more than tripled during that same period from 25% to 90% of the population.

Many Ceará watchers and insiders attribute the change in these two indicators to a radical transformation in the state's governance, starting with the late-1986 election of the reformist and modernizing governor, Tasso Jereissati. He succeeded in electing his protege and successor, Ciro Gomes, four years later, and then won re-election himself to a second term in 1994, still unfolding.[11] Though each governor had a quite different style, they are both seen as having run a serious, honest, and modernizing state government--in sharp distinction to what went before and to many other state governments of the Northeast.

The most significant accomplishments in Ceará's governance fall into three following areas. *First* was fiscal adjustment and reform in a state where payroll commitments consumed 87% of the state's receipts when Jereisatti first took office.[12] *Second* was a set of three innovative programs--in rural preventive health (clearly responsible for the decline in infant mortality[13]), in transferring 30% of the state's public procurement to small firms in the interior, and in "declientelizing" the administration of large food-relief and public-works employment-creating programs traditionally mounted during periods of intermittent drought.[14]

Third, the state government aggressively and successfully recruited investors from Southern and Southeastern Brazil, and from outside the country, to set up manufacturing plants there and, to a lesser extent, tourism ventures. Dozens of new plants have located in Ceará in the last four or five years--mostly from the South and Southeast--in the traditional industries that previously constituted Ceará's manufacturing sector--footwear, garments, textiles, agro-processing, and tourism. (This is not to say, however, that these industries are using traditional technology--many of them, as the state proudly claims, are using the latest technologies.) Ceará has been quite aggressive in offering tax exemptions, facilitating infrastructure investments, and other subsidies to the firms it courts. These incentives probably do not add up to more than those offered by other Brazilian states, at least according to my interviews with firm owners. They point to as key, rather, the "credibility" of the new governance.

Fourth, and related to the state's ability to attract new investors, the state government has successfully pursued international-donor funding for major infrastructure investments (most importantly, a new port and airport improvement, major sewerage investment in the capital city, Fortaleza, and various other sanitation and road investments related to private tourism investment). These investments are a more recent phenomenon, based on the credibility the state gained with international donors for its governance in the early years of the reforms. Remarkably, in fact, none of the reforms listed above had outside donors behind them or assisting them. In fact, the one sector in which there had been a large donor presence was also the sector in which both production and the administrations of the new governors performed poorly--agriculture.[15]

Misperceptions on Ceará

Before proceeding to the contrast between Ceará and Kerala, and how it relates to the contrast between Latin America vs. East Asia, it is necessary to correct three widely held misperceptions, especially among the international donor community, about the nature of Ceará's accomplishments and governance. These corrections, and the strength of the misperceptions, are relevant to the themes of the workshop in that they illustrate some of the difficulties and inaccuracies of the LA/EA comparison, and how one might move beyond it.

Misperception I: growth before and after 1987. Ceará's higher-than-Brazil and higher-than-NE growth rates during the 1987-1993 period are a striking achievement for a poor Northeast state. At the same time, however, these rates were significantly *lower* than the state's growth rate of the earlier 1980-1986 period and even during the 1970s. Like Brazil and the Northeast in general, growth rates in Ceará were almost 2-1/2 times *higher* in the previous period, 1980-1987, when average annual per capita GDP growth rates reached an impressive 8.1% per year--as compared to the 3.4% of the post-1986 period. The earlier period of much higher growth, then, *preceded* the entry on the scene of two young reformist governors, the first in 1987, who are credited with the state's turnaround from "backward" and "clientelistic" to "growing" and "modernizing." The comparison of these two periods on growth alone, in short, shows that if one wants to relate the state's economic performance to the two reformist governors--as is the claim of Ceará admirers--one cannot point to the state's growth in relation to the immediately preceding period, because growth was much higher then. Rather, and as the state government itself customarily does, one must point to the fact that Ceará's growth rate after 1987 *fell much less* than that of Brazil and the other Northeast states.

I point out this misperception not to detract from the achievements of the current period of good governance, but to lure the attention of researchers of good policies to that immediately-preceding period. The current attempt to attribute Ceará's good relative growth performance to the policies of its reformist governors, that is, obscures and deflects interest from a question of considerable importance to those interested in understanding the policy determinants of economic growth: if good policy characterizes the post-1986 period, and bad policy or lack of any policy ("clientelism," "backwardness," lack of "public-minded vision" by elites, lack of "public-sector competence") characterizes the previous period, then how does one explain the much more impressive growth of the earlier period? One simple answer is that growth, or the lack of it, may not have much to do with what governments do--particularly subnational governments, and particularly for the short time periods encompassed by Ceará's new governance (10 years). But this is not an interesting response for those looking for the relationship between growth and governance. More significantly, I suggest that discovering the determinants of Ceará's higher preceding growth has not attracted the attention of students of economic development and governance[16] because much of that earlier growth, it turns out, was the fruit of a set of regional and state policies that are now thoroughly discredited in the development community--partly through the EA vs. LA contrast itself.

Ceará's higher growth rates seem to be in part the long-maturing result of an interventionist industrial policy by the Northeast regional authority (SUDENE) and the Northeast Regional Development Bank (BNB) that started in the mid-1960s. These policies included a central-government tax-credit scheme for large, mainly manufacturing firms and, in the case of Ceará, the creation of industrial estates particularly in--interestingly enough-- "traditional" industries like textiles, apparel, and shoes. The policies, and their complementary subsidies, are now discredited, not only by commentators on policy in general but by non-Northeast Brazilians, and even by some Northeasterners themselves: the "massive" subsidies for Northeast industrial development and their attendant capital-intensive, unemployment-perpetuating results; the persistence of poverty and inequality 30 years after the policies were initiated; the "bloated," "ineffective," and "politicized" bureaucracies of SUDENE and, to a lesser extent, the Bank of the Northeast; the interventionist "industrial policy" and failed policy of "industrial estates;"[17] and, finally, the "clientelistic" and "traditional" administrations of Ceará and other Northeast states.

How do we explain Ceará's impressive *pre*-1987 industrial growth against this background, where the by-far strongest policy influence around was a set of policies that are now discredited? If "clientelistic" and "rent-seeking" is the wrong description of public-sector administration in Ceará and the rest of the Northeast, then what is a more accurate description? Is it that the discredited policies were not that bad in their time, but now need reforming for the new era that has commenced? Or is that things could have been even better with better policies and better governance--a contention that, though common in such cases, seems to take us into a counterfactual never-never land and away from trying to understand what actually happened. Similarly, can "good" pieces of this set of policies be extracted, in terms of lessons for their present, from their larger "bad" context? Finally, Ceará has shown particularly outstanding performance in the textile sector (the single largest benefactor of the state's share of regional subsidies). (The same is true, even more strongly, for the Northeast state of Bahia's petrochemicals sector, similarly, benefitted.) We could describe these two sectoral successes as a difficult-to-explain result of discredited "old" policies; or, without much twisting of the facts, they could be described as looking eerily like the now-fashionable "picking-of-winners" currently advocated by Michael Porter for developing and newly industrializing countries and a host of his admirers and industrial-policy consultants. Which explanation is correct, and which determines the lessons to be learned from these successes?

Without doing more research on such cases, it is difficult to answer this question and to tell the difference between the two contrasting explanations. But a stylized regional comparison of East Asia vs. Latin America has been built on an assumed difference--East Asia picks the winners with the right policies, and Latin America indiscriminately targets losers, as well as winners, with bad policies. With this mental template, little attention can be paid to the variations away from this stylized view, and the lessons to be learned from them.

It is difficult for us to notice, in sum, the pre-1987 economic growth of Ceará, let alone to attribute it to an environment of governance in that state (and in the Northeast), and to a set of policies and programs, that we now have pronounced as disabling rather than enabling. Hence, our tendency to point to the post-1986 Ceará state governments, whose agenda fits better our present-day conceptions of what works and what does not. The point is not that the prior policies were "right," or that the current Ceará governance has nothing to do with it.[18] Rather, we obviously need to do more homework on this and other similar cases, lest we get the lessons wrong.

Misperception 2: human indicators. It is generally acknowledged by the Ceará state government that its impressive progress on infant mortality noted above has not been matched-- at least yet--in educational indicators, life expectancy, or relative or absolute poverty indicators. The percent of the population below a poverty line continues at one third, unemployment has not declined significantly, and literacy remains roughly the same as the pre-1987 level of 56%. With respect to the newly reduced level of Ceará's infant mortality rate, in turn, it should be noted that 44 per thousand is still almost twice that of the developed South and Southeast of Brazil (28)-- and it is two-and-half-times that of Kerala's low IMR rate of 17.

This is not to discredit the state's impressive achievement in reducing infant mortality, or the seriousness with which it is taking on other problems. It is simply to show that the state's success in reducing infant mortality does not bespeak a broader pattern of successful public provisioning of the type that shows up in the human indicators.

Misperception 3: good governance and civil society. The third misperception about Ceará illustrates our inclination, recently, to interpret good governance as having to do with civil society--on the basis, in many cases, of rather slim evidence. With respect to Kerala and in seeming confirmation of that assumed relationship, a substantial body of grounded research firmly establishes the extent to which the effective public provisioning of that case was driven by a densely associational civil society (and party mobilization, later, by the Communist Party), and its demands of government for reform and accountability. Many admirers of and participants in the Ceará experience also portray it as a story, in part, about civil society--or, at least, about reformist administrations that were "participatory" and "consultative," that forged "partnerships" with "civil society." (A small book on the Ceará experience written by some of those who managed it was entitled *Shared [Public] Management: The Ceará Pact.*) But this image is not accurate--at least not in terms of the literature on civic associationalism and governance--and makes it difficult to explain how that outstanding governance emerged, the nature of it, and what lessons can be drawn from it.

In many ways, Ceará's story is the opposite of Kerala's in terms of civic associationalism. In contrast to Kerala's complex interactions between civil society (including unions), party organizing, and governance--which led to an effectively public-provisioning state--the Ceará story is remarkably simple: it is about a long linear path of struggle between two small *elite* fractions--the traditional landholding elite and the newer urban and modernizing elite.[19] Contrary to the current image of the Ceará story as being one of a young reformist governor (Tasso Jereissati) bursting suddenly onto a hopelessly clientelistic and traditional scene after the elections in 1986, that gubernatorial election constituted one of the *last* chapters of the struggle of one elite fraction to win out over the other--the modernizing over the traditional.[20]

To be sure, the larger environment of transition from military government to democratization in Brazil during this period of struggle brought this elite struggle out of the closet into the open with a first election in 1982 (the modernizing fraction's candidate won, but his administration turned out to be weak). In addition, Ceará's reformist government has contributed importantly to the *creation* of associations that have then turned around and demanded accountability and reform from the very government that assisted in their birth or strengthening. (This development in itself should place another question on the workshop agenda: government-induced associationalism turns on its head the one-way causal relation between "government-independent" civic associationalism and good government shown in Putnam's study of Italy and assumed by many who think about the role of nongovernment associations in governance.[21])

Once the reformist governor came to power in the beginning of 1987, finally, he did indeed institute a new "partnership" and "pact" with business, which met for breakfasts on Mondays once a month with state-government department heads and often with the governor himself. Sub-groups were created (the textile sector, the granite sector, etc.) and sector-specific Monday meetings were held to discuss problems and plans. But the key actors who attended the breakfasts and participated in the pact came mainly from the original elite fractions. And the "civil society" of the much-advertised pact was mainly business and did not include labor (with some important exceptions, as time went on[22]). (This contrasts with Kerala's pact which, if it erred, did so in the other direction--including labor more than it did business.)

In addition, some of acclaimed ingredients of Ceará's success were explicitly "excluding" rather than "including"--namely of workers, and those who represent them. The success of Ceará in recruiting outside investors (in contrast to Kerala's scaring of them away until recently) has been based on an explicitly cheap-labor, "low-road" approach to global competition. (This sounds a somewhat dissonant chord in the otherwise remarkably modernizing public discourse of this new state administration.) The state government has promoted its advantages to potential outside investors much as did the Southern states of the U.S. when they were wooing textiles, furniture, and other manufacturers away from New England: namely, and as noted above, cheap and docile labor, and an "enabling" environment that helped firms discourage the organizing of workers, the paying of fringe benefits, and the protections of the labor law. (Ceará, in trying to attract foreign investors, also emphasized its dry sunny climate, with year-round sun and warmth, and its greater relative closeness to European and U.S. ports--in comparison to the more developed southern and southeastern Brazil.)[23] Ceará is not unusual in following this path to attracting outside investment. Other similarly low-wage states and countries have often done the same. But the grave concern of not only labor unions but some non-labor elites who concern themselves with how the state should enter the modern world are nevertheless inconsistent with the popular image among Ceará-admirers of an "inclusive" model of governance, broad consultation, and rich civic associationalism.

The contrast of Ceará to Kerala in terms of inclusiveness and civic associationalism is not meant to portray Ceará negatively but, rather, to reflect different paths to development. Kerala, after all, was considered notorious for many years in development circles for scaring away outside investors (and local ones), in contrast to Ceará's success at attracting them. But the contrast raises questions about how to reconcile the current interest among academics in the development field over the connection of civic associationalism to good governance (reflected in the workshop memo) with the grudging acknowledgement (also in the memo) of the "good results" of the autonomous-state/labor-repressive side of the East Asian success stories. One could even say that the new Ceará looks more like the workshop memo's East Asian model--a state government being able to act "autonomously" (which includes the keeping of labor at bay) and, at the same time, "embeddedly" (with business mainly, not labor). This kind of state governs well in many ways, as Ceará has remarkably done, but not in response to a broadly based and rich "associational" civic society that demands accountability.

Ceará vs. Kerala

With respect to the issues of human indicators and public-provisioning, as we have seen, Ceará is no Kerala. In addition to the differences pointed out above, Ceará's much-proclaimed success at reducing infant mortality to 44 per thousand births--for which it received UNICEF's Maurice Pate prize--still leaves infant mortality at more than twice that of Kerala, a state whose population is more than four times the size of Ceará's and whose per-capita income is only 22% that of Ceará's ($260 vs. $1,162). Although Ceará's two reformist governors have given a high and welcome priority in their discourse to primary education, they have as yet made only slow progress in this direction--with literacy at 56% compared to Kerala's 91%. Ceará's performance in preventive health, moreover, was not as dramatically matched in curative health--at least not yet.

The Ceará/Kerala comparison with respect to social indicators and governance is somewhat awkward, and unfair to Ceará, because Kerala has a decades-long history of public provisioning and doing well on social indicators. It is not possible to tell at this point whether Ceará will ultimately come through on primary education, whether the momentum of the initial preventive health decline will be sustained, whether corresponding improvements will be made in curative health, and whether the current plateauing of the infant-mortality rate is only transitory. Much of the above-cited list of Ceará's achievements, moreover, lies in other areas than that of Kerala--namely, fiscal reform and downsizing of public employees in the face of fiscal crisis, and the attraction of outside direct investment (in contrast to Kerala's reputation for seeming to scare off outside investors). Many Cearenses, finally, are genuinely proud of their state, its development, and the notice they have received throughout Brazil and the world about their governance. This kind of confidence and optimism is almost unheard of in Northeast Brazil, and the positive effect of this in terms of self-fulfilling-prophecies is hard to measure with indicators.

A surprise of the Ceará-Kerala comparison, and our perceptions about both states, is that Kerala currently (the 1990s) does better than Ceará on per-capita economic growth--the workshop's theme of "the enlargement of private incomes." In performance that must come as a surprise for those familiar with Kerala's 1980s reputation as a stagnant economy--of "equity at the cost of growth" or, more recently, of "strong labor unions scaring away private investment"--Kerala has grown at per-capita GDP rates almost *double* those of Ceará since 1987--6.4% as vs. 3.4%.[24] Even more impressive, given Kerala's reputation of the 1980s as a slow grower within India, Kerala's post-1987 growth rate has been 28% *higher* than that of all-India--5.0%.

The conundrum for Kerala-watchers, and the caveat of those development thinkers

evaluating its possibilities as a model, are its continued low per-capita GNP--$260 vs. India's

$310 (not to mention Ceara's $1,162).[25] This in addition to the belief or, at least suspicion, of

many that Kerala's "slow growth" and continuing low per-capita income is a result of a highly

unionized and "intransigent" labor force. This kind of explanation of low growth, commonly

heard today in the development field, shares something with Martin Rama's econometric findings

on the association between low growth and high unionization--as well as with the McGuire

workshop memo's characterization of the problematic aspects of the Latin American side of the

LA/EA comparison. Namely, "labor elites" (among others) in Latin America--in contrast to the

labor-repressed East Asia--are identified as making difficult the development of a state that

might otherwise be more effective at public-provisioning. This happens because of a

"misdirecting" to the middle classes of the benefits of the welfare state and the public

provisioning that are meant for the poor.

The Kerala case, in sum, produces a different set of questions that are difficult to either

raise or explore within the confines of the contrasts and categories of this particular kind of

analysis. Why did a state responsive to popular demands produce the opposite result in terms of

effective provisioning (though not in terms of growth) than did the Latin American case?

Correspondingly, how do we reconcile our enthusiasm for civic associationalism's effect on

governance with our distaste for its assumed negative effect, according to the workshop memo,

on growth? I can not answer these questions, but I would hope that they would be taken

seriously by exploring the Kerala case (and others similar to it) more seriously in terms of the

why and the how of public provisioning.

Public provisioning and good outcomes: old cases and new interpretations?

In the development field, many have dismissed Kerala as an exception, albeit laudable. Or, they point to Kerala's persistently low per-capita growth rates of the past, reflected in its low per-capita income ($260), as a reason to dismiss its achievements in high human indicators-- certainly not a model to be followed. This, however, is an "old" interpretation of Kerala. It fails to notice the state's better growth in the 1990s, and its recent evolution of state/labor/business relations in a more business-friendly direction. These recent developments have not brought Kerala back into the lexicon of development stories, not to mention that the state's long-standing story of highly effective public-provisioning does not appear in the currently burgeoning literature of best-practice and how-to cases of public management.

This blind spot in the current attention of the "state-capacity" literature to Kerala (and similar such cases) is testimony to the fact that Kerala does not really fit the stylized portrayal of development traits to which we have grown accustomed in the EA vs. LA comparisons. That is, explanations for Kerala's success have to do, as the memo says, with public provisioning--food subsidies, schools, health programs, agrarian reform.[26] This is what Latin America did a lot of (although not as comprehensive agrarian reforms) and poorly, the EA/LA contrast says, while East Asia did something else--not public provisioning. (I actually think the EA/LA comparison and, correspondingly, the workshop memo, exaggerates the difference between the policies pursued by EA vs. LA of relevance to human indicators; both regions devoted substantial resources and policy attention to health, education, and even agrarian reform. It was the design and implementation of the policies that were different, not their type.) But researchers should be moving on to another set of questions. Why was Kerala's public-provisioning associated with improved human development indicators (and even growth, more recently) and Latin America's just the opposite--"populist," as the memo says? More important, why was Kerala's public provisioning so much more successful than the rest of India's?

The questions I pose are, in part, about state capacity and the quality of governance. But for all the interest in and research on Kerala's social indicators, we do not really know that much about why and how the government in such a poor state like Kerala could distribute food subsidies, run employment programs, and re-distribute land without enormous rent-seeking and leakage[27]--in contrast to so many other places, including the rest of India and Latin America in particular. With all the current interest in "state capacity," "governance," and "institution-building," in other words, the Kerala case is an important and strangely missing example. Perhaps this is because Kerala is an "old" story, and hence less interesting to those on the new governance and institution-building bandwagon--a serious mistake in the choice of cases on which to do evaluation research.[28]

If we want to understand why Latin America's public provisioning was "misdirected" to the middle classes, in contrast to Kerala's, then we should also be looking into similar "off" examples. Costa Rica is an obvious candidate, closer to home than Kerala. Like other Latin American countries, it also had high welfarism and public provisioning. Like Kerala, however, the public provisioning was effective, as witnessed by Costa Rica's high performance on human development indicators for many years relative to other Latin American countries. (Costa Rica, of course, is dissimilar in other important ways to Kerala.)

Costa Rica does not appear on the 16-country list of the workshop memo, but it fits perfectly the memo's category of "providing welfare state benefits excessively, prematurely, or misdirectedly." Indeed, it has been even more welfarist than most Latin American countries and even more "labor permissive," at least in terms of its not having gone through the labor repression of the military periods of other Latin American countries. But, as with Kerala, the provisioning has been more effective than in other Latin American countries, as witnessed by the high social indicators (assuming, according to the memo's argument, that high social indicators are, at least in part, the result of effective public provisioning). If excessive welfarism explains Latin America's problems and inadequacies at effective public provisioning, then what explains the even more "welfarist" Costa Rica's success?

Methodology

The set of questions I have raised about Kerala, Ceará and other places throughout lead clearly to the methodological question posed by the workshop memo: what is the value of within-country as vs. cross-regional (or cross-country) comparisons?

Within-country comparisons (between subnational governments, or between different agencies or programs) do better in many ways at illuminating certain aspects of the questions and quandaries posed in the workshop memo. They also provide more practical and realistic lessons for reformers. At this juncture, moreover, Latin America might learn more from between-country than between-region comparisons of the East-Asia/Latin-America ilk. Cross-country comparisons within a region (or within-country comparisons) allow us to hold certain things constant--surely a

prerequisite for serious hypothesizing. So many things vary in a comparison across countries and regions that it is difficult to arrive at accurate explanations, let alone lessons that are relevant to another part of the world. In addition, many of the country and regional characterizations of the current literature, as reflected in the workshop memo, represent either an "average" of the quality of a country's programs and policies or a representation biased toward the more conspicuous ones--whether good or bad. They fit certain parts of the government and not others, or certain parts of the country and not others.[29]

I find it troubling that such cross-regional rather than cross-country or within-country comparisons seem to have more influence in the development field's analysis of the problems of Latin America today. This bent of mind is clearly reflected in the searches of Latin American governments for new ways of thinking about policy and reform of the state. Many Latin Americans heartily accept the East-Asia/Latin-America comparison as grounds for a general discrediting of their own experiences, and as marching orders for their own reforms--moreso, in some cases, than the very researchers and other observers who have put these comparisons on paper. This wholesale discrediting of Latin America's past development policy and performance makes it difficult to discern and understand the elements of the Latin American past (and present) that actually have worked out well and are worth building on, or imitating elsewhere in the region. The EA/LA comparisons of the last decade, of course, have served an important role in jolting people out of traditional ways of thinking and doing things. But such comparisons often manifest themselves in the form of government officials and agency managers embarking heartily on policies and practices that they *think* constitute the East Asian model of governance (or the New Zealand model of public management, or the Grameen Bank model of micro-credit, or the Japanese model of lean production, or the U.S. model of Total Quality Management). In many cases, the model--or what people think it is--gets adopted on the run and with major pieces missing, or under circumstances that are quite different.

The findings of the EA/LA comparisons are not the problem I am talking about. It is, rather, the absence of an as robust interest on the part of researchers and policy analysts in within-country and cross-country research as a source of guidelines for reform. The results of such research could serve as grounded material for the experimentation we see in Latin America today and the welcome openness to change that it bespeaks.

In closing, I would like to say that the EA/LA contrast troubles me, as posed in the workshop memo and literature it draws on, because it seems to sidestep the issue of "agency" as related to good governance. It does so by focusing on an explanation of problems (generic populism or welfarism) that makes it difficult for good governance (in this case, effective public provisioning) to be explained in the cases where it emerges--like Costa Rica, or Ceará, or Kerala.

Notes

1. Heller compares Kerala's 29 million to California's roughly the same number, with the Kerala population being settled on one-tenth the amount of land.

2. I would guess that this is one of the reasons why the Grameen-Bank "model"--another question raised by the workshop memo--is much more successful in Bangladesh than in many other countries with lower population densities where imitations have been attempted.

3. To help me out, I was fortunate to have participated in two recent seminars in which the Patrick Heller presented his research on Kerala, in which illuminating comments were made by Bish Sanyal and Ani Dasgupta, and to have had some further conversations with Heller. My understanding of the Kerala case is based on those encounters, and his and Amartya Sen's writings. Any misrendering of the Kerala case is my responsibility, not theirs.

4. Kerala is the only bow to South Asia relevance in this workshop, though the South Asia/Latin America comparison may yield more interesting lessons for the workshop's concerns with public-provisioning than the East Asia comparison.

5. Note, however, that despite Kerala's many-times higher survival indicators than Ceará and Brazil, Brazil nevertheless has a higher human development index--0.75 vs. 0.65. This is because of the weight of Brazil's much higher (than Kerala's) per-capita income in the index (I thank Patrick Heller for this clarification).

6. Heller's analysis shows that the typical Putnam-like rich associationalism of Kerala (and India, more generally) tended to be caste, ethnic, or religion-specific. Left on its own, without the more inclusive and cross-cutting mobilizing of the various social movements of Kerala's long history, this kind of associationalism can be fraught with danger, since it lays the groundwork for inter-caste, inter-ethnic, and inter-religious conflicts.

7. An exception in the recent Western development literature being the work of Patrick Heller.

8. From 1991 onwards, this growth manifested itself in a permanent 11% increase in the level of Ceará's per-capita GDP as a percent of Brazil's per-capita GDP (about $1,433 to Brazil's

$3,400)--namely, from a steady 38% to 42%--and a 13% increase in per-capita GDP as a percent of that of the Northeast, from 79% that of the Northeast to 89%. Also impressive, this growth occurred at a time when Ceará's agricultural sector-- traditionally the mainstay of the state's exports (cotton in particular) and accounting for a quarter of the state's output-- declined drastically, partly due to an attack of the cotton boll weevil. Industry, and secondarily services, clearly led this growth performance.

I do not extend the 1987-1993 comparison to a more recent year because my data for economic growth in 1993-1995 (from the state planning agency, IPLANCE) are not clearly comparable with the 1987-1993 series I noted previously. The 1993-1995 data seem to reveal a slight decline during those years to about 2.7%.

9. The Brazilian-government data for Ceará's IMR are quite different from those commonly cited in Ceará (and in my own book)--namely, a drop from 100 to 65, rather than from 77 to 44. To complicate matters further, Brazil's IMR rate of 42 in this paragraph of my text is not consistent with the rates for Brazil of McGuire's memo (his data show Brazil's IMR at 57 in 1993, rather than the 41.6 of my data). His are taken from the United Nations Development Report and mine from Brazilian government sources--namely IBGE, Censos Demográficos, and PNADs. I chose these latter sources for this particular paragraph--as against McGuire's/HDR's or the state of Ceará's--because they are the only ones that allow a state-by-state and regional breakdown.

10. In comparing IMR declines in Ceará vs. other places starting with lower rates, it is important to keep in mind that a big decline from quite high initial rates is considered rather "easy" by the public health field, in comparison to subsequent reductions, because of the dramatic effects brought about by the introduction of oral rehydration therapy for diarrhea (as Ceará did in its preventive health program)--the largest single killer of infants in underdeveloped regions, particularly rural areas.

11. As of this writing, Brazilian governors are not allowed to immediately succeed themselves, although there is a constitutional amendment that proposes to allow re-election now under consideration and highly likely to be passed. In the 1994 gubernatorial election, it should be noted, Jereissati lost in the state capital--doing much better in rural areas. The candidate he backed for mayor of the state's capital and largest city in the 1996 municipal elections also lost.

12. The fiscal reforms involved (a) expunging the payroll books of 40,000 ghost workers or double salaries for those working one job, (b) aggressive collection of taxes, assisted by extensive computerization, (c) reducing real wages among public-sector workers by not giving cost-of-living adjustments (this

contributed more than the termination of ghost workers to reducing payroll obligations); and (d) insisting that new employees be hired only through competitive exams. This set of reforms succeeded in reducing the share of salaries in total receipts from 87% of expected receipts in 1987 to 45% in 1991 (all this during a time when federal transfers were decreasing)-- leaving the state for the first time with a budget for investment, not to mention non-salary operating expenditures.

13. Some give equal credit to economic growth and a federal milk-distribution program administered by the state.

14. The most broadly-based and enduring was the rural preventive health program, involving an "army" of 7,300 newly-hired paraprofessional health agents, earning the minimum wage and often semi-literate, who were hired by the state government from the communities where they were to work and paid the minimum wage. The public-procurement program represented an unusual and imaginative redirection by the state government of 30% of its public-sector procurement of goods and services from traditional urban suppliers and distributors to small and micro-firms throughout the interior of the state. The program resulted in a 30% reduction in cost of these items, which were delivered at comparable quality and within comparable time periods. (The public procurement program was temporarily suspended two years ago because of a challenge from the courts [inspired, some say, by the program's and the governors' opponents] that questioned the legality of the program's waiving of open bidding regulations [the state expects to win this case, but it requires a change of law at the national level].) Finally, the state was successful at "de-clientelizing" the administration of its intermittent public-works programs in the interior, employing thousands of rural males in these emergency programs during the region's periodic droughts. The programs also involve massive distribution of food supplies and water from trucks. The drought programs, though continuing to be less clientelized than those preceding 1987, never reached the degree of non-political allocation that they did in 1987--at least according to citizens of the affected communities.

An extensive discussion of these programs can be found in the author's *Good Government in the Tropics*, Johns Hopkins University Press (1997); the health program is also treated in Judith Tendler and Sara Freedheim, "Trust in a Rent-seeking World: Health and Government Transformed in Northeast Brazil," World Development 22 (No. 12, December 1994):771-1791; and the procurement program in Judith Tendler and Mônica Alves Amorim, "Small Firms and Their Helpers: Lessons on Demand," World Development 24 (No. 3, March 1996):407-426.

15. Since the late 1970s, and pre-dating the new governance, the World Bank heavily supported the agricultural sector and the state's agricultural institutions with a succession of large integrated rural development projects. Agriculture, however, has stood out during this period for its lackluster performance, its fading significance in the state's output and, particularly, the state's inability to deal with a major attack of the boll weevil (starting in the mid-1980s) on its traditional export crop--cotton--which is also the major input for its textile industry. The textile industry, in ironic contrast to the production of cotton, *is* one of Ceará's major modernizing successes--having outperformed that of Southeastern Brazil in competitiveness, technological modernity, and exports.

16. With the exception of a small group of Northeast economist-researchers, such as Katz and Policarpo, who have pointed out Ceará's better economic performance starting in the 1970s. They have not drawn attention, however, to the 1986-1987 divide and the new good governance (most obviously, because the rates fell during that period). They have tried to understand the difference between Ceará and other states, particularly the previously better-off and more-industrialized Pernambuco--attributing this difference to some interesting factors relating to the differing natures of the industrial elites of both states, and the extent to which industrialization management came from inside or outside the state.

17. A remarkably similar set of critiques and disappointments have been expressed about Italy's policies and institutions to develop its lagging region, the South. Certain aspects of Brazil's Northeast policies were modeled on the Italian case.

18. Although it must be said that econometric studies would be hard put to demonstrate the effect of Ceará's recent governance on growth rates, let alone within such a short period of time. In the 1980s, a remarkably similar set of admiring allegations about the relationship between the economic performance of the state of Massachusetts in the 1980s and the administration of Governor Michael Dukakis were shown to be not verifiable, even by the economist-admirers of that administration.

19. The struggle between these two elite fractions took place over a period of ten to 20 years preceding the 1987 election, and within the realm of a business association--the Federation of Industries of Ceará and, more particularly, the Ceará Industrial Center (CIC), which was a part of it. The more modernizing, "young-turk" faction won control of the CIC years before the 1987 election, and sponsored a series of public lectures and ensuing debates about how to bring their state out of poverty and backwardness--to which they even invited, among others, well-known "left" and sometimes exiled intellectuals such as Celso Furtado and Maria da Conceição Tavares. This was quite

remarkable for an elite business group during a period of
repressive military government, and in a part of the country
known for most supporting that government.

Jereissati, part of that group and 35 years old when he first ran
for election, was the candidate the group decided to put up for
election against the "clientelistic" three families of rural
landholding wealth that had dominated previous administrations.
Significantly, and less commented upon, this young-turk fraction
had similarly put forward another candidate chosen by them four
years previously, a government "technocrat" from outside their
group who won but who ultimately, they decided, did not have the
power or the capacity to stand up to the more traditional elite.

20. Jeffrey Paige's new book comparing Costa Rica, Guatemala, El
Salvador, and Nicaragua recounts the origins of Costa Rica's
success as a peaceful, relatively open and successful welfare
state also in terms of the winning out of the more modern
fraction of the elite--in his cases, the agro-industrial as vs.
the agricultural elite.

21. I make this argument at greater length, and present evidence
from Ceará, in *Good Government in the Tropics*, The Johns Hopkins
University Press, 1997.

22. Both governors were known to be more open informally on
certain occasions, in comparison to previous governments and to
many neighboring Northeast governments, receiving delegations of
representatives of labor and other excluded groups--associations
of rural workers, protestors to proposed dam projects, etc.--and
to negotiating their demands with them.

23. The state government worked with the firms to make it
possible to create labor "cooperatives" or "associations"--a form
of labor contractor--which would allow the firms to contract the
associations rather than hire workers directly. It introduced a
bill in the state legislature to facilitate this form of
contracting and lobbied successfully for its passage. It also
encouraged firms to locate outside the capital city in rural
areas, and gave them more subsidies for doing so. This policy
was meant to provide more rural employment by "decentralizing"
industry but also, as reported by state officials and firms, was
considered desirable because it made it more difficult for
workers to organize in that decentralized location scattered the
new jobs spatially.

24. Kerala and India data from Patrick Heller, Ceará data from
Brazilian state and central government sources (IPLANCE and
IPEA).

25. The per-capita GDP figures for Brazil and Ceará used here are
quite a bit lower than those used in the text above for purposes

of comparability with India and Kerala. For the former figures,
I am using data developed by Patrick Heller from the *World
Development Report* of 1994, the *UNDP Human Development Report* of
1994, and Government of Kerala data from 1992. For the
Ceará/Northeast/Brazil per-capita GDP figures used previously, as
noted above, I used government of Brazil sources, which give
higher figures. I did this in order to make possible comparisons
between Ceará and Brazil and the Northeast. In order to arrive
at this paragraph's [lower] per-capita GDP figure for Ceará, I
took Ceará's per-capita GDP as a percentage of Brazil's per-
capita GDP from my data and applied this percentage (38) to
Heller's/World Bank's per-capita GDP for Brazil of $2,770.

26. In contrast to the well-known foreign imposition of the
agrarian reforms of many of the East Asian cases--which often
disqualifies them as models for Latin America and most other
places--it is important to note that Kerala's agrarian reform was
the result of *internal* and broadly inclusive mobilizing carried
out over many years by the state's Communist Party. The CP was
able to build and draw on various already organized groups of a
dense civil society, all of which also helped to keep it in
check. Although Communist-Party mobilizing may be just as
irrelevant for Latin America today as foreign-imposed agrarian
reforms, the broader phenomenon of widespread mobilizing around
agrarian and other poor-oriented reforms is not at all unfamiliar
to what is happening today in some places in post-authoritarian
Latin America today. In Brazil, for example, the rise of the
Landless Workers Movement (and earlier, the Workers' Party) and
its demands for agrarian reform, have clearly played a role in
the seriousness with which the government is currently facing
that issue.

Just as India's respect for democracy and procedure created space
for the Communists to mobilize around this and other
redistributive issues, Brazil's new respect for democracy has
made it more like India--in contrast to the previous
authoritarian period--in terms of the kind of mobilization it
will tolerate. And just as the Congress Party's involvement in
the struggle for liberation from the British contributed to its
reluctant willingness to tolerate Communist-Party organizing, so
Brazil's struggle to free itself from a repressive military
regime also created a new environment of tolerance for
mobilizing.

27. I owe this observation to Patrick Heller, in response to my
question about where I might find some literature from a public-
administration or institution-building view of how the state
government actually did it, and why so well.

28. One explanation may lie in the fact that researchers of
Kerala who publish in Western development journals--whether pro
or con--have been captured by other issues: first, that low per-

capita incomes could be associated with high social indicators (a lot of research effort went into establishing and measuring these outcomes); second, a later-emerging view that doubted the sustainability of a low-growth model (the same doubts fell on the similarly touted Sri Lanka case), a view that was augmented later by those who pointed to the mobilizing and empowerment of labor as the culprit (in certain ways, similar to the negative judgments on "populist" Latin America); and third, a more mobilization-sympathetic set of researchers who were fascinated by what happened *outside* government, rather than inside.

29. Mark Granovetter provides an interesting example of the shortsightedness caused by characterizing whole countries--in the case of his example, the East-Asian style of government as "good" and South Asian as "bad." He attributes this overly general characterization, and the attribution of "good" to one and "bad" to the other, to the fact that "business groups" are hardly studied in the non-Indian literature on India, but yet they are a hot scholarly topic for students of East Asia. There, the particular pattern of relations with them are said to have been an ingredient of "good government" which results in not noticing their importance, let alone touting them, in a place like India normally used as an example of "bad" policies and "rent-seeking" governance.

Comments on *Partnership for Capacity Building in Africa*
For PREM Public Sector Group, The World Bank
8 March 1998

Judith Tendler
Massachusetts Institute of Technology
tendler@mit.edu

The ***Partnership for Capacity Building in Africa*** (PCBA) is to be commended for its serious attempt to understand the problems inherent in existing relationships between the donor community and African countries, for the long process of consultation with Africans that accompanied and informed the exercise, and for the extent to which it boldly commits to an approach that breaks significantly with the problematic aspects of the existing relationship and gives more say to African participants in determining how such a new approach is to be structured.

I start by listing some aspects of the draft PCBA report that could be improved, and then make some suggestions as to how the improvements might be made. I divide my comments into two sections: (1) raising questions, and (2) suggestions. I add a few minor observations at the end. In developing these comments, I have kept in mind the Questions for Reviewers provided by Cheryl Gray.

I - Questions

1. The analysis

Despite the report's call for a new approach to Africa's problems, its analyses of them (as well as the proposed solutions--more below) have an "old" quality to them. Even though I am not an African specialist, I have seen them many times in WB and other writings. This is not consistent with the report's claim to a "new" approach. In particular, the characterization of the African development experience seems too monolithic--painted as a failure, as rife with corruption, administrative and political incompetence, and with civil society nowhere to be seen, either because it is repressed or too weak to make a stand. I will leave it to the African specialists to argue with such a monolithic portrayal on the grounds of accuracy.

What is problematic about the monolithically negative portrayal for the PCBA is that such an initiative needs to be built on an understanding of why some things have worked (within countries, as well as between countries) and others have not. For example, the report states that "management, poor policies, and weak institutions" have prevented African agriculture from achieving "high levels of growth leading to poverty reduction and improved living standards." But we know that there are significant exceptions in some countries and/or in certain regions. Cases like these should provide us with the lessons that feed into the strategies and remedies proposed in the report. For an exercise like this--especially one that seeks to escape from the imposition of foreign models--the more positive outcomes cannot afford to be neglected because they should form the basis of an argument about what is *likely* to work.

The monolithically negative portrayal is also problematic because it is like typical donor portrayals of Africa that many Africans have found insulting. In that sense, it is somewhat jarring in a report claiming to represent a more African view. Correspondingly, the portrayal of such unrelieved incompetence and corruption could be self-defeating, because it may not inspire much confidence in donors being asked to commit more than a billion dollars to an undertaking that puts so much decision-making capacity in African hands.

The "systemic" nature of the portrayal of Africa's problems--all bad things go together in an analytically neat and closed circle of underdevelopment and incapacity--hinders one's ability to figure out how to intervene, to identify the point of entry. The similarly "systemic" nature of the report's recommended approach--"integrated" and "not piecemeal" (p. 3)--also seems unrealistic in light of what has been learned from past experience with "integrated" approaches. If the analysis of Africa's problems could show contrasts, contradictions, and jagged edges, including some bright spots, this would help indicate paths of entry into the problem.

The negatively monolithic portrayal of Africa also creates trouble for some of the suggestions the report makes. For example, the proposed scheme bars from participation those countries that do not have "good governance, open society, the rule of law, and proper accountability" (p. 59, note 6). But this would seem to exclude most African countries, at least as characterized by the report's own analysis.

I find these criteria for excluding certain countries from participation confusing for other reasons as well. First, the stated purpose of the PCBA is to contribute to the *building* of these very qualities--proper accountability, good governance, strengthened civil society, etc. Second, there are always islands of institutional promise in badly-governed countries. Isn't it important to see them as opportunities to at least set those countries on a path toward good governance? In this sense, it is something more like the "piecemeal" approach that one wants, though it would be more accurately described as an "incrementalist" strategy of bringing about change--distinctly not "integrated." Third, such broad grounds for exclusion, because their vagueness allows considerable room for interpretation, could simply open the door for capricious and idiosyncratic selection, depending on whoever was in charge at a particular moment.

Could a set of criteria for judging grant proposals be devised that would favor those activities that seemed to be on the path toward improving governance, accountability, etc.? These kinds of selection criteria would also act as incentives to movement in the desired direction.

Judith Tendler, "Comments for WB on African Capacity-building Partnership," 3-8-98

Finally, the portrayal of the African continent as basket-case implies a kind of African "exceptionalism" that, regardless of its justifiability, makes it difficult to learn from and apply lessons being learned in other, non-African countries. If Africa is so uniquely bad, and so resistant to development as a continent, then the solution must also be unique. There's not much to be learned, that is, from the experience of other continents.

While reading the PCBA report, for example, I was reminded of an article written some years ago by Uma Lele, which looked into the reasons for poor performance of rural development projects in East Africa. Bringing to bear on this case the experience of the Indian case, she pointed out that the Indian successes in dramatically increasing agricultural productivity were preceded by years and years of patient and unglamorous investment of funds and technical assistance in the building of agricultural research institutions. During this long period, of course, there was no immediate return in increased agricultural productivity.

Lele criticized the unsuccessful African experience with IRDP programs, then, not for its peculiarly "African" elements (endemically corrupt and inadequate administration, etc.), but for the fact that the governments and the World Bank had invested heavily in rural development projects without first investing in the building of capacity of the agricultural research institutions. This is the kind of lesson that the PCBA should be able to draw from the experience of other continents. The African "exceptionalist" perspective precludes the learning of such lessons.

I am not suggesting that the report go to the other extreme and project a monolithically rosy view of the African scene--but only that it reflect the variety of bad *and* good that exist within and between countries, in which opportunities for improvement inhere.

2. The remedies

Most of the report's priorities and suggestions to remedy Africa's problems are perfectly acceptable. But they are too numerous, too vague, and have a "Christmas-list" quality to them (see, e.g., pp. 15-17). (Many are also "boilerplate"--I have seen them in many WB and other donor reports, even for countries outside Africa.) In some ways, they remind me of the justifications and proposals for the integrated rural development projects of the 1970s and 1980s: donors, along with governments, were capable of doing *everything* at one time, and had to if they were going to make any impact on the problem--namely, health, education, micro-enterprise assistance, roads, drinking water, electrification, irrigation, and agriculture credit, research, and extension.

It's not that any single one of these interventions would not improve things markedly, or that it would not be desirable to achieve all these things at once. Rather, experience has shown that the all-together-at-once approach does not work because it's too complex and too organizationally demanding. One needs an incrementalist *strategy*, which is quite different from the piecemeal-ism that the report rejects.

Judith Tendler, "Comments for WB on African Capacity-building Partnership," 3-8-98

The report should explicitly choose to include some actions and objectives and *exclude* others, and indicate the reasons for such decisions and such a ranking of priorities. There are various clear criteria one could choose for supporting some activities and excluding others: for example, (a) some are easier than others and therefore more likely to actually work, (b) the problems that some of the proposed goals are meant to remedy are of greater urgency than others, (c) some initiatives create conditions that make other interventions easier to carry out, or even contribute toward reducing the lower-priority problem itself, (d) some initiatives are better suited to the kind of organization that the PCBA proposes to set up.

After reading initially of the extensive consultations in Africa that led up to this report, I expected that the report would provide a sense of the varied commentaries and suggestions, grounded in different country experiences, that would have emerged from these consultations. It was difficult to believe that such an extensive set of consultations among Africans would have yielded an analysis of the problem and a set of suggestions that sounded like so many other World Bank and other donor reports I have read. Perhaps the quality of those findings was lost in the attempt to generalize. Couldn't that source be better mined?

3. The new entity and the size of the program

After reading about the major inroads that the PCBA hoped to make in Africa's problems, and the comprehensive and ambitious listing of fundable activities and objectives (from creating civil society to mending Africa's universities to increasing accountability of government institutions to microcredit programs for small businesses), I was surprised to see that the initiative involved funding of only $8 million per year in each country for five years. It is not that the ability to have an impact is related to the amount of money spent. Rather, this relatively low level of spending in each country would seem to dictate a highly strategic and focused approach to grant-making that would clearly specify (a) certain areas of priority, and/or (b) types of interventions where the marginal impact of a small amount of funding was likely to be high, *based on past experience*, and/or (c) activities for which the need to monitor would be relatively lower (more on this below).

Take the example of helping sick universities. Even if only partially successful, this would constitute a significant contribution to Africa's development, and would be an appropriate area for such a grant-funded program. What would be the way to focus on this problem, given this particular level of funding and time-span? (Or is it not feasible?--in which case, this particular task should be excluded?) What is the relevant experience that can be brought to bear on such an endeavor? Could this be one of a few priorities, at least in the first years? If not, why not? With respect to the need to focus, I cannot imagine such a funding initiative being successful at putting some universities on its feet *and* creating free-standing "centers of excellence" within the initial five-year period. A choice would have to be made.

Judith Tendler, "Comments for WB on African Capacity-building Partnership," 3-8-98

David Leonard published a proposal some years ago in *World Development*, which aimed to help bring highly trained (and highly-earning) African professionals back to their countries. I don't remember the details, but it was clever and was widely circulated. Though the PCBA might not necessarily be interested in this particular proposal, this kind of thinking is an example of a kind of focus, concreteness, and proposal-making that would help improve the report.

Similarly, I was rather confused about what the proposed institution would do, in terms of its grantmaking. It seemed that the new entity would fund a large number of different types of things--from helping civil society to funding and supporting microcredit programs. But these are highly different activities, requiring different kinds of projects and support. Also, much of the text gives the impression that the PCBA would fund mainly "soft" initiatives--restoring sick universities to health, strengthening judiciaries and public auditing departments, building civil society. But the monitoring-and-evaluation section emphasizes rates of return and economic impact analysis (p. 71), which is not suited to these kinds of interventions. Some explicit clarifications are necessary

The suitability of the grant (vs. loan) mechanism, of course, depends on the type of project. Grants were preferred, I assume, because they are much less administratively demanding--a good enough reason, in my view. But if that is the case, then this requires excluding activities that are suited to loan funding--like micro-lending and other services where charges are normally levied or where increased production lends itself to measurement.

I also wasn't clear as to what the proposed institution would be *like*. First, I thought it was like a small regional development bank, without the investments in infrastructure; then, like a technical assistance agency; then, like a foundation such as Rockefeller or Ford; then, a small donor giving myriad grants to NGOs without much overall impact. Would there be a few projects of $1 million apiece, or many projects of $50,000 apiece? It would help if the report specify what other existing institution this proposed entity would be roughly like, and *not* like. Given the need to narrow down, moreover, it might make sense to propose a first experimental phase during which only one or a few particular types of activity would be funded--perhaps a suggestion emerging out of the many consultations. Then decisions could be made about subsequent phases, based on the results of that first phase.

For the level of funding proposed for the PCBA, and the seeming large number of small projects, the reliance on monitoring, evaluation, and accountability that was projected seemed unrealistic--particularly given the low percentage of the funding projected for administration. Most organizations administering grants of this size simply do not have the capacity to engage in the kind of monitoring and verification of results portrayed in the report. This is even true of respected organizations in the United States like the Ford Foundation, let alone a new agency in a continent that is said to be rife with problems of accountability. All this suggests that activities for funding should be selected that either have a respectable record of accountability already (the report should list some), or that suffer less from lack of monitoring than others. This latter

Judith Tendler, "Comments for WB on African Capacity-building Partnership," 3-8-98

characteristic will be determined by (a) the nature of the activity, (b) the track record of the organization, and/or (c) the propensity for "natural" monitoring in the project's environment.

One example of the latter would be subprojects that have a kind of "built-in," "natural" monitoring coming from outsiders in the community where the project was located. The Bank itself has had some experience with encouraging or even formally contracting outsider local groups to monitor the programs it funds--providing them with the information necessary to do this. Many civic associations and NGOs complain precisely of the lack of this kind of information about what government or other powerful actors in their world are planning to do. The provision of such information to groups outside a funded organization is unusual, in short, and often elicits the kind of monitoring one needs--often in informal ways and often without expending additional resources. As a by-product, of course, this kind of approach would also contribute to the civil-society-strengthening objectives of the program. The point is not to argue for any particular proposal here, but to suggest that the report itself could be more concrete in making such suggestions.

The report praises the "success" of three already-existing regional capacity building initiatives in Africa (p. 53)--ACBF, AERC, and AMSCO. It would be useful to know what had been learned about building effective regional African agencies from these three experiences. Why, moreover, is none of these agencies appropriate to manage the new initiative? If the existing entities are not effective agencies, what would be different about the proposed one that would make the proposed entity more effective, or would avoid any problems now afflicting these existing regional initiatives? Why is it necessary to create a separate institution at the regional level and in each participating country (the national capacity secretariats), rather than placing this initiative in an existing one?

In this sense, it is somewhat ironic that the report goes into some detail about the Bank's having learned from the past "mistake" of creating separate project units in the past, rather than trying to figure out how to make programs work in existing entities. Since the report provides considerable detail about why these separate units had been a mistake, and what had been learned from this experience, this cannot help but place into the reader's mind a parallel set of reservations about the proposed separate and new facility.

It is not that new entities are necessarily always unwise, but that there seemed to be no clear justification for creating them in a case where so little funds were being managed--at least at the national (as opposed to regional) level. The report should say what it is about these particular proposed new entities that makes them less subject to the problems familiar to us from other such cases.

II - Suggestions

1. New vs. old

Judith Tendler, "Comments for WB on African Capacity-building Partnership," 3-8-98

224

The report could be more explicit and detailed about what is "new" about what it is proposing. It actually promises to do so, at least implicitly, by saying that it "seeks to avoid the approaches and attitudes by African development partners that have proved to be faulty in previous efforts..." (Box 4.1, p. 54). It needs to elaborate these criticisms (the only one I remember relates to expatriate technical assistance), and to show how its recommendations represent distinct improvements over the way things have been done in the past.

For example, the report mentions in several places its critique of expatriate technical assistance. This led me to expect an interesting proposal in this area, which nevertheless did not emerge. The only proposal of this nature, in fact, was the "basic tenet" of using technical assistance "sparingly" (p. iii). But this seems to be throwing away the baby with the bathwater. Technical assistance provided by experienced people from the country or the region--especially people who have been intimately involved in successful African experiences, at local as well as national levels--can have quite powerful impacts, and is not necessarily costly.

2. Monolithic vs. mixed results

In order to be realistic, an exercise of this nature must convince the reader by building on an understanding of what has worked better in Africa in the areas of interest to the PCBA. If it wants to build universities, for example, what African experiences can it look to that have worked better and that could be used as guidelines for how to proceed? If it wants to make government agencies more accountable, what strategy would it follow that has worked somewhere in Africa? If it wants the CGIAR centers to integrate more closely with the national centers, what experiences can it point to where this actually happened, even if only partially, and what were the lessons learned that could be applied to other cases? After all, this latter objective (regarding CGIAR centers)--and the critique of the existing situation that it implies--has been on the to-fix list of donor evaluations for many years. If it hasn't been fixed by now, what is different about the PCBA approach that would lead the reader to believe that it can be fixed this time around?

To win the confidence of funders for such an initiative, it would seem, the PCBA would have to lay something on the table that was convincing because it was somehow different than what is usually proposed, and was grounded in positive African experiences.

3. Donor vs. non-donor initiatives

The report could strengthen its claim for a more Afro-centric institutional base and decision-making power by citing cases of improved agency performance or other such initiatives that had little to do with donors. For example, the report stresses the need to get away from expatriate technical assistance and donor dominance in other forms, but many of the better-working initiatives it cites seem to be donor-funded and with heavy donor involvement, including technical assistance (e.g., AGETIP/World Bank [Box 3.11, p. 29]; Kenya Enhanced Commodity Distribution System/USAID [Box 3.21, P. 51]; Tanzania Improved Management of

Environmental Information/UNDP [Box 3.17, p. 44]; Uganda--Building Capacity of Small Private Firms/IDA [Box 3/10, p. 28]).

I remember being struck, when working on an evaluation for the South African government of a set of 110 squatter upgrading and sites-and-services projects, that the South African government was so strongly behind such a program (as opposed to 'low-cost housing') without any serious involvement of the World Bank. (This set of programs started with the de Klerk government, three years before Mandela's election, and continued thereafter.) Few countries had ever undertaken the sites-and-services and upgrading approach to low-cost housing without Bank insistence and funding; and the Bank-funded projects usually involved one or only a few such projects in any particular country, not the dozens of the South African case. Indeed, the South African projects were implemented unusually rapidly, at least in comparison to many Bank sites-and-services projects; they went further in decentralizing project administration and incentives than any Bank project; and they represented an unusual commitment to labor-intensive construction, something the Bank has tried very hard to do in other African countries, particularly in rural roadbuilding. Might this homegrown South African experience have any bearing on such attempts in other African countries?

The three most important factors in understanding these impressive developments in South Africa were: political (the de Klerk government was worried about the upcoming elections and the demand for housing was quite politically salient), fiscal (the government was able to sell off strategic reserves because of the end of the economic boycott and therefore had windfall resources), and administrative (there was a long history--within and outside government--of working on this issue and becoming familiarized with these kinds of approaches).

These are the kinds of examples (though many of them may be more modest than this one), and the lessons learned from them, that should form the basis of the recommendations of such a report. Those who carried out such programs, and understand why they worked and what parts worked better than others, should also be drawn upon for technical assistance on similar projects in other countries. (I thought that this recommendation was one that the report might be leading up to when it made its initial criticism of expatriate technical assistance.)

As I wrote the above South African story, I could imagine the readers saying, "But South Africa is an exception, so...." Although South Africa, or this story, may be an exception, seeing it as such is to deprive this kind of exercise of the value to be learned from such cases of better performance. Calling them exceptions is to dismiss their value as examples to be learned from. This contributes as much to an outsider-dominated approach to development problems in Africa as donor power itself.

Linking suggestions to existing positive experiences in Africa, in sum, would be a way of saying something "new," and of avoiding the "old-sounding" and all-encompassing suggestions of the report.

Judith Tendler, "Comments for WB on African Capacity-building Partnership," 3-8-98

III - Other suggestions

1. I was confused about the purpose of the boxes. Some of them, about specific projects, seemed to indicate the type of project that would be funded under the initiative--AGETIP, for example, and a small-firm program in Uganda, BUDS. They also seemed to represent examples of successful projects, or at least to imply that. But some, like the Uganda project BUDS, reported only one year of operation, long before one could claim success for a particular intervention of this nature (Box 3.10, p. 28).
The AGETIP example, as detailed in the box, seemed questionable as a model for this new approach--at least according to the PCBA's stated goals with respect to donor-African relationships. The AGETIP-type projects have had strong donor funding and involvement, including non-African technical assistance--from the World Bank *and* ILO. In other ways they may not represent--at least up to now--a model that fits the PCBA's objectives.[1]
The subprojects of the PCBA's proposed program, finally, would seem to be too modest for an AGETIP-type effort, with its costly investments in physical infrastructure. So what was AGETIP supposed to be an example of? If there are indeed positive African experiences without heavy donor involvement that could be built upon, they should be an integral part of the text because the suggestions should flow from them.

2. I disagree with the guiding suggestion that appears in a few places that Africa's problems are a result of "priority of politics over economics" (p. 6)--and that economics should have a priority over politics. Many of the goals of this initiative, if they are to be achieved, will be deeply embedded in political processes. To fail to understand how the political piece contributes to successful outcomes, and to attribute achievements to "apolitical" processes, is to misread the lessons to be learned from such cases. In addition, an argument that associates bad outcomes with politics and good outcomes with "a-politics" is implicitly anti-democratic. Politics is an essential part of an effective democracy, and it is always a part of any story of good government performance, as well as bad. For similar reasons, and in the spirit of the report's concern about governance in Africa, I would not have omitted "elected officials" from the list on p. ii of a "continent transformed...by African technical, professional, and managerial personnel...."

---

[1]For example, according to a recent OED Evaluation Brief (which was otherwise quite positive), little maintenance of this newly constructed physical capital was forthcoming, nor were institutional arrangements for maintenance in place. Although this is a serious problem, it is quite "old," having afflicted all kinds of infrastructure projects in developing countries, particularly roads and water; it long pre-dates the AGETIP model. The infrastructure department of the Bank itself has recognized the seriousness of this kind of problem for many years: failure to maintain seriously compromises the rates of return of road and water construction projects because of premature deterioration and even loss of the facility. A successful model, at least for the kinds of objectives stated in the PCBA report would, by definition, have solved this problem--or at least be pointed in that direction. Routine maintenance and repair, it might be added, generates significant employment activity--another important goal of the PCBA report.

Judith Tendler, "Comments for WB on African Capacity-building Partnership," 3-8-98

3. There seemed to be some assertions in the report that could not be justified or were not true. On p. 57, for example, a "key attribute" of the Trust Fund was said to be a "high rate of return" on the funds. I was not sure what this meant, since the proposed Trust Fund seemed to be a *grant*-making agency; also, many of its funded activities would not lend themselves to measuring rates of return. Also, the "cost-effectiveness" of the proposed fund was attributed to its "bypass[ing] government" and the targeting of funds to "specific individuals." But there is no prima facie evidence that this would lead to high rather than low rates of return in any particular case.

4. This is quite minor, but it wasn't clear why the term "business" plan is being used. The operation seems to have more in common with public-sector or nongovernment/nonprofit operations than with a business.

5. It would be useful to know why only 12 countries participated in the consultations, and why those particular countries.

Judith Tendler, "Comments for WB on African Capacity-building Partnership," 3-8-98

Transforming Local Economies: Lessons from the Northeast Brazilian Experience

Judith Tendler
Massachusetts Institute of Technology
tendler@mit.edu

Prepared under the auspices of the MIT/BN Project (Massachusetts Institute of TechnologyDepartment of Urban Studies and Planning/Bank of the Northeast)
4 August 2001 (draft–coments welcome)

Presented at the OECD/State of Ceará State Government Meeting on Foreign Direct Investment, Fortaleza, 12 December 2002

Abstract

This research started with an attempt to find and explain cases of competitiveness and upgrading among particular sub-sectors, firms, and micro-regions in the textile, garment, footwear, furniture, and irrigated fruit (for export) sectors in the nine states of Northeast Brazil. In searching for explanations for good (and poor) performance, and the policy implications therein, our fieldwork led, time and again, to matters relating to training, technical assistance, and research. This came as no surprise, particularly given the last decade's findings and related policy advice on the importance of upskilling of the workforce, of "soft" and other process improvements in contrast to "hard" improvements like equipment and production technology, and of the key role to be played in this process by large sophisticated buyer firms–often outsiders–in a tutelary and "tough-love" relation to their smaller-firm local suppliers. These concerns were being taken seriously in all of our cases, but there was a clear *absence* of advancement in some of them in contrast to clear progress in others. Four factors help explain this contrasting pattern of outcomes. *First*, despite the fact that much of the policy advice and the literature on which it draws focuses on the transformative effects of large *buyer* firms, the most impressive effects were sometimes associated with large *input-supplying* firms–and for reasons that seemed obvious, once they were discovered. *Second*, the otherwise laudable public-private partnerships and informal networks around training, technical assistance, and research that evolved between government actors, training-and-research institutes, and the large firms in a particular locale, sometimes *excluded* small and medium firms (SMEs) from the web of support, though not deliberately. The exclusion was driven in part by a mutual attraction between professionals of these institutions and their large-firm counterparts–an attraction that proved fatal to developmental impacts. The exclusion was sometimes driven as well as by governors and other powerful politicians who construed their political fortunes as depending on the "landing" and good treatment of a large outsider firm. In the less excluding outcomes, powerful political leaders found it in their electoral interests to go against this grain and push for more "inclusive" institutional actions and styles. *Third*, the literature tells us that while large outsider firms in developing countries generally invest liberally in training their workforce, SMEs in developing countries do *not*–with the latter firms therefore often requiring, paradoxically, more experienced workers than the former. This leads to a classic case of "market failure," and hence one of the few remaining strong rationales for public subsidy and support in the local economic-development field. Working in the opposite direction, however, the eagerness of state governments and training institutions to cooperate and partner with large firms led them to generously subsidize the workforce training–usually customized to the particular firm–of firms that were likely to invest in training anyway. This exacerbated the market failure, rather than remedying it. *Fourth*, though the current concern about upgrading local economies focuses on the building of ongoing *formal* institutions of training, technical assistance, and research within a region–and bringing single sophisticated outsider firms to the region as benefit-spreading "Trojan horses"–one of our cases of a footwear cluster rested partly on the importance of longstanding *in*formal networks reaching from local SMEs to advanced firms, clusters, and institutions *outside* the region–and the bringing back into the region of advanced practices by these myraid firms themselves.

Small Firms, the Informal Sector, and the Devil's Deal[1]

Judith Tendler

Massachusetts Institute of Technology
Cambridge, Massachusetts 02139
tendler@mit.edu

IDS Bulletin [Institute of Development Studies], Vol. 33, No. 3, July 2002

Abstract

These days, everybody loves small firms and their clusters–donors large and small, governments and nongovernment organizations, left and right. Some characterize small firms (SFs) as the proper subject of social policy and safety nets, and house SF programs in departments of social welfare or labor. Others see SFs as the stuff of "serious" economic development, and focus on upgrading their collective efficiency, productivity, and market access. Unfortunately, the combination of the social-policy view with the inevitable local politics of SFs generates a brew that inadvertently undermines not only the upgrading agenda, but certain aspects of the social-policy agenda itself–namely, better environmental, labor, and health-and-safety practices and protections. This article explains how this happens, and shows that things don't always need to turn out that way, especially if donors and others pay attention to the histories lying behind today's thriving SF clusters in developing countries.

Everybody seems to love small firms. Whether big donors or small, bilateral or multilateral. Whether left or right, government or nongovernment, practitioners or academics, myself included. Small firms have even gained a prestigious place in the firmament of social policy, where microcredit and other small-firm programs are seen as forming a safety net into which the poor can gently fall. But this is exactly where the trouble begins, and that's what this article is about.

Over the last decade or so, myriad programs, projects, and policy reforms have focused attention on informal-sector (IS) firms and small firms (SFs) in general, as part of a broader social-policy agenda of reducing poverty and unemployment.[2] Despite this welcome attention, many planners in developing countries nevertheless continue to view SF/IS programs as "only" welfare, rather than the stuff of "serious" economic development. The particular form taken by SF/IS support in many countries reinforces this view, as explained below, as does the way SF/IS support is often embedded in politics. This jeopardizes certain benefits, ironically, that we hold crucial to the current agenda of reducing poverty and unemployment: greater observance by firms of environmental and labor regulations, sustained increases in efficiency and productivity in local economies and, as a result, improvement in the quantity and quality of jobs.

I was first struck with the darker side of small-firm and informal-sector support when interviewing economic-development officials in the Brazilian state of Pernambuco. I was curious to know why they had not included, in a new program of support to a handful of small-firm clusters in the state, a particularly vibrant and longstanding garment cluster about a two hours' drive from the capital city. They explained that it would be quite awkward to elevate a cluster of firms to "growth-pole" status that was notorious for not paying taxes and not observing other government regulations.[3] At the same time, however, they did not see themselves as having the option to enforce these regulations, even as a *quid pro quo* for providing public support, because the cluster was concentrated in two municipalities that contained more than 30,000 electors.

After visiting some other places and reading about cases in other countries, I came to interpret what I was observing as a kind of unspoken deal between politicians and their constituents–myriad small-firm owners, many in the informal sector. If you vote for me, according to this exchange, I won't collect taxes from you; I won't make you comply with other tax, environmental, or labor regulations; and I will keep the police and inspectors from harassing you. I call this tacit understanding "the devil's deal" because it causes informality to become *more* attractive, and formalization *less* attractive, than they otherwise might be. Once the deal is made, it is difficult for either side to get out of it, as the above-mentioned comments of the Brazilian officials reveal.

In certain ways, then, the devil's deal can pose just as significant a barrier to formalization and upgrading of small-firm clusters[4] as the actual costs themselves of formalization and regulation. Much of the policy advice on this subject, however, focuses on the "burdens" themselves as the source of the problem–particularly, the costs of formalizing and observing tax, environmental, and labor codes. It advocates reforms, in turn, that grant special relief from these burdens to small firms in the form of exemptions from or reductions of taxes and other costs associated with environmental and labor regulation. In addition, the SF literature is strangely silent on the politics in which SF support is so firmly embedded.[5]

The dynamic of the devil's deal also reinforces the distinctly dismissive attitudes held by many economic-development planners and by development-bank managers toward smaller and informal-sector firms. To the extent that these managers and civil servants acknowledge the importance of SF/IS assistance, they often view it as a "welfare" measure that belongs in "social" rather than economic- development agencies–in ministries or departments of labor or social welfare, or special small-firm agencies. In their eyes, SF support will help mop up the unemployment resulting from the necessary reforms and initiatives meant to restructure the economy and institutions of government for a trade-liberalized world.

In these terms, the SF sector becomes mainly an instrument for preserving and even creating *jobs*–albeit often poor-quality jobs in poor-quality firms–rather than as an opportunity to stimulate economic development. This frees policymakers to dedicate their economic-development attention elsewhere, by reducing for them the political cost of the job losses that ensue from the modernization of industry and economic-policy reforms. From this perspective, and more generally, SF-assistance programs do the important work of helping to maintain the "social peace," rather than necessarily to modernize the local economy.[6] Contributing to this same perspective, many international donors and non-government organizations couch their current support for IS/SF assistance, such as micro-credit and other programs, in terms of "safety-net" measures for poverty reduction.

The devil's deal offers more to IS/SF clusters than just looking the other way from their violation of regulations. Governments often grant small firms a particular kind of support in which there is something for everyone–special lines of cheap credit, blanket credit amnesties when times are bad, and blanket exemptions for small firms from certain taxes and regulations. The exemptions are "burden-relieving" in that they reduce the costs of small firms (or keep them from increasing) in a way that requires no effort on their part. They are also "universalist" or "distributive" in that they benefit *all* small firms–whether they want to grow or not, whether they are seeking to improve their efficiency or not, and regardless of sector.[7]

In maximizing the number of satisfied constituents, this kind of support to small firms is ideal for maintaining and increasing electoral loyalty. It is less than ideal, however, for stimulating local economic development that is sustained and employment-enhancing. Today, that is, the most widely agreed-upon forms of public support for local economic development do not have this universalist and burden-relieving character. In some ways, in fact, they are just the *opposite*. They strategically identify and try to remove bottlenecks to improved efficiency, productivity, and marketing for the sector as a whole. Before any significant support is rendered, they often require or elicit broad involvement of the sector in a process of discovering exactly what the problem is and what to do about it. And they may benefit directly–at least at first–only those firms most capable and most interested in upgrading their production which, in turn, often leads to the latter's formalization. The histories of dynamic small-firm clusters often reveal this particular kind of strategic public support which, in turn, has been central to the formation of strong local economies and the reduction of unemployment.

Once the "devil's deal" has been made between firms and politicians, it becomes politically awkward for governments to carry out the above-mentioned strategic and sector-specific support because it does not automatically benefit all small firms. To the extent that it does benefit the region as a whole–as in the breaking of important infrastructure bottlenecks or the linking of local producers to outside buyers through trade fairs–the benefits may be longer in coming and more diffuse, and their effects may be felt by many firms only indirectly. These traits are just the opposite of those characterizing the relief provided by the burden-reducing exemptions and subsidies–immediate, automatic, universal, conspicuous, and directly available to each firm as an individual unit.

Classifying firms by their size (small, medium, or large) for purposes of public policy, rather than by their product or sector, reinforces the tendencies toward the burden-reducing approach. "Small," that is, can encompass a quite diverse set of firms–rustic and sophisticated, producing in different sectors, and located in different places. For purposes of lobbying for burden-reducing measures, for example, "small" can even be meant to include a rustic brick-making operation in the countryside or a sophisticated software firm in the city. With such heterogeneity, the only way an association can serve a majority of its members is to appeal to the broadest common denominator–namely, size. But the kind of support that best fits the size denominator is the burden-reducing subsidies and exemptions because of, as seen above, their universal and distributive benefits. That is why we often find small-firm associations pressing more for the universalist exemptions than for the strategic supports. In this sense, then, size is

234

also the *lowest* common denominator, in that its associated subsidies and exemptions are the least likely to lead to sustained development.

No one would deny the importance of SF associationalism in the histories of many dynamic clusters. Organizing and lobbying according to firm size, moreover, may be the only way small firms can hope to compete with larger and more powerful firms for the attention of policymakers. At the same time, the attention paid by governments and donors to firms according to their (small) size–and to small-firm associationalism–can also work inadvertently in the same direction as the devil's deal.

The large volume of research on small firms and their clusters does not tell us much about the circumstances under which universalist concerns and demands will dominate strategic ones in SF associations, let alone the sequence by which universalist concerns and their burden-relieving support sometimes miraculously give way to more strategic episodes. Complicating the story, the two approaches may coexist within the same association.[8] Putting together and lobbying for a strategic agenda, moreover, requires harder work over a longer period of time–more deliberation, analysis, and consensus–than lobbying for the burden-reducing exemptions and subsidies. In this sense, the universalist exemptions of the devil's deal will be more appealing to SF associations because they are *easier*, just as they are more appealing to politicians because of their greater *political* yield.

Focusing on the difficulties small and informal firms face in meeting the costs of environmental and labor standards distracts our attention from pursuing opportunities for firms to, indeed, rise to the occasion and meet these standards, rather than be exempt from them. Though we are used to thinking that SFs need protection from these "excessively" burdensome costs, there are many cases in which SFs have actually met those costs and, contrary to the burden-relieving scenario, have been better off for it. They became more efficient, produced higher quality goods, and gained new access to more demanding markets.

How did such dynamic clusters get from where they were before–when they were the pathetic, low-productivity small firms of the welfare scenario–to where they are today? Much of the research on small-firm clusters fails to ask this particular question, dedicated as the research has been to understanding how these clusters function at any particular moment in time or drawing best-practice lessons for practitioners. It is the evolutionary sequence of these cluster histories, however, that will reveal lessons on how to promote SF dynamism while not compromising–in contrast to the burden-reducing approach–our concerns for increasing the rule of law, reducing environmental problems, protecting worker rights, and upskilling labor. The histories will also provide insights into the sequences of events and other circumstances under which local actors make the transition from burden-relieving to more strategic and transformative deeds.

Offhand, five recent cases come to my mind of major advances in improving the efficiency, productivity, and other sector-wide aspects of partly small-firm clusters in which standards were increased rather than waived. In three of these cases, the advances were triggered in part by suddenly-imposed bans of importing countries on a developing country's export. Germany banned the import of leather goods produced with certain chemicals, all used by the Tamil Nadu leather-goods cluster in India; the U.S. banned the import of precision surgical instruments from Pakistan, made in the Sialkhot cluster, because of problems with the quality of steel; and El Salvador banned the import of Nicaraguan cheese because it did not meet the importing country's new hygienic standards.[9] In each of these cases, the importing country had been a major buyer of the export of that product for some time. The firms, acting through previously existing collective, public, and public-private institutions, rose to the

occasion–meeting the costs of the new standards, resuming exporting, and becoming more

competitive. One would not want to count on such wrenching import bans, of course, as a "best

practice" for upgrading small-firm clusters.

The remaining two examples did not need the import bans by customer countries to fuel

them, and hence show another possible path to similar results. These two cases were also

triggered by problems in the international market–namely, increasing competition to SF clusters

caused by the entry of cheaper or better products into the international market from other

countries. One case involved a footwear cluster in southern Brazil and the other, a marble cluster

in Andalucian Spain.[10]

In both these cases, importantly, the SF associations first lobbied government for the

typical burden-reducing measures–tax exemptions, credit amnesties and subsidies. But,

unusually, the government explicitly *rejected* the burden-reducing approach as a way of coping

with the crisis provoked by the outside competition. Making its own counter-demand, the

government agency involved offered a *different* kind of deal in exchange for support: it required

that the firms gather together and engage in a time-consuming and difficult exercise that

identified problems and proposed sector-specific solutions.

In the Andalucian case, the marble cluster had declined through the years partly because

of increasing competition in the international market from the Italian marble industry. The

Planning Ministry offered the following deal: the firms would themselves have to get together,

decide what the problems were and how they might be overcome, and then arrive at a proposal

on what to do. In addition, the Ministry required 100% consensus among the sector's firms, in

return for which it offered technical and facilitating assistance for this process, and the promise of financing for whatever proposal for upgrading that might emerge. This was a deal also, then, but in certain ways it was just the opposite of the devil's deal: what it demanded in return was not political loyalty, but a set of behaviors that would lead to greater economic dynamism.

In the Brazilian case, similarly, the association of small footwear producers–faced with a crushing increase in cheap footwear imports in the late 1990s–lobbied the state government of Rio Grande do Sul for tax relief. The government denied the burden-reducing relief, but proposed a different kind of exchange. It offered to finance and assist in other ways the participation of these firms in an important major trade fair, an annual event held in the shoe-producing Franca region of Brazil, so as to increase their exposure to the large Brazilian market. As a result, their sales increased significantly, which also increased the state's sales-tax return by more than the amount expended for this support.

The Brazilian story also shows that such strategic deals can yield political returns as robust as those of the burden-reducing measures. The state's footwear cluster, located a few hours from the capital city, had typically voted against the party in power at the time of this offer–the left-wing Workers' Party. Many of the smaller firms who benefitted from the trade-fair experience, however, subsequently shifted their allegiance to that party, in a first-time split of the political loyalties of the footwear-producing sector as a whole.

Obviously, not all small-firm clusters would be able to respond as successfully as happened in these cases. But the general sympathy in the SF/IS agenda for protecting small firms as a group from various burdens–often in the name of protecting the "only" source of employment in particular local economies–distracts our attention from possibilities among such firms to meet these costs in a way that leaves them and the local economy better off. Such an economically robust outcome might provide more sustained employment, let alone better

238

environmental and labor standards and tax collection, than would protecting small firms as a category.

I am arguing, then, that the widespread sympathy for small firms as a special category–and in particular their "inability" to pay taxes and conform to environmental and labor standards–tends to undermine other important concerns about appropriate strategies for reducing poverty, increasing employment and development, and improving governance. These include reducing environmental degradation (to which small-firm clusters can be major contributors); protecting worker rights to organize, and improving health and safety in the workplace; expanding the coverage of social security, health, and other social insurance to poorer workers; increasing the tax yield of governments so as to better finance public services and, in so doing, drawing government and firms together in a contract–in this case, to promote a more inclusive style of economic development.

Researchers and funding institutions could contribute to breaking the stranglehold of the devil's deal by exploring the paths by which SF/IS firms or sectors actually grew into formality, treated workers better and upgraded their skills, and worked toward improving their environmental practices. These kinds of cases–where firm agglomerations succeeded in meeting regulatory requirements, became more competitive, and were better off for it–need to be sought out and chronicled, such that lessons for policy can be learned from them. This would help to show policymakers–particularly at the subnational level, where such enforcement and economic-development support increasingly takes place–another path and another set of possibilities. Showing that such outcomes are perfectly imaginable, and familiarizing planners with the felicitous outcomes of actual cases and the paths that led to them, might also contribute toward reducing the generalized antipathy in the economic-development sector of many countries toward the enactment or enforcement of environmental and labor standards.

The policy sympathy for small firms as a category of assistance, in sum, is desirable on many grounds. At the same time, the concern about protecting SFs from reasonable regulations–let alone from the vicissitudes of the market–can become toxic when combined with the political dynamics of the devil's deal. The waiving of tax, labor, and environmental regulations that results from sympathy for the "plight" of small firms may hinder rather than help local economies if it condemns them to low-level economic stagnation, degradation of the environment, and violation of worker rights. The latter all clearly increase unemployment and poverty, as well as burdening unnecessarily the task of poverty-reducing social policy.

Endnotes

1.This note was developed from Section 3 of my chapter, "Why social policy is condemned to a residual category of safety nets, and what to do about it: thoughts on a research agenda for UNRISD," in the forthcoming volume, *Social Policy in a Development Context*, edited by Thandika Mkandawire (copies of the chapter can be obtained from tendler@mit.edu). I thank UNRISD for supporting the larger paper, and for helpful comments on an earlier draft at a seminar on the topic of social policy that it sponsored in Sweden. For comments on this or previous drafts, I thank Mansueto Almeida, Éverton Chaves Correia, Alberto Criscuolo, Jacob Lima, Nichola Lowe, Mick Moore, Lisa Peattie, Lant Pritchett, Rémy Prud'homme, and Hubert Schmitz, as well as participants in seminars sponsored by the Institute of Development Studies at Sussex, Cornell University, Duke University, the Harvard Center for Population and Development Studies, the World Bank, and the Brazilian Center for Applied Research in São Paulo. Support for part of the research contributing to this article is gratefully acknowledged from the Brazilian Bank of the Northeast (BN), through the MIT/BN project.

2.By specifying the subject to be firms that are small and/or informal, I am not excluding from the universe of firms discussed herein some small firms that are partly or fully formal, and even some firms that are producing in the same sector and in the same locality as the small firms, but tending toward medium size. Though this fuzzy definition ignores important distinctions, it is necessary to reflect the fact that SF demands often emerge from a set of firms defined by the space they occupy together and the same product or value-chain in which they produce. Just as important, the loose definition serves the purpose of brevity, and is also consistent with the language used by the international development community in describing and justifying the kinds of policy objectives and programs discussed in this article.

3.The non-payment of taxes in this region has been no secret in Brazil. A national news magazine reported—in an article on the dynamism of the cluster entitled, "Taxes not paid here"–that "this [cluster] wouldn't even exist if firm owners had to pay taxes." The chief of the state's Treasury Department, in turn, said that the taxes collected there did "not even represent 1% of what could be collected." "Aqui não se paga imposto: conheça Santa Cruz do Capibaribe, a cidade que se transformou numa das mecas da informalidade no brasil [Taxes not paid here: welcome to Santa Cruz do Capibaribe, the city that transformed itself into one of the meccas of informality in Brazil]," José Maria Furtado, *Revista Exame* [Brazil], Vol 35, Edition 733, No. 3, pp. 96-99, 7 February 2001. [Translations from the Portuguese are mine.]

4.With apologies to today's cluster specialists, I will use the word "cluster" throughout more loosely than it is sometimes defined, partly for lack of a better single word and to avoid the more ponderous "agglomeration." In its more carefully-defined form, a small-firm "cluster" usually means a set of small firms located close together geographically with significant inter-firm relations among them, with an at-least evolving associational dynamic, and usually some history of success in growing, and in improving efficiency and productivity; in more recent definitions, other parts of the supply chain to which those firms belong also have to be present to qualify as a "cluster." My less demanding use of the term requires only that a particular region has a significant number of small firms producing the same product or in the same value chain, which may also include an admixture of medium and even large firms. Again, my sloppier definition is in some ways more consistent with the way the term is used in the world of policy and practice.

5.There are some exceptions, though they tend to come from outside the small-firm literature, involving country studies by political scientists; some take place in the now-industrialized countries. For example, one study that actually narrates an analogous deal between government and informal firms is John Cross' *Informal Politics: Street Vendors and the State in Mexico City* (Stanford, California: Stanford University Press, 1998); Cross documents how continued informality, in this case, was central to the government's willingness to support the vendors' organizing efforts, and to negotiate a series of their demands. In a study of taxation in Zambia, Lise Rakner notes that the government "may have refrained from broadening its tax base to include the emerging informal business sector in order not to jeopardise its support among the Owambo-speaking majority; "The Politics of Revenue Mobilisation: Explaining Continuity in Namibian Tax Policies," *Forum for Development Studies* (No.1, June 2001, p. 142).

Italian political scientists studying Italy's postwar period have pointed explicitly to the importance of "[c]lientelist generosity–in the form of regulation to protect small business, a lax approach to tax collection for the self-employed, and so on–was systematically directed at these groups"; see Jonathan Hopkin and Alfio Mastropaolo, "From patronage to clientelism: comparing the Italian and Spanish experiences," Chapter 7 in *Clientelism, Interests, and Democratic Representation: the European Experience in Historical and Comparative Perspective*, edited by Simona Piattoni (Cambridge: Cambridge University Press, 2001). Suzanne Berger's work on this same subject in Italy and France is cited in the following note, #6. For an interpretation of small-firm politics in the U.S. economy as affecting viewpoints and policies, see Charles Brown, James Hamilton, and James Medoff, *Employers Large and Small* (Cambridge, MA: Harvard University Press, 1990).

6.Using the small-firm sector to maintain employment and the social peace is not unique to the current period, or to less-developed countries. In work on the political economy of industrial policy in France and Italy, published more than 20 years ago, the political scientist Suzanne Berger explicitly linked the pro-SF programs and regulations that developed in France and Italy during the 1970s to the simultaneous pursuit of a *large-firm* industrialization strategy by those very same governments. She had posed the question of why two countries that had so explicitly pursued a large-firm modernization industrial policy could at the same time have enacted such pro-SF legislation and assistance. It is from her work that I take the term, "keeping the social peace." See, "The Uses of the Traditional Sector in Italy: Why Declining Classes Survive," in: *The Petite Bourgeoisie*, edited by Frank Bechafer and Brian Elliot, pp. 71-89 (New York: Saint Martin's Press, 1981); and "The Traditional Sector in France and Italy," in: *Dualism and Discontinuity in Industrial Societies*, edited by Suzanne Berger and Michael Piore (Cambridge: Cambridge University Press, 1980), Chapter 4, pp. 88-131.

7.I apologize for any confusion I may create by borrowing the term "universalist" from the social-policy literature. In the social-policy literature, for both developed and developing countries, "universalist" is conveyed as the opposite of targeting. It is portrayed as more inclusive of beneficiaries–usually, middle class as well as lower class–than is an approach that, although more accurately targeting the poor, causes the left-out middle class to deny political support for the measure. Recently, many researchers–of both developed as well as developing countries–have argued that targeted approaches, though in some ways ideal in terms of restricting benefits to the intended beneficiaries, are quite cumbersome to administer (means-testing, etc.). They therefore end up alienating the middle classes whose political support is needed to enact such measures in the first place. In applying the term "universalist" here to economic-development-related matters and pointing out its problems, then, I am not thereby criticizing the universalist approach with respect to social policy. Rather, I borrow the term for its usefulness in conveying the same sense of an initiative being more politically appealing when it more conspicuously and efficiently benefits a larger number of voters, even at the cost of diluting program intentions.

8.I thank Nichola Lowe for pointing out these possibilities to me–based on a case from Jalisco state in Mexico. "Trainers by Design: Small Firm Upgrading and Inter-Firm Learning in Jalisco, Mexico," Ph.D. dissertation, Department of Urban Studies and Planning, Massachusetts Institute of Technology, 2002 (forthcoming).

9.For the German/Indian case, see Poonam Pillai, "The state and collective action: successful adjustment of the Tamil Nadu leather clusters to German environmental standards," Master's Thesis, Department of Urban Studies and Planning, M.I.T., 2000; for the U.S./Pakistan case, see Khalid Nadvi, "Collective Efficiency and Collective Failure: The response of the Sialkot surgical instrument cluster to global quality pressures," *World Development* (27, no. 9:1605-1626, 1999); and for El Salvador, see a forthcoming study by Paola Pérez-Alemán, "Decentralized Production, Organization and Institutional Transformations: Large and Small Firm Networks in Chile and Nicaragua," Paper presented at the Third Meeting of the Institute for Latin American and Iberian Studies, Columbia University, International Working Group on Subnational Economic Governance in Latin America from a Comparative International Perspective, San Juan, Puerto Rico, 25-28 August 2000. Note that, in the U.S./Pakistan case, Nadvi reports that there was more cross-cluster success in improving the quality of the precision steel than with respect to labor and environmental standards.

10.For the Andalucian case, see Michael Barzelay [2000], "Managing Local Development: Lessons from Spain." *Policy Sciences* 24 (3 August):271-290; for the Brazilian case, I thank Luiz Miranda of the Economics Department of the Federal University of Rio Grande do Sul.

The Fear of Education

Judith Tendler

Massachusetts Institute of Technology
tendler@mit.edu

14 July 2002

Background paper for
Inequality and the State in Latin America and the Caribbean
(World Bank, Fall 2003)

Presented at the 50th Anniversary Meetings of the Banco do Nordeste,
Fortaleza, 19 July 2002

Abstract

The "new economy" of the 21st century, as we have come to understand it over the last decade, requires a more literate workforce. Firms and countries without it are advised that they will have increasing trouble competing in a global economy. It is this concern, in part, that has led to the appeals of the last decade to developing countries to take basic education more seriously, by dedicating more attention and resources to the sector. In the research conducted for this paper, however, owners and managers of large modern manufacturing firms in the textile, garment, and footwear sectors of Northeast Brazil reported, to their pleasant surprise, that they have been able to live with illiteracy without compromising their ability to compete. They did not prize an educated workforce and, indeed, sometimes worried out loud that "too much education was a bad thing." This "fear" of education also pervades the thinking of politicians and governments, particularly the departments that support economic development–and particularly at the subnational level, where decisions to fund and improve education are often made. These actors often construe their region's "only" comparative advantage in economic development as one of cheap labor; they worry that a more educated labor force may diminish that advantage by leading to a general increase in the region's relative wage, and by reducing the prized "docility" and "gratefulness" of the region's labor force; they also expect to lose the returns to their investment in better education, because of the fabled out-migration of the best workers. The above-noted experiences of firm owners and managers, in turn, seems to translate into a *lack* of pressure on governments by important local elites for improved education–a kind of fatal absence of demand-driven pressures. These various perceptions, it is important to note, are eminently rational in both private and economic terms. Together, they contribute to a kind of "low-level education trap," which may help explain the stubborn persistence of low literacy and poor schooling in many poorer regions (or countries) today. The new wisdom about workforce literacy and global competitiveness, then, may be accurate for only some sectors, regions, countries, and periods of time–but not for others. For this reason, the appeals for improved education should perhaps be grounded in rationales other than the 21st-century "need" for significantly higher workforce literacy. To this end, researchers of political economy and policy reform might explore the historical experiences of other countries–including in other times–to find ways out of the trap.

The rule of law, economic development, and modernization of the state in Brazil: lessons from existing experience for policy and practice

Research Proposal to:
World Bank Office, Brazil (Brasília) and
UK Department for International Development (DfID/Brasília)

Judith Tendler

Massachusetts Institute of Technology
Department of Urban Studies and Planning (DUSP)
tendler@mit.edu
17 January 2007

Today, Brazil faces the twin challenges of rekindling economic growth while, at the same time, stepping up or at least continuing the same pace of reducing poverty and inequality. This proposal focuses on two key means to fulfilling these ambitions: (1) transforming them from tradeoffs–as they often are, or at least perceived as such–into positive-sum strategies and outcomes, and (2) modernizing the institutions of the public sector to better meet these goals in a post-ISI[1] and trade-liberalizing world. These challenges are particularly relevant to the WB's Brazil-program strategy at a moment when, *first,* it is re-crafting its support to this now-middle-income country that has become a significant player on the international scene, and doing so within the context of the Bank's reduced relative significance (albeit high in absolute terms) in Brazil's public investment (including of parastatals) and operating expenditures. *Second,* they lend themselves to lesson-learning evaluation research that builds on the country's growing number of positive experiences and improving public-sector capacity. I couch the proposed project in terms meant to narrow it down to a set of researchable themes and questions within this larger framework. (I am grateful to John Briscoe and Salo Coslovsky for providing detailed feedback on an earlier draft of this proposal, and other helpful suggestions and examples.)

In choosing the experiences and the style of research, the proposed project's purpose is to:

(1) Yield findings of practical interest to the WB/DFID and the Brazilian public sector over a two-year period, with interim discussions with Brazilian actors and WB/DFID staff on emerging impressions, draft papers, and next-step questions throughout the period.

(2) Identify certain opportunities–sometimes missed–for a public-sector role based on existing experiences and their histories, which often would not require significant increases in resources or radically different ways of doing things–hence could generate significant impacts at the margin for a small investment of resources and time.

(3) Follow a process throughout that–in addition to field interviewing and data collection–engages with small groups of public-sector managers and "front-line workers," as well as relevant business and NGO groups, around what they judge to be their better examples of positive-sum outcomes and, equally, of less positive ones–addressing the "why's?" for these contrasts in outcomes, and the processes of organizational learning by which they identified mistakes (or did not) and corrected them.

(4) The project would be carried out by myself and a small team of researchers (3-6) over a two-year period. Methodologically (and substantively), it would build and improve upon my prior experience in four similarly applied research projects in Northeast Brazil over a ten-year period starting in 1992, in which I supervised small teams (5-8 each) of MIT graduate students trained by me in coursework and at fieldwork sites–as elaborated further in Section 5 on methodology, which also identifies the research team.

---

[1] ISI refers to the import-substituting-industrialization policy regimes that characterized Latin America and many other developing countries around the world, which have been dismantled gradually starting in the 1980s in Latin America, and later for particular countries. Many of the debates about economic development policies have been couched in these terms–ISI and post-ISI. In Brazil, the process started in the 1980s, and many of today's current economic-development advances had significant roots in that earlier policy regime.

In what follows, I identify four themes together with research questions, implications, and case illustrations. In addition, and for purposes of brevity, I use the term "regional economic development" and the acronym RED (or simply ED) to distinguish my subject from macroeconomic policies and outcomes, which are not treated here. RED outcomes and related policies and actors operate substantially at *subnational* levels (regional, state, micro-regional, and municipal, as well as related central-government actors–the latter being the central-government part of federated structures with strong subnational presence).

There is significant overlap between the themes presented, with almost every one of them present and of relevance in each of the others. They are strongly influenced by markets and civil society–including firms and their associations, nongovernment organizations, and social movements–all of which fall within the study's analytical lens. At the same time, the proposal's central focus is the public sector, its modernization, and lessons to be learned from existing experience. Finally, I suggest how and why some currently popular interpretations of existing experiences–including some of the well-known cases noted below–are actually *mis*readings or, at least, incomplete. To help interpret the lessons of such cases more accurately, the proposal identifies some examples of particular cases and institutional actors that would be suitable objects of research attention.

The proposal is organized according to the following set themes and related questions. Several of the themes overlap with each other, and each theme appears in almost all the case examples illustrated in the proposal, as do several of the same institutional actors:

Section 1: Linkages and spillovers. What explains that–when looking across cases of regional economic development–some show significantly greater linkages, spillovers, and employment and/or income-distributing effects? Given that almost no such comparative studies on the Brazilian experience now exist as a basis for informing state-government policies to promote economic growth, how can the findings of such research meet this need?

Section 2: The intersection between the rule of law and economic development. Why do some cases of improved implementation in the rule of law jeopardize competitiveness and economic development, while others co-exist easily with it and even advance it? What does the Brazilian experience show with respect to transforming the so-called zero- or net-negative outcomes to positive-sum outcomes?

Section 3: Institutionalizing the mediation of conflict. What can be learned about experiences and environments in which the generic conflicts between differing interest groups and even different factions within public agencies are successfully mediated?–given the extent to which increasing democratization and decentralization has brought these conflicts more into the open.

Section 4: Modernizing the state: discretion, commitment, and reform fractions. Running across all the themes, why do some public agencies and programs perform better and produce better outcomes, while others working under seemingly similar conditions do not? Why, in some cases, have reform fractions of dedicated civil servants with a strong collective identity as professionals been key in advancing reform and "modernizing" the state and, in other cases, not? In addition, under what circumstances is greater autonomy and discretion of civil servants associated with better performance in some cases and, in others, just the opposite?

Running clearly across these four themes and cited cases are *politics and political-economy* factors. They are often central to outcomes, whether for the worse *or* for the better–but are often not taken into account. When they are, the tendency is to focus on their negative side, and to see them as exogenous and random. When politicians are centrally behind better outcomes, then, why in these cases and not in the others, and what are the patterns that run across them? In turn, how do agency managers and professionals succeed in attracting political support–or even mold existing interest by politicians into forms that help, rather than hinder?

Section 5 addresses research methodology; *Section 6* lists the research team with bios. *Annex A* summarizes across themes some cases and institutional-actor examples; and *Annex B* briefly summarizes and cuts across the preceding sections with case examples.

5. Methodology

This project would be carried out by myself and a small team of researchers–starting first with three or four researchers–identified in the next section–and perhaps evolving to five or six over the course of the two-year project. Methodologically, it builds on an approach I have developed in doing my own field research in Brazil and elsewhere over the last 30 years.[2]

The methodology also builds and improves upon my more recent experience during the 1990s and early 2000s in four similarly applied and comparative research projects within Northeast Brazil, over a ten-year period starting in 1992, during which I supervised teams (six to nine each) of MIT graduate students trained by me at MIT in prior course work and research methodology, and then in the field in Brazil.[3] The first three projects were funded by the state governments of Ceará and Maranhão–partly out of funds for evaluation research in WB projects, though not dedicated to these projects exclusively; the last and Northeast-wide project was funded by the Bank of the Northeast.[4]

My book, *Good Government in the Tropics*, was based on these first two projects; the same with my four or five monographs and publications from the fourth project with the BNB. (On two separate occasions, MIT awarded these research projects and their methodology, for combining research with graduate education to produce outstanding applied research and practical findings.) The current project would not be Northeast-specific, given the additional learning to be gained from a cross-regional perspective–for example, the relevance of lessons learned in the Northeast for the North; or patterns of public performance that run across poorer and richer regions. (I have considerable fieldevaluation and other research experience in Brazil outside the Northeast, as well as outside Brazil.)

[2] An example of the type of practical and WB-relevant results from my individual research can be seen in OED's publication in the early 1990s of my *New Lessons from Old Projects: Lessons from the Northeast Brazilian Experience*. The executive summary and Chapter 2, "Reinventing the projects," are of methodological relevance to the current proposal. Another example, from outside Brazil and the WB, is my *World Development* article, "Whatever Happened to Poverty Alleviation," based on my field study for the Ford Foundation of lessons to be learned for their programming in the future of their most successful grants in terms of widespread impact in India, Bangladesh, Kenya, and Egypt. This, and a subsequent exercise in interviewing Ford project officers in New York on what worked and what didn't through the years and why, plus the ensuing report and meetings with staff and management around both exercises–had an impact on Ford's programming, and the reports were also used as orientation materials for new program officers.

[3] I considered only the following types of researchers to participate in the team for this project: (1) advanced doctoral students or post-docs who have participated in my previous Brazil projects, plus those whose training and fieldwork in Brazil I have supervised subsequently; (2) only Brazilians (and other Latin Americans who speak Portuguese, and have lived and carried out field research and Brazil); and (3) those who have a track record of producing well-written papers, providing grounded evidence, data analysis, and findings with practical implications, and who have considerable experience outside academia.

[4] A list of the papers and publications by the graduate researchers that resulted from these four projects is available on request. The list of papers and publications for the fourth project with the BNB–project proposal–entitled *Rethinking regional development after trade liberalization* (also available on request)–includes abstracts of all the monographs, theses, and publications, including my own.

The methodology involves looking into and across cases through the analysis of existing data and intensive interviewing of actors and clients, focusing at least as much on the build-up of capacity through the years, as on current comparative judgments. Akin to a "natural experiment," it compares what has worked and what has not across various cases, and identifies patterns running across similar kinds of public agencies, programs, and projects with outcomes that vary remarkably across regions (states, municipalities, microregions), types of activity, and types of bureaucracy. My WB/OED evaluation study–the *New-Lessons* study noted earlier is one example of applying such a methodology to WB projects: the same type of project (the Northeast rural-development projects after a ten-year history), within a roughly homogeneous region (the semi-arid and relatively poor Northeast), and the same strong funder and funder presence (WB)–nine similar projects in nine Northeast states.[5] The Ceará-state research that gave rise to *Good Government in the Tropics* used a similar comparative approach–this time looking for patterns across different *sectors* (preventive health, drought relief, agricultural extension, small-business programs) *within* one state, as well as looking within each sector.

The process of case selection and development, and the questions to be asked, will be–as in the previous studies–highly iterative. Our interview and other research questions attempting to understand better outcomes will be forged partly out of a prior understanding of the reasons usually put forward for *less* impressive outcomes. We ask specifically, for example, why a particular problem like corruption or political interference or change in government did *not* occur in a particular case; or, if it *did* occur–as is often the case–why it did *not* prevent improved outcomes. In asking such questions, we often refer to other places–like the neighboring *município* or state–where the problem *did* occur and *was* undermining (either in the same program, same agency, and/or in the neighboring town or state, etc.).

Another interviewing challenge lies in the typical explanations given by those interviewed of positive outcomes. They often give short-term and idiosyncratic explanations, pointing to the presence, for example, of a "dynamic," "charismatic," or "visionary" program director or elected leader. In so doing, they focus on the *dis*continuity with previous government, explaining how the new one had to "start from scratch." Interviewing methodology requires getting beyond this "firewall" in perceptions between the current and past government, by going back in time. We also ask, for this reason, a set of questions about *process*, given that learning from experience is often key to learning lessons from better programs. For example: what did you do in the past that you don't do now and why? What mistakes were made that you corrected and how were they identified? How did you know that something was not working?

With respect to the focus of questions on local and regional economic development, an analogous methodological challenge relates to the common complaints by business about government presence–whether they concern a too-heavy presence, regulatory or otherwise–or the opposite in terms of desired support, namely, little or no presence. Many analysts of government policy and programs, in turn, often point to a "*too*-supportive" presence in the form of costly subsidies and heavy-handed intervention. In the more nuanced picture, even though subsidization may have been heavy–often generating

---

[5] The starting point of this previous study, of course, was WB *projects*–which would not constitute the starting point of the proposed study. In the three 1990s projects funded by Brazilian state governments, they were interested in casting a broader net over experiences and history in a way that would help them think out future policies and programs within the WB-project context, and more broadly.

economically perverse results–it is sometimes the unnoticed "lighter" forms of support that turned out to be key in generating enduring impacts, often long after the heavier policy regime was dismantled. Looking at a longer historical trajectory, finally, does not mean that outside support requires equally long time periods to bear fruit. In many cases, however, the lessons to be learned from the past experience can be easily "dis-embedded" from the broader policy regime under which they occurred.

The methodology is meant to allow each researcher to develop his own set of cases, while at the same time embedding the individual research in the questions running across the larger project and the themes that define it. To this end, the process will involve periodic meetings among the members of the team and myself during the research–in the field and at MIT–to elicit emerging questions, puzzles, impressions, next steps, and patterns. I also selectively accompany each of the researchers in some field interviews–partly for me to understand directly, partly to point out next questions to ask or, afterward, to mention questions that should have been asked following up on a response to a prior question–the common "missed opportunity" in interviewing.

Another interviewing challenge lies in the typical explanations given by those interviewed of positive outcomes. They often give short-term and idiosyncratic explanations, pointing to the presence, for example, of a "dynamic," "charismatic," or "visionary" program director or elected leader. In so doing, they focus on the *dis*continuity with previous government, explaining how the new one had to "start from scratch." Interviewing methodology requires getting beyond this "firewall" in perceptions between the current and past government, by going back in time. We also ask, for this reason, a set of questions about *process,* given that learning from experience is often key to learning lessons from better programs. For example: what did you do in the past that you don't do now and why? What mistakes were made that you corrected and how were they identified? How did you know that something was not working?

With respect to the focus of questions on local and regional economic development, an analogous methodological challenge relates to the common complaints by business about government presence–whether they concern a too-heavy presence, regulatory or otherwise–or the opposite in terms of desired support, namely, little or no presence. Many analysts of government policy and programs, in turn, often point to a "*too*-supportive" presence in the form of costly subsidies and heavy-handed intervention. In the more nuanced picture, even though subsidization may have been heavy–often generating economically perverse results–it is sometimes the unnoticed "lighter" forms of support that turned out to be key in generating enduring impacts, often long after the heavier policy regime was dismantled. Looking at a longer historical trajectory, finally, does not mean that outside support requires equally long time periods to bear fruit. In many cases, however, the lessons to be learned from the past experience can be easily "dis-embedded" from the broader policy regime under which they occurred.

www.ingramcontent.com/pod-product-compliance
Lightning Source LLC
Chambersburg PA
CBHW051334200326
41519CB00026B/7422